OWNERS, OCCU
SEVENTEENTH C

Best 2
Tony Barton

Owners, Occupiers and Others:

Seventeenth Century Northwich

*The fourth Wonder is the salt springs found there,
from which salt is boiled, wherewith various
foods can be salted; they are not near the sea,
but rise from the ground.*
(Nennius, *The Wonders of Britain, c. AD 810*)

Tony Bostock

In memory of
JAMES CYRIL BOSTOCK
(1922 - 2003)
My father:
a Northwich man – born and bred.

ISBN
1 901253 37 6
First published February 2004

© Tony Bostock 2004

The moral right of Tony Bostock to be identified as the author
of this work has been asserted by him in accordance with
the Copyright, Designs and Patents Act 1988.

All rights reserved. No part of this publication may be reproduced,
stored in a retrieval system, or transmitted in any form or by any means,
electronic, mechanical, photocopying, recording or otherwise,
without the prior permission of the copyright owner.

A catalogue record of this book is
available from the British Library.

Published by:
Léonie Press an imprint of
Anne Loader Publications
13 Vale Road, Hartford,
Northwich, Cheshire CW8 1PL Gt Britain
Tel: 01606 75660   Fax: 01606 77609
e-mail: anne@leoniepress.com
Website: www.anneloaderpublications.co.uk
www.leoniepress.com

Printed by:
Anne Loader Publications
Collated and bound by: B & S Swindells Ltd, Knutsford
Covers laminated by: The Finishing Touch, St Helens

Tony Bostock

ABOUT THE AUTHOR

Tony Bostock is an accomplished local historian. He holds a B.A. in History (Manchester, 1991) and an M.A. in Local History (Keele, 1994). He is the author of many articles on various aspects of Cheshire History; is on the editorial team of *Cheshire History* and was editor and writer of the *Winsford Record*. He is a regular speaker/lecturer to local history and family history societies and has had posts as a part-time lecturer in these subjects with Liverpool University's Centre for Continuing Education, Mid-Cheshire College, the WEA, and most recently Sir John Deane's College, Northwich.

As well as being a member of a number of academic societies in the region, he has been an active member of the Executive Committee of the Cheshire Local History Association and its predecessor the Palatine Local History Committee for many years. For three consecutive years he chaired the CLHA and is now its Secretary. He is also an active committee member of the Winsford Local History Society, of which he was chair-person for many years. Having retired from a professional life in public service, Tony now applies himself more to the study of local and family history.

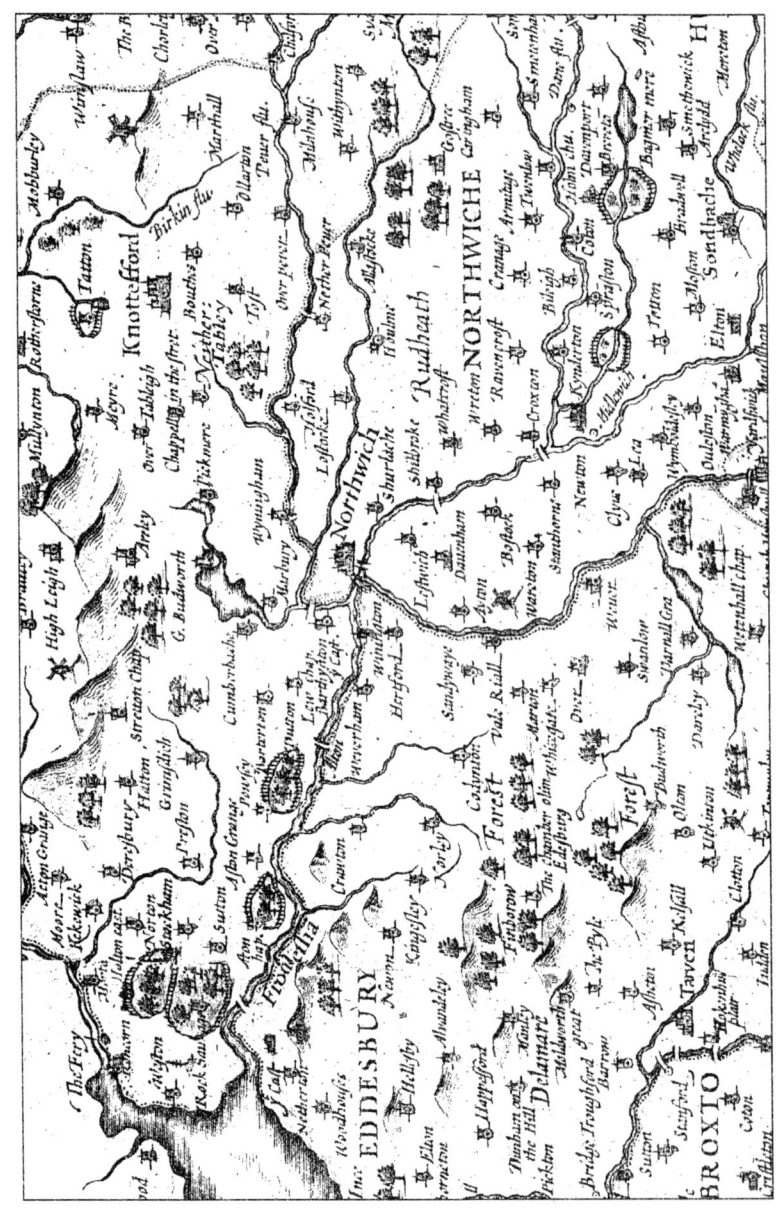

Figure One: **Northwich and its Environs**
(From Speed, 1662, CRO: PM1/11)

TABLE OF CONTENTS

List of Illustrations	ix
Preface	xi
Acknowledgements	xii
Abbreviations, Conventions and Glossary	xiii

INTRODUCTION — 1

1 A MEDIEVAL MISCELLANY — 6
Domesday 'Norwich' and 'Witune'
The Medieval Town
The Tudor Period

2 THE TOWN — 30
The Town of Northwich
Witton
Continuity of Landscape

3 THE PEOPLE OF NORTHWICH — 49
Population
Poverty and Wealth
Lifestyles
Earning a Living

4 NORTHWICH TOWN GOVERNMENT — 92
The Lord of the Manor and the Burgesses
Local Rivalries
Courts
Town Officials
The Customs

5 THE WICH-HOUSES — 114
The Wich-houses
The Salt Making Process

6 OWNERS, OCCUPIERS & OTHERS	137
The Owners	
The Occupiers	
The Others	
7 RELIGION, POLITICS & CIVIL WAR	164
Religion	
Politics	
Civil War	
Later 17th Century Events	
8 CONTINUITY AND CHANGE: THE DAWN OF A NEW ERA	182

APPENDICES

One:	**17TH CENTURY RESIDENTS OF NORTHWICH & WITTON**	188
Two:	**ELIZABETHAN OWNERS & OCCUPIERS**	190
Three:	**REFERENCES TO THE NORTHWICH TOWN PLAN**	194
Four:	**POLL TAX RETURNS, 1660**	197
Five:	**HEARTH TAX RETURNS, 1664**	202
Six:	**SIZE OF HOUSES FROM NORTHWICH INVENTORIES**	205
Seven:	**WICH-HOUSES AND THEIR OWNERS**	208
Eight:	**OWNERS AND THEIR ALLOCATION OF LEADS**	214

BIBLIOGRAPHY	218
INDEX	222

LIST OF ILLUSTRATIONS, FIGURES AND TABLES

Fig. One:	Northwich and its environs	vi
Fig. Two:	Townships with links to Northwich	10
Fig. Three:	Seventeenth Century Northwich	31
Fig. Four:	Late 18th century Northwich	35
Fig. Five:	18th century Witton	36
Fig. Six:	Urban Continuity	38
Fig. Seven:	The Carpenter and the Cooper	71
Fig Eight:	The Shoemaker and the Tailor	75
Fig. Nine:	The Husbandman and the Blacksmith	79
Fig. Ten:	17th Century Wich-houses in Northwich	116
Fig. Eleven:	A 16th Century Salt Town	120
Fig. Twelve:	A 16th Century Wich-house	123
Table One:	Some of the Farmers and Valuations of Medieval Northwich	17
Table Two:	Summary of Population Estimates	52
Table Three:	Hearth Tax Returns, 1664	55
Table Four:	Occupational Structure, 1660	64
Table Five:	Burgess Families	95
Plate One:	The Town Centre from Winnington Hill	43
Plate Two:	The Bull Ring looking towards Town Bridge	43
Plate Three:	The site of the 17th century Court House	44
Plate Four:	The Bull Ring and High Street	44
Plate Five:	The site of the House of Correction	45
Plate Six:	Apple Market Street formerly Yate Street	45
Plate Seven:	The site of the 17th century Swan Inn	46
Plate Eight:	The site of the Leadsmithy	47
Plate Nine:	The site of the 'Gripyard' behind the Leadsmithy	48
Plate Ten:	The open yard at the rear of High Street	48

PREFACE

Why a book about Northwich? Why the 17th century? One answer to the first question, a purely selfish reason, is that many generations of my family have lived in the area of Northwich, Witton and Leftwich since the late 17th century, having moved from just along the road in Davenham. The other reason is that for many years I have been intrigued by the whole business of the Cheshire salt industry and, whilst much has been written over the years in books and journals about Cheshire's salt industry, there seems to be little about Northwich's part in that, nor as regards its status as a market town and borough. Early in the 20th century Calvert produced a book called *Salt in Cheshire* which contained in its 1,200 pages a good deal of interesting information but in essence much of it consisted of transcriptions of ancient sources with little or no interpretation of them and added to which it is not an easy book to pick up and read. On the other hand Brian Curzon's *The Book of Northwich* (1995) is a much easier read. Marjorie Cox refers to something of the town's history in her excellent *A History of Sir John Deane's Grammar School, Northwich* (1975). As for the other two wiches – Middlewich and Nantwich – there is more to be found in print. *A Middlewich Chartulary*, published by the Lancashire and Cheshire Record Society in 1944, has a very useful introductory chapter written by Mrs J. Varley on the organisation of the town and its salt industry, and A.L. Earl has written *Middlewich 900-1900*, published in 1990. The main work on Nantwich is James Hall's *A History of the Town and Parish of Nantwich*, published in 1883. Almost a century later, Eric Garton published a series of books based on his studies of life through various periods of the town's history.

Whilst this book deals with Northwich and makes occasional references to the other two salt towns, I believe that there is a need for a comparative study of all three towns for they are of particular relevance to studies on urban history being three industrial towns of a pre-industrial

PREFACE

age, and three towns with complicated administrative structures – each different in its own way and yet having much in common. The similarities are perhaps more obvious as regards Middlewich and Northwich. Between these two there is a direct road link stretching only six miles and along it there was much coming and going between the communities, especially since a number of families owned property and had influence in the affairs of both towns.

As to the question of the period of study, this is due to the fact that until the late 16th century there is little surviving evidence upon which a history of the town can be based and what there is I have used in my initial chapter. On the other hand the 17th century is a period during which much information becomes available, added to which this is a particularly interesting period of history: an era of social, economic, political and religious change that affected the lives of every individual in some way. Another reason is that the final decades of this century saw the demise of the traditional operational practices and customs of making salt in Northwich: processes that had probably existed previously for many hundreds of years.

This book enlarges upon my article of the same title published in Volume 41 of *Cheshire History* (2002). Much of what I said in that essay is repeated, I have added new material and on occasion I have revised some earlier opinions in the light of new evidence and corrected errors.

Today Northwich is a typical Cheshire town with a mix of commercial and industrial sites surrounded by numerous residential estates. Its name is that of the whole district that includes the neighbouring townships of Witton, Leftwich, Hartford, Castle, Winnington, Barnton and Rudheath. The core of the area is so built up with housing estates, shops, offices and commercial sites that it hard to tell where one township ends and another starts – indeed Northwich and Witton have for centuries been seamlessly welded together. Ancient Northwich was a very small town of about six acres, concentrated on a small plot of low-lying flat land at the confluence of the rivers Dane and Weaver and surrounded by the fields and meadows on the slopes of neighbouring townships. It is this picture of the town the reader should hold in mind whilst reading this account.

ACKNOWLEDGEMENTS

In compiling this study I have used the archives held by the Cheshire and Chester Record Office on a regular basis. Accordingly I must thank Jonathan Peplar and his staff for their help and consideration, but particularly the search room staff who have tirelessly retrieved so many original documents for my perusal. I should also thank the following who have read initial drafts of this work and offered advice, comment and corrections to the typescript: Dr Alan Crosby, Marjorie Cox and Stephen Mathews.

The illustrations used in figures Seven, Eight and Nine are from Comenius' *Orbis Sensualium Pictus* and are reproduced here by courtesy of the Director and Librarian, the John Rylands University Library of Manchester. Finally thanks to the Cheshire Record Office for permission to reproduce the maps used for Figures One, Four and Five. Figures Eleven and Twelve are from Georgius Agricola's illustrations of salthouses in Saxony.

Thank you all.

Tony Bostock

Swanlow, Winsford
December 2003

ABBREVIATIONS, CONVENTIONS AND GLOSSARY

Abbreviations

BPR:	*Register of Edward the Black Prince.* Four volumes. Ed. M.C.B. Dawes (1930-33)
Calvert:	Calvert, A.F., *Salt in Cheshire* (1915)
Cantab:	Venn, J and J.A., *Alumni Cantabrigienses* (122-54)
CCAM:	*Calendars of the Committee for the Advance of Money*
CCC:	*and of the Committee for Compounding..*
C Cl R:	
C Ch R:	*Calendars of Close, Charter, Inquisitions, and Patent Rolls*
C Inq:	
CPR:	
Ch Ch Acc	*Chester Chamberlain's Account*
CRO.:	Cheshire County Record Office
CS:	*The Cheshire Sheaf*
Chet Soc:	Chetham Society
Cox	Cox, M., *A History of Sir John Deane's Grammar School, Northwich* (1975)
DB:	Morgan, P. (ed.), Domesday Book: Cheshire, Phillimore (1978)
DKR:	*Report of the Deputy Keeper of Public Records.*
DNB:	*Dictionary of National Biography*
DRO:	Derbyshire Record Office
Gastrell:	Francis Gastrell, *Notitia Cestriensis* (Chet. Soc., viii)
Harl Mss:	Harleian Manuscripts, British Museum
HSLC:	Historic Society of Lancashire and Cheshire
HT:	Lawton, G.O. (ed.) *Northwich Hundred: Poll Tax 1660 and Hearth Tax 1664*, Lancashire & Cheshire Record Society, cxix (1979).
LCAS:	Lancashire and Cheshire Antiquarian Society
LCRS:	Lancashire and Cheshire Record Society
L & P:	*Letters and Papers, Henry VIII*
Lib Rolls:	*Liberate Rolls.*

OWNERS, OCCUPIERS AND OTHERS

Ormerod:	Ormerod, G., *History of the County Palatine and City of Chester*, second edition, ed. T. Helsby (1882)
Oxon:	Foster, J., *Alumni Oxonienses* (1887-88 and 1891-92)
Par Reg:	Parish registers of St Helen's Church, Northwich, formerly Witton Chapel
PCC:	Prerogative Court of Canterbury
Pipe Rolls:	Stewart-Brown, R. and Mills, M. (eds) *Cheshire in the Pipe Rolls, 1158 – 1301*, L.C.R.S., vol 92 (1925)
PRO:	Public Record Office
PT:	Lawton, G.O. (ed.) *Northwich Hundred: Poll Tax 1660 and Hearth Tax 1664*, L.C.R.S., cxix (1979).
VRLB:	Brownbill J., (ed.), *The Ledger Book of Vale Royal Abbey*, L.C.R.S., vol. 68 (1914).

Conventions

For ease of reference footnotes are added at the end of each chapter.

Unless in italics or quotation marks all spellings of names and places have been modernised. All contemporary abbreviations have been expanded and modern punctuation and capitalisation has been adopted. Roman numerals have also been modernised.

The use of '*de*' and '*le*' in personal names has been omitted.

Dates given are in accordance with the modern calendar. Numbers in brackets following mention of a particular building in Northwich relate to the key to the early 17th century town plan, see *Appendix Three*.

Instead of the term 'salt house' I have adopted the more ancient term 'wich-house' throughout: the two terms are synonymous.

ABBREVIATIONS, CONVENTIONS AND GLOSSARY

Glossary

Many of the terms contained in this glossary will be explained fully in appropriate sections of the text, however, as some of these unfamiliar terms do occur in earlier sections a brief explanation of some of them is appropriate.

Barrow:	A conical wicker basket in which the damp salt was hung to drain and dry.
Borough:	A town which had been allowed freedom from normal manorial control and which had its own government and administration performed by the freemen of the borough – burgesses.
Burgess:	A freeman of the borough who had particular rights and exemptions. The privilege was granted to individuals by the lord of the manor and was hereditary.
Brine:	A strong solution of salt and water from which salt can be extracted by the process of boiling and evaporation.
Court Baron:	A manorial court which all tenants of the manor were obliged to attend. It would oversee the customs of the manor, transfer property rights, enforce payments of dues and services and appoint manorial officials.
Court Leet:	A manorial court presided over by the lord's steward with jurisdiction over petty offences and civil matters. It also took a 'view of frankpledge' by which the working of a mutual responsibility among the local people for good order was maintained.
Heriot:	Due paid to the lord of the manor on the death of a tenant.
Hundred:	The ancient administrative division of a shire.

OWNERS, OCCUPIERS AND OTHERS

Inquisition post mortem: An enquiry made after a freeholder's death to enquire into what lands he or she held, from whom and as to who was the heir.

Lead Looker: A town official who had responsibility to ensure that everyone had a proper share of the right to produce salt and to determine when and for how long that person might continue to do so.

Leads: The usual term for the lead pan in which the brine was boiled to produce salt. Even after iron pans were commonly used they were still known as 'leads'. As a usual rule each wich-house contained, or had the right use, four leads. Leads were made to a standard size so that everyone boiled the same amount of brine.

Manor: An area of land belonging to a lord, over which he had full economic and legal jurisdiction.

Peecing: The right to boil brine continuously in four leads for two days and two nights. The number of peecings granted to an individual was based on the number of leads held as a proportion of the total.

Steward: The representative of the lord of the manor who would preside over the manorial courts and otherwise act in an executive capacity.

Walling: A word stemming from the Anglo Saxon term meaning to boil. The process of producing salt.

Wich-house: A salt-house. This might not mean a structure but rather a piece of land in Northwich to which was attached a right to a share of brine and to produce salt.

INTRODUCTION

John Leland visited Northwich during his epic perambulation of the kingdom in the 1530s but does not seem to have been very impressed, describing the place as a 'prati market toune but fowle' – small and dirty[1]. He continues by saying:

> ... and by the salters houses be great stakkes of smaul clovyn woode, to seethe the salt water that thei make white salt of. The salt water pitte is hard by the brinke of Dane river, the wich, within a good but shott, runnith in to Wyver. Apon the Bank, betwext the saltspringing pitte and Dane River, I saw Congleton a market town 10 miles of and Maxwell Forest thereby.

The comment about being able to see the town of Congleton and Macclesfield Forest, some 14 miles as the crow flies, from his vantage point on the bank of the River Dane, seems today to be somewhat incredible. It is an interesting comment and indicates the open nature of the landscape along the Dane Valley and perhaps much of the Cheshire scenery at this time.

Half a century later William Smith was somewhat more detailed with his description:

> Northwich standeth where the River Dane falleth into the Weever, twelve miles north-east from Chester, and ten miles north from Nantwich; and is a proper town, having every Friday a market, and yearly two fairs: that is to say, on the day of Mary Magdalen, and on St Nicholas' day, being 6th of December. Here also is a salt-spring, or brine-pit, on the bank of the river of Dane; from which the brine runneth on the ground, in troughs of wood, covered over with boards, until it comes to the wich-houses, where they make salt, as before in Nantwich hath been declared. The town is (as it were)

> divided into two parts; one part thereof is called Cross, which belongeth to sir Thomas Venables; and without the town's-end standeth a very fair church of stone, which although some call it Northwich church, yet is the proper name thereof Witton, and is but a chapel; which causeth me to think that the town was named first Northwich, after the finding of the salt.[2]

The 17th century writer, William Webb takes a more romantic view:
> And now where this wedding is kept between Weever and Dane, the one as the groom, embracing the other in his bosom as his bride, and entering both names into the one of Weever, we see Northwich, the third of those salt making Wiches, so renouned for that commodity, a very ancient town, as the buildings and situation may well testify. The chief lordship whereof appertaines to the right honourable the earl of Derby, a market town well frequented, gives name to the Hundred, and seated so near the middest of the county, and so well for travel every way, that it seems fit, and is oft allotted to the meetings of the chief governors of the county, for their great affairs. One street thereof called Wytton, yields obedience to the fee and barony of Kinderton the chief owner of them and the whole town, within the chapelry, for so they term it, though it hath a very fine church called Wytton, the name of that lordship, mounted aloft upon a bank, that overviews the town of Northwich, and is their church, though a member, as I take it, of great Budworth parish.[3]

A far more pragmatic view is taken towards the end of the century (1694) when the well-travelled Celia Fiennes wrote:
> ...so to Northwich.... its not very large, its full of Salt works the brine pitts being all here and about and so they make all things convenient to follow the makeinge of salt, so that the town is full of smoak from the salterns on all sides.[4]

Both Smith and Webb suggest that Northwich was a grand and important town and yet this was a very small town, perhaps the smallest in the county, consisting of only six or seven acres. What then were the reasons for the town's importance? The chief reason has to be that it was one of the centres for the production of that indispensable product – salt. This industry, based on a brine pit on the banks of the River Dane, was fundamental to the prosperity of the town and, as one might expect of a business that was of considerable importance and of great value to those

INTRODUCTION

fortunate to share in it, the salt-making process was highly organised and regulated. But there were other aspects that contributed to the town's prestige.

Northwich was concentrated on a small plot of low-lying flat land at the confluence of the rivers Dane and Weaver and surrounded by the fields and meadows on the slopes of the neighbouring townships of Leftwich, Witton, Castle and Winnington. The town's underlying solid geology comprises of Lower Keuper Saliferous Beds from which brine was extracted. Above this, alluvium deposits run alongside the two rivers. The surrounding land comprises of deposits of boulder clay and glacial sands and gravels with alluvial and loamy soils once suited for grazing lands.[5] These soils meant that Northwich was surrounded by lands used primarily for pastoral activities and dairy farming: in fact the characteristic farm of the Cheshire countryside consisted of small dairy herds which from the late 14th century were kept for the purpose of producing cheese on a commercial basis. Northwich was encircled by an agricultural landscape, which was dotted with numerous small villages, hamlets and farmsteads, and so it was ideally situated to act as a focal point.

Geographically it was in the very heart of the county and at a point where the old Roman road from Chester to Manchester intersected routes to the north and south: in fact in 1654 the town was described as being 'a great thoroughfare'.[6] A mile or so to the east ran King Street, a Roman road connecting Wilderspool in the north with Chesterton in the south and having a direct link to London, which would have been an advantage to the many Northwich men who had business links with the capital. At this time the River Weaver was only suitable for small craft and goods of any substance had to be transported by road, but its importance as a transportation route to the port of Frodsham was being recognised in the 17th century.[7] Bills were introduced to make it navigable in 1663, 1670 and 1699, though work did not begin until 1732.[8] The town's position at the confluence of two of Cheshire's major rivers and a reliance on good road communications resulted in concerns for its bridges over the Dane and Weaver and also the bridge over the Witton Brook in Witton, such that local people often left bequests for their maintenance.

The central position of Northwich, as a hub of road links to other parts of the county, made it important as a trading centre. As an urban centre it had developed during the medieval period with a market and two annual fairs. Also, Northwich was regarded as a borough and had been since at least the 13th century, though the nature of its status and privileges is uncertain as no charter survives.[9] Apart from Chester, Northwich was one of 11 market towns. Considering the nature of the products sold at the market in the 14th century it does seem that it was a significant trading centre, and there is no reason to suppose that this was not still the case in the 17th century.[10]

The town was located in the north-west corner of the Northwich Hundred, one of the seven former administrative districts of Cheshire, and bordered the hundreds of Eddisbury and Bucklow. Within the hundred there were three other towns – Middlewich, Sandbach and Congleton, but Northwich's central position in the county and the fact that it was the hundredal town meant that it was 'oft allotted to the meetings of the chief governors in the county'. Indeed this was one of five locations at which Quarter Sessions were usually held throughout the century and until 1760.[11] Being a manor held by the powerful Earls of Derby, who for much of the 17th century held the post of Lord Lieutenant for the county, was probably another important factor in the town's reputation.

The 16th and 17th century writers seem to be correct in suggesting the importance of Northwich. But what was Northwich really like in those times? Who lived in the town and how did they earn their living? Who controlled the town's affairs and how were the townspeople governed? How was its famous salt industry organised? In the chapters that follow I hope to answer, at least in part, some of these questions.

---

[1] J. Leland, *Itinerary* (1769), vol. v, f.82.
[2] William Smith, in *King's Vale Royal*, quoted in Ormerod, i, p.137.
[3] William Webb's 'Itinerary of Northwich Hundred' (1621) published in King's *Vale Royal* (1656) may be found in G. Ormerod, *History of Cheshire*, iii,

INTRODUCTION

p.10.

[4] C. Morris, (ed.) *The Journeys of Celia Fiennes* (1947), p.224.

[5] Cheshire Historic Towns Survey, Vale Royal Borough, Part 1.

[6] *Calendar for the Committee for Compounding*, 1643-60, part I, 685.

[7] 'And if Encouragement were not wanting it might be made Navigable to the Sea by a river running through the Town there.' J. Collins, *Salt and Fisheries* (1682), p.2.

[8] J. Howard Hudson, *Cheshire 1660 – 1780: Restoration to Industrial Revolution* (1978), pp.129, 132.

[9] With some Cheshire towns these questions can be answered: Altrincham received a charter from Hugh de Mascy in 1290; Frodsham was founded by Earl Rannulf III of Chester in the first quarter of 13th century; Knutsford had a charter from Lord Tabley in 1292; Macclesfield received its borough charter in 1261 from Prince Edward, Earl of Chester; Stockport in the late 12th century from Robert de Stockport; and Tarporley had a charter in late 13th century. The people of Middlewich and Nantwich claimed burghal rights of ancient tradition, see Varley, J, *A Middlewich Chartulary*, Chetham Society (1941), p.105.

[10] The goods included corn, flour, cattle, sheep, goats, pigs, fleeces, hides, skins, fish, wine, clothing, nails, horseshoes, ploughclutes, tin, brass, copper, white glass and coloured glass. D. Sylvester and G. Nulty (eds.) *The Historical Atlas of Cheshire* (1958), p.26.

[11] The others being Chester, Knutsford, Middlewich and Nantwich.

1

A MEDIEVAL MISCELLANY

To place 17th century Northwich in context it is appropriate to consider what we know about the area during the medieval period. Overall there is little information so that what I have included in this chapter does not give a full picture. Rather it contains somewhat separate items of interest – hence, a medieval miscellany.

Before commencing one needs to remember that in mentioning Northwich I refer only to that small tract of flat land at the confluence of the rivers Dane and Weaver; a hundred yards or so around what we refer to today as the Bull Ring. Much of what is known as Northwich town today lies in what was the township and manor of Witton.

Domesday 'Norwich' and 'Witune'

The history of Northwich stretches back into Roman times. A fort, to control both the crossing of the River Weaver and the salt workings at the confluence with the River Dane, was established in the 70s AD on the high ground we now call Castle Hill. Archaeological excavations in the area have uncovered Roman artefacts including the remnants of Roman lead salt pans and a complete pan and other materials suggesting occupancy during the late first century and again during the second half of the second century.[1] It is not until the time of the Domesday Survey (1086) that we have any documentary evidence concerning the town. Whilst to reach back further is a matter of conjecture, the pages of the

Domesday Book do allow a retrospective glance at Northwich immediately before the Conquest. It seems that in the days of Edward the Confessor the salt industry in Cheshire was well established with a strict set of rules and regulations and significant penalties for those who transgressed. The clauses of Domesday record in particular detail the arrangements that governed this business and the revenues payable to both the King and Edwin, Earl of Mercia, who shared them in the ratio of 2:1. The main conditions applied to all three salt towns – Nantwich, Middlewich and Northwich – but Northwich had some laws that were peculiar to it.[2]

As a general rule between Ascension Day (40 days after Easter) and Martinmas (11 November) anyone who occupied or owned a wich-house was allowed to convey salt home for domestic use without any payment, but if he or she were to sell any of it then a toll had to be paid. Summer and autumn were times when salt was much in demand for salting slaughtered meat for preservation through the winter months. During the remainder of the year toll was paid whether or not it was to be used in the home or sold, probably in an effort to restrict the making of salt to particular times of the year and safeguard supplies for when it was most needed, or else to conserve winter fuel supplies. Additionally, and probably for similar reasons, between Martinmas and Ascension Day a payment was made by the owners or occupiers for each week that a wich-house was at work boiling brine, whereas for the rest of the year this was not normally the case. Payment was made every Friday in kind, amounting to 16 boilings, or just over one packload of salt and worth about 1s. However, those who worked wich-houses belonging to either the King or the Earl had to make this weekly payment throughout the year. Northwich though was somewhat different. Here those 'thanes' who held wich-houses were fortunate to be exempt from paying 'Friday boilings'.

Trade in salt was subject to a variety of tolls. Carriers who visited Middlewich and Nantwich paid 4d in toll for a large cart-load of salt (that is one with four or more oxen) and half as much for a smaller cart with two oxen. As regards using pack-horses a distinction was made between men from the local hundred and those from elsewhere, so that a local man paid ½d and the other 2d, likewise men on foot from the local hundred paid 1d for eight man-loads whereas a man from another hundred paid 2d. Again Northwich was somewhat different and specific mention is made of people coming from other counties rather than from another hundred. Such 'foreigners' paid 4d on a cart-load with two or more oxen, whereas a Cheshireman paid half this amount and was given three days' grace to make the payment or else incur a penalty of 40s. Likewise a packhorse load going outside Cheshire was charged at a penny whereas a Cheshire man paid ¼d by the third night. Any man from the Northwich Hundred who carted salt for sale in Cheshire paid a penny for each cart as he loaded it, but if he worked with horse-loads then he paid a penny for each load at the end of the season (11 November); failure to pay by that date cost him 40s.

The size of a load of salt was of crucial importance and the taking of excessive amounts was penalised. If a cart was so overloaded that the axle broke within a league (2½ miles) and the carter was caught then he was fined 2s. Similarly, if a horse was so overburdened that it collapsed, the same fine was charged. However, if anyone managed to get beyond the specified distance then he got away with it. If it could be proved that anyone departed from the salt town without paying what was due he or she could be brought back and fined: a freeman could be fined 40s and an unfree person 4s. If an individual managed to get beyond the county boundary then he was not brought back, but could be charged and penalised wherever he was found. So far as penalties for criminal offences committed within the bounds of the town were concerned, these were limited to 2s or 30 boilings of salt. Serious offences of murder and capital theft were dealt with as in the rest of the county, which might involve being condemned to death.

The differences between Northwich and the other two salt towns are somewhat puzzling. Part of the answer may lie in the fact that at Northwich ownership of salt-making rights had traditionally extended to men from manors in different hundreds – Dudestan (Broxton), Roelau (Eddisbury North), Tunendune (Bucklow West) Bochelau (Bucklow East) and Ati's Cross (just in North Wales but then part of Cheshire). (See *Fig. Two.*) Perhaps it was considered unreasonable to make a distinction between men from different hundreds; reasonable though to charge a higher rate for men from other counties. At both Middlewich and Nantwich ownership seems to have been limited to 'local' men, and therefore those coming from other hundreds were required to pay more. Also the income from these two salt towns was accounted for along with the hundredal revenues and seems to have been an integral part of the hundredal financial administration which might account for 'outsiders' being treated differently. It is also possible that Northwich had the more plentiful supply of brine and was regarded as being the main centre of distribution for Cheshire and elsewhere. If this is so, then that might be reason to restrict use in Middlewich and Nantwich by higher and seasonal tolls; certainly there were more restrictions on salt-making in those two towns in the 17th century.

The Cheshire saltways traced by means of place-name evidence seem to focus on Northwich and may also offer support to the theory that Northwich was the main trading centre in the early medieval period.[3]

From Northwich the route towards Chester and on into Wales crosses Saltersbrook by Saltersbridge at the bottom of Kelsall Hill. The route to Whitchurch passes Salterswell House at Tarporley. Saltersway and Salterswall in Over may equally refer to a route from Middlewich to Chester as any route south from Northwich. To the south-east there is a location known as Saltersford Bridge near Holmes Chapel. This crossing of the River Dane is referred to in 1331 when Edward III granted 'pontage' for five years on wares passing over the River Dane between Macclesfield and Middlewich to build a stone bridge at Saltersford.[4] This route not only went on to Middlewich but forked to lead across Rudheath to Northwich. From Stockport, Macclesfield and Congleton there are routes across the Pennines into Yorkshire and Derbyshire, indicated by places such as Saltersway, Saltersgate and Saltersford.[5] To the north there are locations known as Saltersgate and Salters Ford at Hindley and Pemberton near Wigan, where a man named Adam the Salter is recorded in 1291. Sixteenth century financial records of a family from the Wigan area show that there were regular trips to Northwich for salt.[6]

Returning to the Domesday clauses – the incomes from the salt trade and the many rules and regulations were not insignificant. Northwich

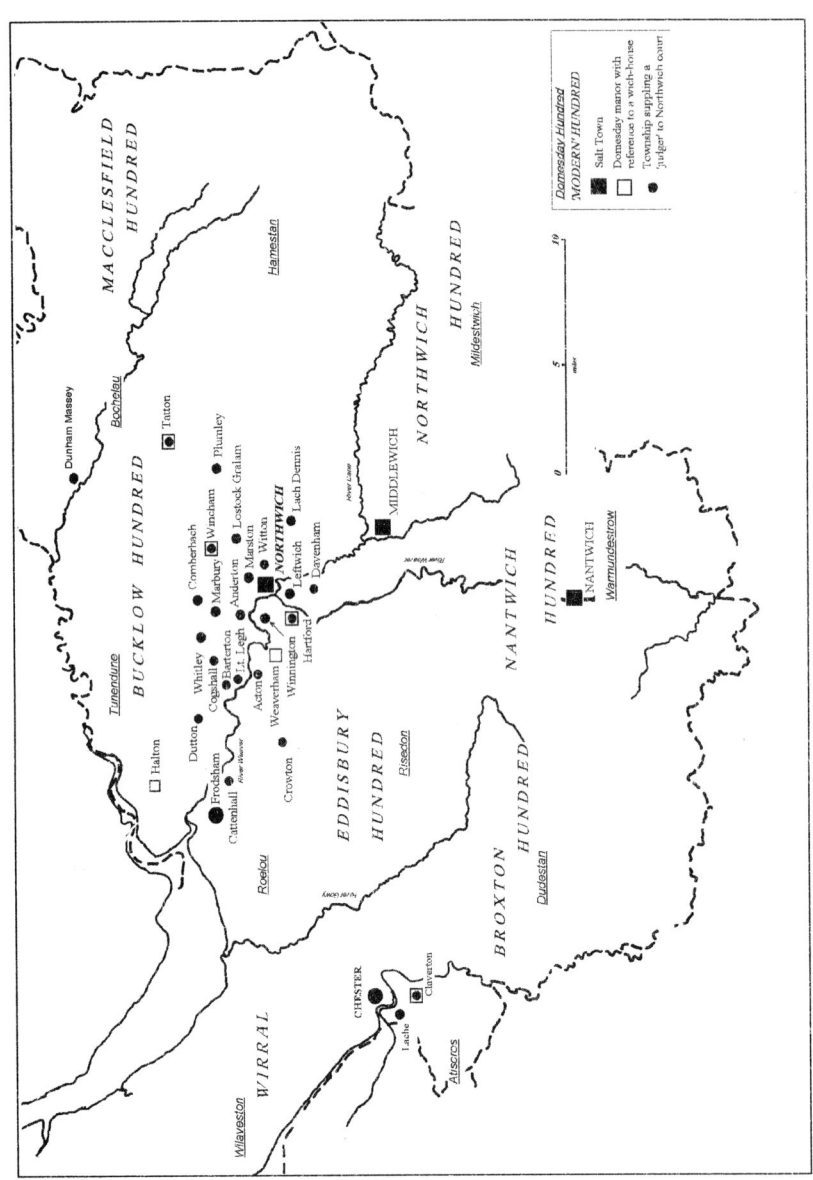

Figure Two: **Townships with ancient links to Northwich**

was said to have been worth £8 in the days of King Edward the Confessor, but was derelict or 'waste' when acquired by Earl Hugh, the first Norman Earl of Chester; by 1086 it was worth 35s. The town of Middlewich similarly rendered £8 in the days of King Edward, found to be waste by the Earl and then worth only 25s and two cartloads of salt. It is difficult to assess Nantwich's pre-Conquest value as it is given in conjunction with the pleas of the hundred as a total of £21. When Earl Hugh took possession of the town it was also described as being derelict, but there was one wich-house working: subsequently the Earl granted the town to one of his companions, William Malbank, for £10 a year. The references to the salt-towns being derelict needs some explanation. The term used in Domesday is 'waste'. Exactly what is meant by the scribe is uncertain and could mean anything from being devasted or derelict to the less drastic situation of simply being unproductive or unprofitable. A popular theory is that an estate which was 'waste' when acquired by its new Norman lord had suffered from King William's punitive raids through Cheshire in the winter of 1069-70. It may be the case that Northwich and Middlewich were destroyed by the Conquerors' army, with Nantwich less so, though I am inclinded to think that such a vital industry would not have been completely destroyed and that the term really means that there was no profit to be had from the salt-trade when acquired by the Earl.[7] Particularly interesting are the references to the ownership of the *salinae* – the wich-houses. At Nantwich we are told that the King and the Earl had between them eight *salinae*, that the Earl had another one to himself and that many local men had them too, but at Middlewich it seems that although these two great lords shared the revenues of the town they did not themselves hold any wich-houses. Likewise, at Northwich there is clear reference to the houses being held by 'thanes' – local lords. Whilst we are not given the names of the owners or occupiers of any of these wich-houses they may be inferred from other passages. Earl Edwin had seven houses in Northwich associated with his large manor of Weaverham and a further right to ½ a house with his manor of Frodsham. The lords of the manors of Halton, Hartford, Wincham, Tatton and Claverton had between them 5½ wich-houses, some of which are described as being unoccupied. It is quite likely that other local lords had interests in Northwich too for a number of wich-houses were associated with certain functionaries known as 'judgers'. These individuals performed service in the Earl's courts to advise and deliberate on legal and procedural matters, and their ownership of wich-houses was dependent upon performing this service. Later sources suggest that there were 'judgers' from the townships of Acton, Barterton (alluding to either Bartington or Barnton), Cattenhall (often listed incorrectly as Tattenhall), Claverton, Cogshall, Comberbach, Crowton, Dunham Massey, Dutton, Eaton, Hartford, Lach Dennis, Lache, Leftwich, Leigh, Little Witton, Lostock Gralam, Marbury, Marston, Plumley, Tatton, Winnington and Witton[8] (see *Fig. Two*). Of these, as already noted, three are specifically referred to in Domesday as having wich-houses, and of the others, Acton, Barterton, Dutton, Leigh and perhaps Lostock, formed part of the Weaverham estate; Comberbach, Dutton and Plumley were part of the Halton estate; and Crowton was part of the Frodsham estate. A similar situation existed at Middlewich for here there were judgers of Bostock, Brereton, Clive, Cranage, Croxton, Kinderton, Minshull Vernon, Newton, Occleston, Sandbach, Sproston, Stanthorne, Sutton, Tetton, Weaver and Wharton. Nantwich too had judgers.[9] Northwich then had at least 23 wich-houses in the immediate pre- and post-Conquest periods, but there is every reason to suppose, as with later times, that this was not the total number.

Despite the detailed entry there are omissions. Domesday does not tell us whether there was anything else besides wich-houses. Were there any dwellings? Was there a mill? Were there any people living here? The pages of Domesday are tantalising as they do not always give a complete picture, rather they tell us what the scribes needed to know about taxable property and who owned what. It is my belief that at this time Northwich consisted predominantly of wich-houses, or rather plots of land on which salt-making was carried out, with perhaps a few dwellings and workshops – it was in essence a small industrial enclave. The anonymous working population probably lived in neighbouring townships, such as Witton. In fact the place-name suggests just this – the *wīc-ton* – the wich-settlement.

The Domesday description of Witton is much simpler and follows the pattern of other Cheshire manors. Here a Saxon thane named Dot held 1½ hides of taxable property in the days of Edward the Confessor. A hide was originally a measure of land, some say about 120 acres, but by the time of King Edward it was an hypothetical unit of taxable wealth. The estate consisted of two ploughlands (a ploughland being a unit of land sufficient for working with a single plough) of which an anonymous Frenchman held one ploughland along with the services of a ploughman and a smallholder (*bordarius*): this suggests that half of the manor was unproductive. During Edward's reign the manor had been valued at 7s, but when acquired by the Earl of Chester and subsequently granted to its new lord, Gilbert Venables, it was described as 'waste' and no monetary value is given for 1086. Here in Witton there was a mill worth 3s; doubtless this was on the site of the one that existed right up until the 19th century. There is no reference to a wich-house here despite the fact that later sources refer to a 'judger's' house associated with the manor. However neighbouring Wincham, a manor also once held by Dot and then by Venables, did have a wich-house and it may be that this right was transferred or that there was some confusion at the time of writing the Domesday clauses: it is likely that the Wincham wich-house and the Witton judger's house were one and the same.

Of course Domesday only gives us glimpses of Northwich and Witton during the 1060s. There is every likelihood that a different picture emerged following William's accession and the rule of the Norman earls of Chester. For example, those who had wich-houses in Northwich prior to the Conquest may not have been so fortunate afterwards with many of the properties being given to new lords such as the local barons of Shipbrook (the Vernon family) and Kinderton. Although some tolls remained the same for centuries, there may have been some changes to the customary dues paid, especially since now the revenues were entirely in the hands of the Earls of Chester, rather than being split with the King as they were in pre-Conquest times. The very fact that the Domesday entry tells us that Northwich was 'waste' when acquired by the Earl and that by 1086 was worth 35s, suggests that re-organisation had been necessary and was achieved to some degree: the same is probably true of both Middlewich and Nantwich. The exact nature of the developments in the Norman period are not known to us now but there can be little doubt that reparation of such an important business as salt production would have been a priority. The development of Northwich from being a small industrial enclave to becoming a town with a resident population and a community of traders and craftsmen was in all probability a part of this same process.

The Medieval Town

Throughout the medieval period Northwich was regarded as a borough and its chief residents as burgesses; this had been so since at least the late 13th century. As there is no known charter – if there ever was one – the date of creation and the exact nature of its status and the privileges the people obtained is uncertain.[10] Boroughs were founded by either the crown or manorial lords in order to benefit from regular rents and other income associated with trade. So far as the residents were concerned they obtained a number of freedoms, or privileges, setting them apart from those subject to normal manorial controls. For example, burgesses had the right to sell or exchange their burgage plots or tenements, which enabled them to leave the town if they wished, unlike manorial tenants who were bound to their holdings and could not leave without the lord's consent. Burgesses had a degree of local government through their own assembly, or court, at which they were able to control affairs within the town and to elect their own officials. In some towns, especially the larger towns and cities, the burgesses were able to pay 'fee farm', an annual lump sum to cover the lord's income from rents, tolls and the profits of the courts and thus obtain full control over their own affairs. Certainly some borough aspects existed in Northwich, but the question is how long had this been so?

It may be the case that Northwich was regarded as a borough in Saxon times, and there are two reasons for this. First, in Domesday we are informed that the revenues were divided between the King and the Earl of Mercia in the ration 2:1 – a recognised burghal characteristic. Second, as already mentioned, a number of local lords had manorial appendages in pre-Conquest Northwich, which is another feature common to ancient boroughs. During these times it is likely that whilst the lord of

Northwich retained the mineral rights to the brine, he leased out the valuable manorial rights to make salt and freed the salt-makers from the manorial system, granting them special privileges and the right to trade. However, it is also likely that the creation of the borough was part of the post-Conquest improvements and re-vitalisation. During the rule of the Norman Earls of Chester, Northwich was part of their demesne and kept for their use and profit, and it is likely that borough status was granted during this time, perhaps during the time of the sixth Earl, Randolph Blundeville (1181-1232). It may have been created in order to keep tighter control on the production and trade in salt as it is apparent from later evidence that only those resident in Northwich were permitted to make salt. Additional franchises – the freedom to bake bread and to brew ale without licence – seem also to have been included.

A further alternative to these hypotheses is that both are true, in that burghal stutus existed in the pre-Conquest period for the purpose of salt production and its trade, with additional franchises being granted during the Norman era to enhance trading opportunities. It may be that Northwich was laid out during this latter period as a planned town and based upon the earlier semi-urban settlement associated with the salt industry. Only from the time of the borough's foundation did the market place become established along the main road leading from Castle to Witton, and following this the administrative buildings, shops and domestic dwellings would have been built.

It might be appropriate to suggest that Northwich's development mirrored that of Middlewich.[11] It has been suggested that Middlewich's history as a borough went through three phases. The first phase was in the late Saxon and early Norman period when the town was recognised as a place of importance as an urban and industrial enclave with different and specialised customs to those pertaining on the surrounding manors. During the second phase, which lasted for much of the medieval period, the traditional customs were formalised, perhaps with the issue of a charter which has been lost, or else through a series of occasional grants of privileges giving some immunity from normal manorial burdens: it is during this phase that the town's limited military obligation was recorded. The third phase extended from the late 14th century through to the

17th century. During this time the burgesses increased their trading privileges and gained a considerable degree of self-government in connection with the salt industry. The burgesses' power was however limited due to a controlling influence which could be exercised by the lord or his lessees, the farmers of the town. Whilst the burgesses may have at times held the farm for themselves and thus gained full independence, their failure to maintain the position allowed other interests to prevail. The burgesses of this period can be likened to the guilds which existed in many boroughs at this time – as a body of townsmen who were more interested in regulating the salt industry for their own benefit than seeking relief from seigneurial interference. As a result of this narrow interest with affairs of the salt industry full self-government was never achieved. What autonomy the townspeople had dwindled and died as the medieval organisation of the salt industry became no longer viable, due to external competition and new processes.

The first mention of burghal status is in 1288 when it was declared that Northwich was obliged to find twelve foot soldiers for war in Wales.[12] In 1376 the Black Prince, as Earl of Chester, granted burgesship to Richard Wirrall.[13] A weekly market (on Friday) and two annual fairs (22 July and 6 December) are known to have been held in the town and these would normally have required the issuing of a charter granting such rights – but none survives. In 1353 goods coming into the market were liable to tax in order to raise money for the rebuilding of the town bridge that had been destroyed by the floods two years earlier.[14] The goods included carcases of ox and cow; hides of horses, mares and bulls; fleeces and skins of lambs, kids, hares, rabbits, foxes, cats and squirrels; herrings, large fish, eels, lampreys and salmon; wine, cider and mead; cloth, canvas, worsted, tapestry and silk; iron, pitch, resin and tallow; fat, butter and cheese; onion seeds; shingles, timber, bark, roof nails, other nails; horseshoes; wooden dishes and platters; tin, copper, brass, lead; hemp and flax; jars of oil and salted herrings; coloured and white glass; and millstones and plough-clutes. Whether all of these goods appeared on the stalls at Northwich we do not know – it may have been a theoretical list covering all possibilities.

As with many manors and towns of royal or seigneurial estates held

Year	Value	Farmers
1295	£67	Hugh Northwich, Roger Toproud, Alan Acton
1301	£76	
1310	£73	Alan Acton, Roger Toproud, John Legh, William Gerard, William Venables, John Coton, Robert Bulkeley, James Weaverham
1318	£76	Roger Toproud
1330	£52	Hugh Venables, John Domville, Robert Huxley, Robert Bulkeley, Adam Bostock, Robert Wodehouse
1335	£58 13s	Richard Bulkeley, Adam Parker, Peter Calveley
1339	£60	William Glasebrook, Richard Roer
1343	£57	Richard Bulkeley, Roger Bulkeley, Hugh Toproud
1346	£60	Roger Starkey, Richard Bulkeley, John Winnington, Hugh Toprod
1350	£37 3s	Not let to farm
1353	£46 8s	Not let to farm
1354	£64 9s 5½d	Not let to farm
1358	£66	Granted to Sir Richard deStafford for life
1376	£66	Granted to Sir John Holland for life

Table One: **Some of the Farmers and Valuations of Northwich**

in demesne the revenues of Northwich were 'farmed', or leased, to anyone prepared to take on the responsibility for a fixed payment over a fixed period of time. During the reign of Edward the Confessor the 'farm' was valued at £8. Occasionally there are references to Northwich in the royal records of the time. Northwich is referred to in the Pipe Rolls as being let to farm along with Middlewich for £18 9s in 1184/5, but by 1237/8 Northwich rendered £50 whereas Middlewich realised £67.[15] In the following year the accounts refer to pardon for payments by the people of the town amounting to £10 on the grounds of their poverty. With the death of John le Scot in 1237 the earldom of Chester with the lordship of Northwich passed to the crown and eventually became part of the demesne of the successive Princes of Wales. From time to time the town, with the profits from the mills and courts was leased out to various local families. In 1239/40, Northwich raised only £12 10s and

Middlewich £16 15s, with further mention of £8 17s and £8 6s respectively. The reason for this decline in value is not recorded but may be due to some disaster befalling the towns such as major flooding or fire, both of which were regular threats to the salt business. The first of these two dangers occurred frequently (and still does) when heavy rainfall causes the waters of the River Dane to flow over the banks just prior to the confluence with the River Weaver. The other danger – fire – was as a consequence of the salt-making process which necessitated many fires burning in order to boil the brine, and the closeness of the numerous wattle, daub and thatch buildings in which the process was carried out. Other aspects of Northwich's normal business were also affected by these disasters. In 1240/1, 8s 10d was spent on repairs to the lord's bake-house, or oven.[16] Occasionally, the constituent parts of the manor – tolls, mill, court, oven – were divided and separately farmed. During periods when the town was administered directly by the Earl, either because no suitable farmers had come forward or it was expedient to do so, these aspects were individually accounted for. For the year 1350/51 the water-mill produced £8 10s 9½d; court perquisites, from the twenty-five sessions held, realised £13 18s 7d; various tolls brought in a further £21 17s 2¼d; and lastly the oven a modest 2s 5d: a total of £44 8s 11¾d. The previous year the total income had been some £4 less and this we are told was in part due to the mill being in need of repair and that only a few people were using the oven 'as the tenants are dead from the pestilence' – the Black Death.[17] The tolls charged in the town have some curious names: 'Axstuth' and 'Carterstuth' which by their names seem to be a throw back to the Domesday tolls on the carriage of salt by packhorse and cart; 'stuth' a more general form of toll paid by carters who brought turf and brushwood into the town for sale; 'ernesilver' paid by merchants buying salt and 'kingesmol' a chief rent paid on the occupation of wich-houses.

Who the farmers of the pre-Conquest and early Norman period were is lost to us, as what few records there are merely list the income generated. Whilst, early on, the townspeople may have obtained the farm of Northwich for themselves allowing them an amount of self-government, it is apparent that this did not remain the case, though the local farmers of the 14th century may well have been later representatives of that body. A little is known about the various early farmers, or lessees, of the town from the reign of Edward I. In 1274/5, the farm of Northwich was held by Geoffrey Biron, who gave the nuns at Chester an annuity of 24 marks (£16) out of the issues of Northwich. When Biron took religion and became a monk, the farm was passed to Vale Royal Abbey and the King consequently assigned the alms due to the nuns from the profits of Middlewich instead.[18] In 1294/5, James Pull and Richard Bradwell were named as the King's bailiffs for the town and in the following year Hugh son of Geoffrey of Northwich, Roger Toproud and Alan Acton had a lease of the town for £67: in 1301 this figure rose to £76. Ten years later, nine men – Alan Acton, Roger Toproud, John Legh, William Gerard, William Venables, John Coton, Robert Bulkeley and James Weaverham, jointly had the farm for one year at £73. The value of Northwich declined somewhat as the 14th century progressed, maybe due to the general economic decline of the period, but there can be little doubt that in Northwich, as before, the ever-present threats of floods and fire were the cause.[19]

On 16 March 1308, the Abbot of Vale Royal 'former farmer of Northwich' (in fact he was farmer from at least 1301 until 1307) was acquitted a debt of £25 2s by reason of damages he had sustained, 'through no fault of his own' caused by the burning of his wich-houses.[20] Further information on this matter states that the fire broke out between two wich-houses and due to a strong north wind quickly spread to engulf a total of 65 houses.[21] Conflagration is also known to have struck in 1438 and again in 1583 when Northwich was 'most miserably consumed with fire'. In 1347/8 measures were taken to safeguard the salt workings from the rising waters of the Dane.[22]

During the first half of the 14th century the name of Bulkeley frequently occurs as farmers of the lordship of Northwich in conjunction with representatives of the local families of Toproud, Starkey, Venables, Bostock and Winnington for sums that normally varied between £50 and £60 (see *Table One*). In 1334/5, the farm of Northwich, together with that of Middlewich was held by Richard Bulkeley, Adam Parker and Peter Calveley.[23] The Bulkeley family was often involved in disputes with the Abbey of Vale Royal. In October 1320, Roger Bulkeley of Northwich along with the Winnington brothers – Robert, John, William, Lawrence and Roger – and others, continuously beset Brother John Lewis, a monk of Vale Royal, threatening to cut his head off.[24] Their disputes may have had something to do with the fact that the Abbey had at one time held the farm of the town and also held property in the town.

During the troubled rule of Edward the Black Prince as Earl of Chester, the town was certainly under direct management in order to gain as much revenue as possible. With the onset of the Black Death (1349) leasing of the Black Prince's Cheshire estates ceased and they were directly administered by his officials and remained under his control during the 1350s including the years prior to the risings against him in 1353: for much of this time William Bateson was the Earl's bailiff and manager of Northwich.[25] The violence of these times is born out by the case of Hugh Feremon, alias Hugh Hammeson, and the Starkey family. Hugh was the Earl's bailiff and chamberlain of Northwich in the early 1350s. His name is interesting for if he was according to his name a ferryman this would suggest a regular service across the River Weaver in addition to the Town Bridge which was often swept away or in need of repair.[26] In the spring of 1353 Hugh was killed by local men – Peter, Richard and John Starkey and John Draper – who were indicted and outlawed for his killing. Following the payment of a fine of 40 marks (£26 13s 4d) these men were pardoned on 12 November 1354. Another member of the Starkey family, William son of Roger, was indicted for the slaying of John Feremon but pardoned in April 1354, and two others, Thomas and John were bound over to keep the peace towards the Earl's ministers and tenants and Hugh's widow, Ciceley, in July 1353.[27] Whilst the reasons behind these killings were connected with the overall political situation in Cheshire, one might suppose that as the Starkey family had been regular farmers of the town they were aggrieved at the new arrangements and violently opposed to any strict enforcement of the rules and regulations aimed at enriching the Earl's coffers. Following Feremon's death, William Bateson was appointed to the office of bailiff and chamberlain and was rewarded for his services to the Earl 'since the pestilence'.[28]

Following these disastrous episodes the policy of granting the farm to local men ceased and on 1 October 1358 the town and all its profits, worth £66 a year, were subject of a life-time grant to Sir Richard Stafford, one of the Black Prince's personal friends.[29] The message seems not to have got through to the Earl's officials in Northwich as quickly as it might for the profits were withheld from Stafford for nearly 12 months. In clarification of the grant to Stafford, mention was made that should the mills be thrown down by flood then they would be repaired at the Earl's expense, but that any improvements were to be at Stafford's cost, though he was allowed to use timber taken from Delamere forest: in fact repairs were made to the 'were', baye' and 'dam'. Where was this mill? Unfortunately almost nothing is known. We do know that the mill in Northwich was a water-mill and that it was regularly in need of repair. In 1349/50 the mill was unserviceable for half a year and £13 had to be spent in repairing it and its pond. Ten years later a further £14 was spent when 'divers carpenters, sawyers and other workmen' were employed on repairs to the mill and pond.[30] There can be little doubt that the mill stood on the banks of the River Dane and not far from the brine pit, for in 1347/8 money was spent 'about the mill pond and for transmitting the water of Davene lest it should destroy the saltpit there'.[31] It is likely therefore, that the mill stood on the banks of the River Dane somewhere in the vicinity of an area known as 'Crume Hill', near the location of the modern Cheshire County Council offices. By the 16th century a horsemill had been established near to 'Crume Hill' – had the regular threat of flooding had caused the water mill to be abandoned? The Town Bridge, which spanned the Weaver, regularly suffered from the pressure produced as the Dane and Weaver converged. In 1351 flood waters carried the bridge away and 14 years later it was described as being in a 'very ruinous state and in need of urgent repair'. On both occasions local taxes, known as 'pontage' and 'pavage', were raised for maintenance purposes.[32]

After Stafford's death, Richard II granted the town to Sir John Holland for life in 1380/1. He was a personal favourite of the King and was made Earl of Huntingdon and, later, Duke of Exeter. The mill seems to have caused this new lord of the town a few problems for in 1390 and

1391 warrants were issued for delivery of timber to repair the mill pond and the mill itself. In 1396 Holland granted the lordship of the town to a local dignitary, Sir Richard Winnington for eight years at £55 a year. He was followed by Hugh Winnington, then, for the remainder of Henry IV's reign, by Sir Lawrence Marbury and then Sir Peter Dutton. Despite one or two complications in the right to title the Holland family remained the paramount lords of Northwich. According to the *inquisition post mortem* of Elizabeth Holland, Countess of Huntington, which was held in 1426, the manor of Northwich included rents from numerous tenements, the profit known as 'kingesmol', various town tolls, court perquisites and the profits of the grain mill and the common oven. Eventually, in 1484, the Hollands were succeeded by the powerful Stanley family when Richard III granted the town to Sir Thomas, Lord Stanley and his son George, Lord Strange. From this time until the 18th century this family, later the Earls of Derby, were lords of Northwich.[33]

So much for the lords of the manor of Northwich. With regard to those involved in producing salt and owning property in the town there is less to tell. There were many burgage properties along what we know as High Street and even more wich-houses in the side-streets, all of which were held by many individuals and religious institutions. Among the lay proprietors were the major land-owning families of Vernon, Venables, Warburton, Bulkeley, Dutton, Done, Winnington and Leftwich. There are a few references to some of the owners and occupiers of these properties in the medieval period. The earliest that I have so far found is dated circa 1295 and refers to a grant made by William Toft (ancestor of the Holford family) to John Tarbock of a wich-house along the banks of the Dane and bordering onto 'gromhyll'(1).[34] In 1321 Margaret daughter of Henry Houghton granted to John Pavor a wich-house for 8s a year.[35] Sixty years later Hugh Rued, chaplain, passed on his rights and interest in a messuage and a wich-house which he had from John Eddeson,[36] and on 6 April 1372, he permitted William Houghton to deliver possession of a messuage and wich-house to Alice, daughter of Robert Twembrokes (no doubt with a name like that he lived in Witton).[37] In 1390 Roger son of Hugh Draper quitclaimed to Roger Houghton a wich-house and a shop.[38] During the 14th century John

Stevene gave John son of Hugh Feremon of Northwich a wich-house that lay between those of Henry, son of Stephen, and Richard Bigge.[39] A John Steven is also mentioned in 1366 as having a wich-house that bordered one granted by Richard Vernon of Lostock to John Tarbock.[40] In 1459 the manor of Kinderton was described as having five houses in Northwich and half the profits of the leadsmithy. Occasionally the descent of some wich-houses can be traced from the medieval period.[41] In 1505 Thomas Fovell of Middlewich granted his son John a wich-house in Northwich which was occupied by Roger Walton. Fifty years later this same house was leased by the Fovells to Richard Walton, his wife Elizabeth and Robert their son for 46s a year. It was described as lying between the wich-houses of Roger Horton of Coole and Lawrence Winnington of Hermitage, and between Yate Street to the south and Little Street to the north. In 1586, by which time the ownership had passed by marriage from the Fovells to the Venables family, John, son of Robert Walton, was granted a 21-year lease following the death of his father. The Waltons remained as lessees throughout the 17th century despite the fact that the ownership again changed hands to the Shakerleys of Hulme.[42]

A number of religious houses had interests in Northwich. These were Norton Priory, Basingwerk Abbey, Whalley Abbey, the Hospital of St John of Jerusalem and nearby Vale Royal Abbey. In 1334 Vale Royal held two wich-houses worth 40s a year which were associated with their manor of Weaverham, another worth 20s which had been purchased from Randolph Swetbrun, and a burgage property worth an annual rent of 8s bought from Hugh Northwich, clerk.[43] Despite fluctuations in value, these same three properties were said to be worth £3 3s in 1509.[44] During the reign of Edward I (1277-1307) Lucas Northwich granted a messuage, which lay between those of himself and Pymme Herneway, to William Dutton, who then gave it to Stanlow Abbey which later transferred to Whalley.[45] About the same time Dutton also gave a wich-house to Norton Priory.[46]

A number of enquiries into the affairs of the town were held during the time of the Black Prince. In 1351 the Prince issued an order to enquire into the holdings of the Hospital of St John which had been subdivided into separate parcels each with a tenant who each claimed a right to the franchise of the whole. The enquiry had to examine whether these tenants might carry out trades such as brewing or baking. At this time the inhabitants of neighbouring townships were going round selling their beer at a cheaper price than that brewed in the town. An enquiry into the damages caused to the Earl's and the burgesses' income by this, and it was declared that no one was allowed to brew ale within three leagues of the town as the lord was entitled to 6d each time beer was brewed in Northwich and 3s 11d a year from each brewster.[47] Similarly bread could not be baked in the surrounding townships either. An enquiry into the bounds of Northwich was also ordered so that it might be clear at what point people entered the town and were then liable to pay various dues and tolls including passage – 4d for a cart and 2d for a loaded horse. The following year there was an enquiry into the payment of toll by merchants visiting 'frewichhouses' who claimed that they were exempt no matter where they came from.[48] The Duke of Lancaster seems to have appealed this matter for he claimed that all who bought salt at his house called 'le Whiteleghwichous' ought to be free from paying toll and this was upheld.[49]

So far as the day-to-day administration of the town and affairs of the people are concerned these are discernible through the few remaining medieval court rolls. In these there are frequent references to the issues from tolls, taxes, use of the lord's oven and mill and market stalls and mention of women regularly paying for licences to brew ale. Payments for the right to take a lease of a wich-house and to brew salt occur often, as do fines paid by the 'judgers' failing to appear at court and of men causing obstruction, along with complaints of debt, trespass and assault. These courts were held before the lord's steward: men such as John Coton in 1329, William Starkey in 1399, Robert Castell in 1402, John Legh in 1403 and Henry Ravenscroft in the early days of Henry V's reign. Serious offences were dealt with by the county court and here again the Starkey family makes an appearance. William son of Lawrence Starkey of Northwich killed Richard Winnington with a club in the town on 20 October 1460: Lawrence and William son of Robert Starkey were also implicated.[50]

The Tudor Period

In the 1520s, whilst the Earl of Derby was a minor, the town was temporarily in the hands of Henry VIII. It came to the attention of the King's ministers that a number of gentlemen and others were making salt contrary to the customs of the town in that they were not residents of the town. An enquiry in the Court of Wards held on 20 July 1527 heard from a number of witnesses who confirmed that the custom was that only residents could produce salt. Even those who lived in neighbouring Witton and Hartford had to become Northwich residents; one witness, Oliver Walton, aged over 60 years, stated that he remembered Hukin Yate of Witton building himself a mansion in the town so that he might make salt. Other witnesses spoke of local people either moving into the town or else transferring the right to make salt to someone who was a resident. Perhaps as contrary argument, a list of ten 'forrayne' occupiers of salt houses from 1492 was admitted into the proceedings. Following this hearing, which upheld the rule, instructions were issued to the effect that anyone who transgressed was to be taken before the county court at Chester to be punished and reformed.[51] If members of the local gentry and yeoman stock, such as Hukin Yate, went to much expense to become Northwich residents, and some were trying to use other means to obtain a share in the business then, clearly, the salt trade was recognised as being a lucrative and profitable enterprise.

With the coming of the Tudors the surviving historical evidence for Northwich improves: there is much more information on the owners and occupiers of wich-houses, of the rules and regulations governing the town and information on the people who lived and worked there. In this period the names of families who occur frequently in the next century begin to appear in the records; names such as Bromfield, Done, Holford, Leftwich, Norcott, Pavor, Pickmere, Tarbock, Walton, Winnington and Yate in Northwich, and Golbourne, Hewitt, Mottershead, Pownall, Rowe, Sudlow and Venables in Witton.[52] Of particular relevance in identifying names are the Muster Rolls and the Subsidy Rolls. The Muster Roll for 1548 lists men between the ages of 16 and 60 who might be liable for military service, the equipment they possessed and whether or not they were fit to serve[53] (see *Appendix One*). The imposition of lay subsidies in 1593 produced records of people over the age of 16 who merited taxation: for Northwich the names of nine individuals are listed and for Witton just three[54] (see *Appendix One*).

A number of grants of wich-houses are evident from this time and during the early years of Elizabeth's reign we get the first list of people engaged in the salt industry – the owners and occupiers of wich-houses (see *Appendix Two*). Henry VIII's dissolution of the monasteries meant that the conventual wich-houses changed hands and enriched those members of the local gentry who were already profiting from the salt trade. In 1544 Thomas Dutton obtained three wich-houses, occupied by Gilbert Dutton and once the property of Vale Royal Abbey, which he subsequently transferred to Hugh Starkey of Olton.[55] Letters Patent dated 3 August 1543 were issued in favour of John Deane, clerk, granting him a number of wich-houses once owned by Basingwerk Abbey.[56] The grant consisted of two wich-houses occupied by first William Sudlow and then by Thomas Sudlow; another two occupied by George Sudlow; the 40 'weightes' of lead in those houses, and a messuage in the occupation of Thomas Bromfield. According to Deane's will dated 16 April 1563, three of these houses were bequeathed to his kinsman, another John Deane, son of Richard.[57] Other grants and transfers of property occur involving the families of Venables, Leycester and Starkey.

Despite the impression one might have of a 'built-up' town consisting of many houses, shops and wich-houses, there were some open spaces. Something of the nature of Northwich's early topography can be gleaned from the fact that in 1448 there is mention of gardens in the town and in 1533 Edmund Peckham, one of Queen Elizabeth's councillors, was granted a croft in Northwich known as 'Shawes crofte', which had once been the property of Norton Abbey.[58] One of the access points to the River Weaver was alongside the 'Kiln Orchard'. The variety of buildings is perhaps indicated by a grant from Piers Leycester to John Starkey of five wich-houses, two shops, two chambers, a stable and a parcel of land.[59]

[1] J.B. Curzon, 'Paying for the Invasion' *Cheshire History*, vol 40 (2001) pp.2-11; *The Book of Northwich* (1993), pp, 17-21.

[2] *DB*, ref. S1, S2, S3. For a full commentary on Domesday Cheshire and transcriptions of the entries relating to the 'Wiches' see Harris, B E. & Thacker, A.T., (eds) *A History of the County of Cheshire*, vol I, (1987) pp. 293-391, hereafter *VCH Cheshire*.

[3] For a discussion on the Saltways: W.B. Crump, 'Saltways from the Cheshire Wiches', *Lancashire and Cheshire Antiquarian Society*, vol. 40 (1939), pp. 84-101.

[4] *CPR (1330-34)*, p. 170.

[5] D. Hey, *Packmen, Carriers and Packhorse Roads* (1980), pp. 152-159.

[6] Crump, p. 89.

[7] *VCH Cheshire*, p. 336.

[8] Cattenhall is a hamlet on the banks of the Weaver, in the township of Kinglsey and near to Frodsham. Tattenhall near Chester is unlikely as in the Domesday period this manor was held by William Malbank, the lord of Nantwich, any service due from this township would be due there and not in Northwich.

[9] *Cal Inq, II*, p. 478.

[10] With some Cheshire towns these questions can be answered: Altrincham received a charter from Hugh de Mascy in 1290; Frodsham was founded by Earl Rannulf III of Chester in the first quarter of 13th century; Knutsford had a charter from Lord Tabley in 1292; Macclesfield received its borough charter in 1261 from Prince Edward, Earl of Chester; Stockport in the late 12th century from Robert de Stockport; and Tarporley had a charter in late 13th century. The people of Middlewich and Nantwich claimed burghal rights of ancient tradition see Varley, J, *A Middlewich Chartulary*, Chetham Society, new series, 105.

[11] What follows in this paragraph is a brief summary of the conclusions of the late J. Varley in *A Middlewich Chartulary* pp 15-34.

[12] R. Stewart-Brown (ed.), *Calendar of County Court, City Court and Eyre Rolls of Chester,1259-1297, with an Inquest of Military Service*, Chetham Soc., N.S., vol 84 (1925), p.111.

[13] Orm. *III*, p.157.

[14] Market goods.

[15] *Pipe Rolls*, pp 13, 35.

[16] *Lib Rolls 1240-45*, p. 21.

[17] *Ch Ch Acc.*, pp. 129, 182, 183.

[18] *Pat Rolls, 1272-81*, p. 246.
[19] H.J. Hewitt, 'Mediaeval Cheshire', *Chetham Society*, n.s. 88, (1929), p.118
[20] *C Cl R, 1307-13*, p. 103.
[21] *C Inq Misc*, ii, 1308-48, p.7.
[22] Hewitt, p. 118.
[23] *36 Rep. D.K.*, app 2, p. 486.
[24] *VRLB* p. 50.
[25] *Ch Ch Acc*, p.129, *et seq.*
[26] *Ch Ch Acc*, pp 207, 222. *Pontage* was charged on persons crossing the bridge to help with the cost of repairs.
[27] *BPR, III*, 1351-65, pp. 104, 155.
[28] *BPR III*, 1351-65, p. 230.
[29] *BPR III*, 1351-65, p. 323.
[30] *Ch Ch Acc*, pp. 129, 251, *et seq.*
[31] *ibid*, p. 124.
[32] *BPR III*, 1351- 65, pp. 47, 475.
[33] Ormerod, III, pp.158-9.
[34] CRO: DCH/J/134.
[35] CRO: DLT/A/2/10b.
[36] CRO: DLT/A/2/11.
[37] DRO: D3155/CROXALL XI.
[38] CRO: DLT/A/2/35.
[39] John Rylands catalogue no. 456.
[40] CRO:DCH/J/134.
[41] CRO: DLT/B/1-7.
[42] CRO: DSS/1/1/50/10.
[43] *VRLB*, p. 113.
[44] *VRLB*, p. 192.
[45] Ormerod, *III*, P.160.
[46] CRO: DLT/B/1-7.
[47] *BPR, III*, p.48.
[48] *BPR, III*, p.55.
[49] *BPR, III*, pp 172, 210.
[50] B.E. Harris & D.J. Clayton, *Criminal Procedure in Cheshire in the Mid-Fifteenth Century, T.H.L.S.C.*, 128 (1978), pp.163/4.
[51] Calvert p. 1075.
[52] See Subsidy Roll, 35 Eliz. CRO: DVE/NIII, 6-10; and Muster Roll, 1548, PRO: SP/10.

[53] PRO: SP10/3.
[54] CRO: DVE/1/NIII.
[55] CRO: DLT/A/2/22-25; CPR, 1547-53, p 270. These printed calendars refer to 'salt pits' whereas there can be little doubt that the translation should read salt-houses, or wich-houses.
[56] CPR, 1547-53, p.57.
[57] CPR, 1563-66, p.19.
[58] CPR, 1553-54, p.153.
[59] CRO: DLT/2/26a. Deed dated 1571.

2

THE TOWN

The Town of Northwich

Seventeenth century Northwich can be described as an amalgam of three distinct areas: residential, commercial and industrial. The first of these, situated on the western bank of the River Weaver and below Castle and Winnington Hill, contained several residential properties, yards, gardens and a stable, all owned and occupied by the affluent Northwichians.[1] This area was connected to the rest of the town by the Town Bridge. Along the highway that ran from the bridge to Witton lay the burgage plots that were the dwelling houses, shops, inns and public buildings that formed the borough and the heart of the town's commercial activity. The industrial area lay to the east and south of this road (High Street) where there were a number of parallel streets along which stood the numerous wich-houses for which Northwich was famous. A map of part of the town drawn in the first quarter of the 17th century, and probably circa 1610, shows a compact area with a rectangular grid based on the Market Place and its extension that led towards Witton to the north-west[2] *(see Fig. Three)*.

The different ways in which the building plots of the town are drawn on the map are somewhat baffling. Some are shown with a gable-end facing the street; some seem to be side-on and drawn in such a way as to indicate a sloping roof, sometimes with a chimney; whilst others are shown as a simple rectangle with a little door or gate; and then there are

THE TOWN

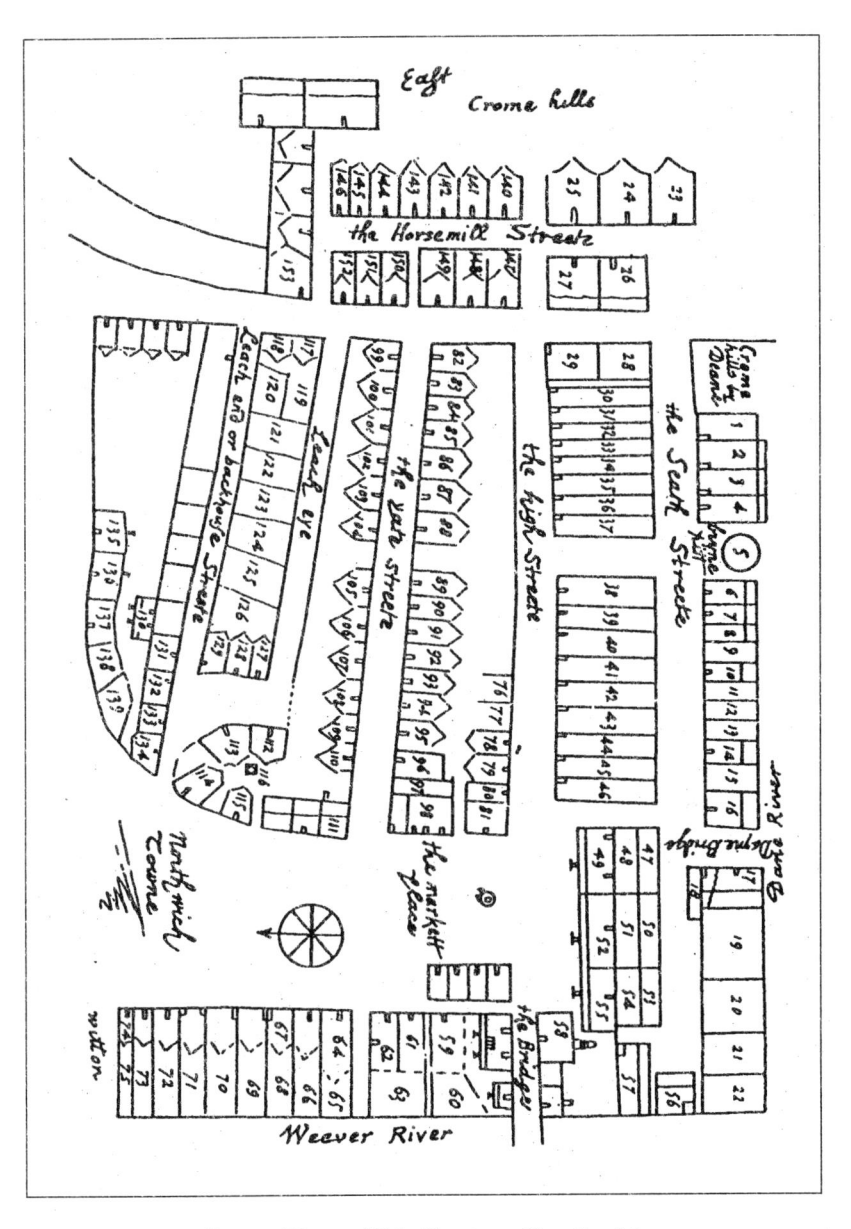

Figure Three: **17th Century Northwich**

what appear to be empty plots of land. The suggestion that those without pointed roofs are the wich-houses is not correct.[3] The 'Leach Eye' depicted on the map was a watercourse that some residents were obliged to keep 'open and purged' alongside which ran a narrow street, later known as Little Street.[4] Some sources suggest that Little Street continued on into what is shown on the plan to be Horsemill Street, and that the parallel un-named thoroughfare was Horsemill Street.[5] By the end of the century some of the street names had changed: the extension of Market Place became High Street, and the old High Street became Church Street; Yate Street became Apple Market Street; Leach End became Swine Market Street, and the Leach Eye became Little Street then Fagg Lane and finally Davies Street.[6] The long, unnamed thoroughfare, running north-south, became Crown Street, and Horsemill Street became Cross Street. All these street names have survived until very recently.

The plan details 170 plots of which 153 are listed in an accompanying schedule (see *Appendix Three*). Particular features of the 17th century town are: the brine-pit (salt-pit) on the banks of the River Dane (5); the Horsemill (23); the Court House (58), the House of Correction (61); the Swan (64); the shops (98); the leadsmithy (114), and the bakehouse (128) (see *Fig. Three*).[7] Of particular note in the Market Place (now the Bull Ring) is an 'island' of four properties – were these shops or market stalls? Also a curious circular symbol – does this represent a market cross or perhaps the town bell?

Northwich's eastern boundary and the banks of the River Dane are marked as areas known as 'Crome hills' (the normal spelling would seem to be 'crum' - heap of earth or rubbish). These were areas of wasteland where ashes from the wich-houses and other refuse, garbage and urban soils were deposited so as to form a barrier against flooding. So important were these areas that town ordinances prohibited the erection of cottages or any other form of improvement.[8] Being sited on the flood plains of the Dane and Weaver, the town has always been very prone to flood in the winter months and until very recently this has been a major threat to property: during the 17th century there are references to damage being caused to wich-houses by flooding.[9] In 1655, due to heavy rain there were great floods in many parts of Cheshire which caused much damage, 'but in Northwiche where Weever and Dane did meete ytt did far more harme'.[10]

Unfortunately the plan and schedule omit the 'residential' area on the west bank of the river. However, extracts from a written survey of dwelling houses made in 1606, about the time the map was drawn, allow a reconstruction of this section of the town.[11]

According to the survey, a traveller entering Northwich from Castle would pass by the 'Lodporne Stone' which marked the boundary. The first house on the left, the west side of the road, was a substantial house held by William Pickmere from the Sutton family; this was later the mansion house owned by Dr Bentley. Next door lived William Leftwich who had a house, yard and garden as well as the next plot on which Justice Peter Warburton had erected a stable and other outbuildings. Next came the house, 'fair yard' and garden owned by Hugh Winnington of Hermitage and let to the Justice. Hugh Winnington also owned the next plot which he let to George Winnington. The next two houses were both owned by Robert Venables of Antrobus and were let to Robert Winnington and William Helsby. The 'Survey' then goes on to mention other dwellings that are on the other side of the Town Bridge, and the points of access through the building plots to the River Weaver. Close to the Town Bridge, to the north of the bridge foot, Peter Venables had three houses: one he let to Raphe Cheney and the other two to William Mere who sub-let to William Swinton and Sir George Leycester. Between these latter two properties there was a 'way leading to the River of Weevir for the Town people to carry Water through at all times and especially in the time of danger of Fyre'. There was another such way between the lands of Ralph Leftwich and the house known as the 'Old Swan'. Another house (53), on the other side of the bridge foot, was owned by Thomas Bromfield of Witton and occupied by a Robert Pickmere and his daughter Joan. Next came the Earl of Derby's court-house (58) with a prison underneath and this we are told was adjoining the 'Town house'. To the south of the court building was another road leading to the river. Near here was a house (49) owned by William Allen of Rostherne and later occupied by John Broome which was then described as being near to the 'Red Lion'. The survey now mentions four properties that are not located along the main highway, but within what I term the 'industrial' area. First of these is Ralph Leftwich's 'antient house' that was once in the ownership of the order of St John of Jerusalem which is likely to be a wich-house along High Street (36). Mention is then made of the leadsmithy (114) held by Peter Venables and Julius Winnington; then the horsemill (23) owned and occupied by Peter Pavor, and finally the Earl's bakehouse (128). The court-house, prison, leadsmithy, horsemill and bakehouse can be identified on the town plan as they are referred to in the schedule (see *Appendix Three*).

The survey is incomplete; indeed the copy says that it is 'observations concerning some dwelling houses'. Another extract from the survey, found among the surviving papers of the Leycester family in the Cheshire Record Office, states that after the Lodporne Stone, on the west side, Peter Leycester of Tabley had a house and a fair garden with a way to the River Weaver and that this property was inhabited by a widow Hickock and then by John Leigh. On the north side of Little Street, Leycester had a house which had been converted into a cow house and used by John Stones who retained a part of it as a bed chamber! Leycester also had a house which had been newly repaired by George Broome (133). Before Broome, this property had once been occupied by Hugh Ditchfield, the husband of the previous occupier's daughter. On the north-west part of Market Street, Leycester owned a shop with a chamber above it occupied by Ralph Bradshaw and his wife.[12] Also among these documents there is a crude late 17th century sketch map of the five streets – Seath Street, High Street, Yate Street, Little Street and Swine Market – all running parallel to the River Dane, and off what is then called 'The Market Stret'.[13]

A map from the next century provides a full picture of Northwich.[14] This map (see *Fig. Four*), drawn to scale in 1793, compares well with the earlier one and would suggest that the total town plan had probably survived in this form for many centuries. Indeed the layout continued on into the 19th century and still exists in the modern town layout[15] *(see Fig Six)*. It shows and names four of the parallel streets as Seath Street, Church Street, Apple Market Street and Swine Market Street. These

THE TOWN

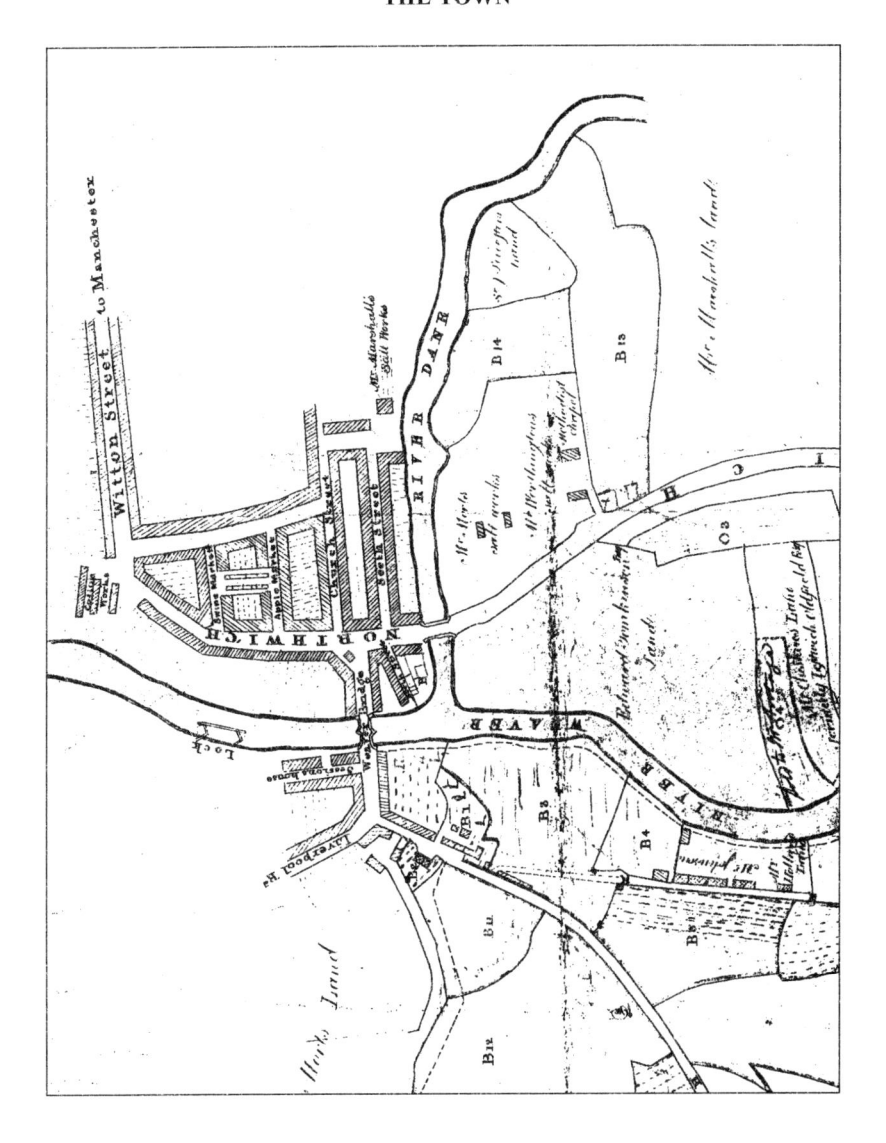

Figure Four: **Late 18th Century Northwich**
*(From a Map of the Tollemache Estate by Fenna, 1798.
CRO: DTW 2477/C/32)*

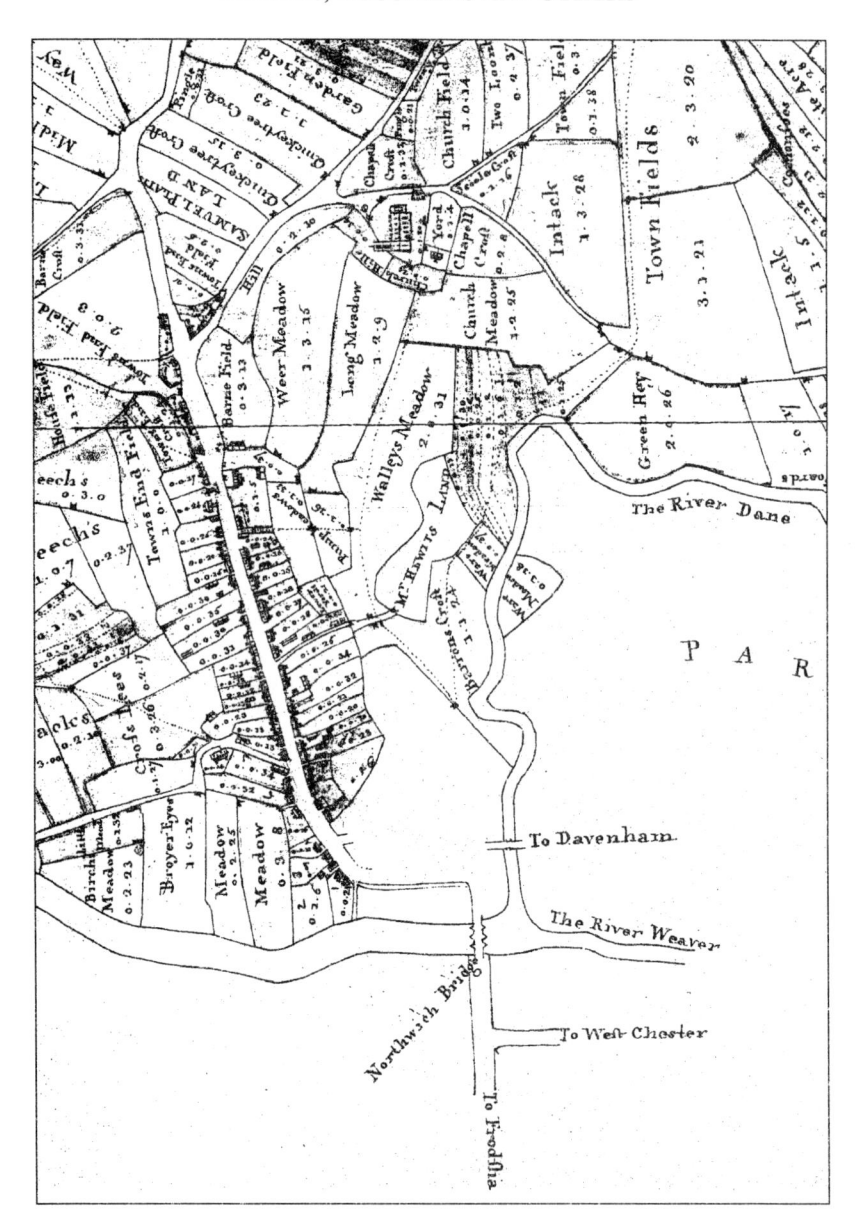

Figure Five: **18th Century Witton**
(From a Map of the Manor of Witton by Billington 1721. CRO: D4360/4).

streets certainly seem to have been very narrow by modern standards for in the 19th century Apple Market Street was described as 'narrow and inconvenient' being only 12 feet wide. Its unsuitablity for trading with the presence of numerous stalls and baskets of wares on market days meant that carts could not pass: this prompted the creation of the purpose built market place.[16]

Witton

What then of Northwich's close neighbour, Witton? Both Smith and Webb allude to Witton as being a part of Northwich: a seamless join where the High Street met with Witton Street. The particular difference between the two was lordship: Northwich on the one hand was a manor held by the Earl of Derby whereas Witton was a manor held since Domesday by the Venables family, who were known locally as the Barons of Kinderton from their home base near Middlewich. This manor consisted of about 450 acres of land set on high ground overlooking the town of Northwich. It is bounded to the north by the Witton Brook and Wades Brook, to the south by the River Dane and to the east by Rudheath Lordship. Running through the centre of the manor is the Chester to Manchester road and branching off this are routes to Great Budworth and Middlewich. The significant buildings of the township during the 17th century were the parochial chapel of St Helen, the grammar school founded by Sir John Deane in 1544, and the corn mill at the junction of the Witton and Wade brooks. The majority of houses in this township were crammed along the 500 yards of highway between the church and the Northwich town boundary: resembling an overspill town. A map of the manor drawn in 1721 *(see Fig. Five)* shows about a hundred buildings in this area with the remainder made up of fields and closes. Since at least the mid-14th century the manor was often referred to as 'Witton Cross' perhaps due to the place of worship on the hill-top being marked by a preaching cross prior to the establishment of St Helen's in the 14th century.

The township or borough of Northwich together with Witton's populated area along the thoroughfare combine to form the town of Northwich and from hereon references to the town shall mean this total area.

OWNERS, OCCUPIERS AND OTHERS

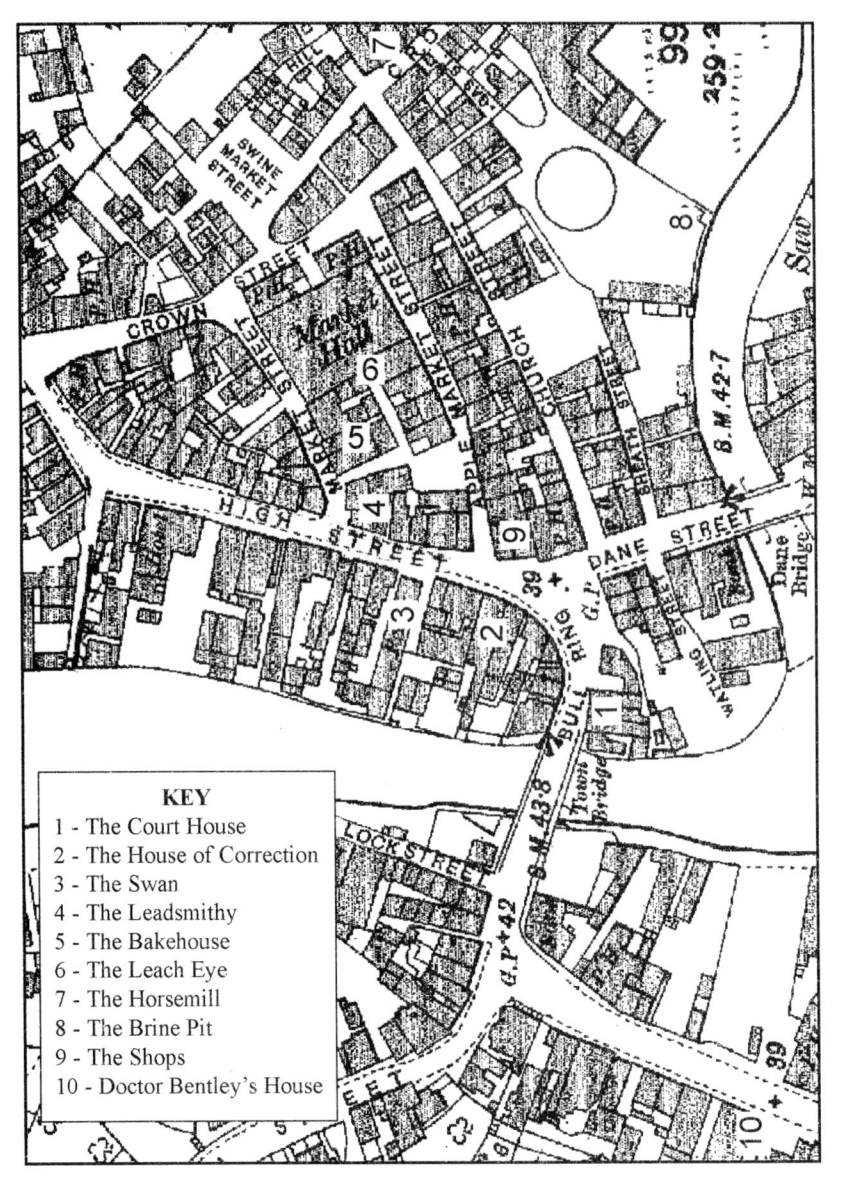

KEY
1 - The Court House
2 - The House of Correction
3 - The Swan
4 - The Leadsmithy
5 - The Bakehouse
6 - The Leach Eye
7 - The Horsemill
8 - The Brine Pit
9 - The Shops
10 - Doctor Bentley's House

Figure Six: **Urban Continuity**
(17th century features on an early 20th century O.S. map)

THE TOWN

Continuity of the Townscape

It is worth spending time considering the continuity of the townscape for whilst admittedly much has changed during the latter part of the last century, a ghost of the ancient town remains.

The area lying to the south-west of the Bull Ring has perhaps altered the least. In c.1610 this area contained a conglomeration of buildings and plots in an irregular pattern. By 1793 this area is depicted as a triangular block of properties together with a small rectangular block adjacent to the Dane Bridge. The early Ordnance Survey map repeats this geometric layout and, importantly, reflects the way in which the main block of property encroached into the line of the road – a fact that adds some credibilty to the 17th century map maker's accuracy. Today the main difference in this area is the shortened central block which allows for a larger Bull Ring. The most notable building in this area was the Court House (58) which fronted on to the Bull Ring and was located where Beresford Adams, the estate agents, have their business premises. The original line of what was Seath Street, now Watling Street, starts in the angle formed by the two rivers and continues eastward along the southern side of Watling Street as far as the Cheshire County Council buildings. Along this narrow street lay a number of building plots (1-4, & 6-16) and the brine-pit (5). The site of what was for centuries the town's foremost economic asset is now marked by the new Watling Street Health Centre; here once stood the lofty gas holder.

The breadth of the carriageway that forms modern Watling Street represents the location of a continuous line of 17th century properties (28-46) which were bounded by Seath Street and High Street. Their remains now lie under the tarmac. The westernmost building was known as 'the Pavement House' (46) which implies that at some time the main roads and the Market Place were paved, though no medieval charter permitting paving is known. This property was once the home of a family whose occupational surname also suggests paving – Pavor. In the early 20th century a Mr Bostock had a chemist's shop in what remained of the Pavement House.

The National Westminster Bank faces into the Bull Ring and stands on a site (41) once occupied by the Angel Hotel which had to be demolished due to subsidence. This in the 17th century may have been the location of the Red Lion. Next door stood 'the Shops' (98) now the premises of the restaurant 'Casa Latina'. Stretching back, between what were High Street and Yate Street, the remains of twenty-one properties (76-80 & 82-97) are hidden by today's market car park. The Market Hall occupies the space between the next two parallel streets: Apple Market Street (the modern name for Yate Street) and Market Street (formerly Swine Market Street and before that 'Leach End or Backhouse Street'). Along the southern side stood twelve properties (99-110) that backed onto the Leach Eye, the stream that ran down into the River Weaver. On the other side of Leach Eye there were 13 properties (117-129) along what we now call Market Street: amongst these was the common bakehouse or 'backhouse' (128) where the townspeople baked their bread. Between the Market Hall and the modern High Street there were several buildings (111-116) in a plot, the overall shape of which has remained virtually unchanged. The building on the corner of High Street and Market Street (114) which is presently unoccupied, was the leadsmithy in which all the lead pans were cast. The triangular parcel of land on the other side of Market Street still retains its original shape. In the centre of this, now an open yard, stood a fairly large house which in c1610 seems to have had two chimneys.

Now we move to the west end of the town. The County Council offices, situated at the junction of Watling Street and Chesterway and alongside Victoria Bridge, are on land that was formerly part of Crum Hills. Immediately in front of the driveway to the office car park stood the horse-mill (23) and, across the other side of Watling Street, where the indoor market is, stood 18 buildings. In fact as you walk along the mall nearest the car park you are walking along the line of Horsemill Street.

Lastly there is the modern High Street – the core of the old town. The Bull Ring corner seems to have had a large house behind which there was a small pathway leading down to the river. This is now Weaver Way, the one-way street leading to the car parks at the rear of Marks and Spencer. On the other corner of Weaver Way and directly opposite Apple Market Street stands a shop which was once the House of Correction –

THE TOWN

the local prison (61). Further on, on the corner of the next access to the river stands the HSBC bank, once a pub called the Eagle and Child and before that the Swan (64). Along the High Street, then the Market Place, stood nine other properties. In total length the building plot probably was somewhat shorter than it is today, that is, not reaching as far as McDonald's (39 High Street), but perhaps as far as the Yorkshire Bank (33 High Street)). Alongside here there may have been a plot of land known as 'Kiln Orchard' at the end of which there was a lane leading down to the river.[17]

With regard to the other side of the River Weaver there is little to be said. The roads follow the same course but the 17th century building plots are now lost under a succession of re-building, especially as a result of the devastating effects of subsidence. However in recent times the majority of buildings that stood between Castle Street and the river have been cleared to create open space and I would suggest that this is the way it was for much of the 17th century for the contemporary survey makes no mention of buildings on this side of the road.

What of Witton's townscape and landscape? There is less in evidence and this is limited to Witton Street, the main thoroughfare and the area around St Helen's church. As for the rest ... the numerous fields and closes have all gone, to be replaced by an urban sprawl.

That there is some continuity in Northwich from the 17th century through to modern times begs the question: just how old is the townscape as regards the street pattern and the location of the wich-houses? The basic layout seems to stretch back as early as the 13th century. In 1295 two wich-houses (1 & 2) were described as being bounded to the south by the River Dane and to the north by the King's wich-house (34), and to the west by the salt-pit and to the east by Crum Hill – boundaries which coincide with the 17th century town plan.[18] If the many wich-houses designated to be 'Judger's Houses' remained on the same site, which they probably did, then there is every likelihood that the history of those sites extends back to Anglo-Saxon times. The fact that these are spread throughout the town, rather than being in a particular area which might then represent an ancient core of the town, again implies a pre-Conquest layout.

OWNERS, OCCUPIERS AND OTHERS

[1] Calvert, p. 1107-8. CRO: DLT/A/2/57.

[2] The town plan is of date c.1610 from Harleian MS 2073 and reproduced in Calvert, A.F., *Salt in Cheshire*, p. 1087.

[3] J. B. Curzon, 'Paying for the Invasion', *Cheshire History*, 40, (2000-01), p. 7.

[4] Calvert, p. 1052-3.

[5] The various listings of wich-house owners (Calvert pp. 1096-99 and 1116-18) when compared to the numbers on the plan and its schedule suggest this (Calvert pp. 1084-87). Also CRO: DLT/A2/54 has a crude sketch which shows Little Street running off Swine Market Street. See also CRO: DLT/A/2/60 and D4360/2.

[6] CRO: A/2/54. According to a small 17th century sketch plan, Little Street ran off Swine Market Street.

[7] Behind the 'leadsmithy' there was a small 'lake', part of the 'Leach Eye'. CRO: DLT/A/2/60, p.34, 44.

[8] Calvert, pp. 1048, 1061/2. CRO: DSS/1/1/11.

[9] CRO: DSS/1/1/50/1.

[10] J. Hall (ed.), *The Civil War in Cheshire*, LCRS, vol 19 (1889), p. 225.

[11] Extracts from the 'Survey' may be found in Calvert, p. 1107-8; CRO: D4360/2, A2/57; and *Biblio Cestrensis*, pp. 204-218.

[12] CRO: DLT/A/2/57.

[13] CRO: DLT/A/54.

[14] *A Map of the Willbraham Tollemache Estate* surveyed by Jos. Fenna, 1793, CRO: DTW 2477/C/32.

[15] The O.S. map of 1876 has been used.

[16] CRO: LuNo55.

[17] CRO: DLT/A/60.

[18] CRO: DCH/J/134.

THE TOWN

Plate One: **The town centre from Winnington Hill**

Plate Two: **The Bull Ring looking towards Town Bridge**

OWNERS, OCCUPIERS AND OTHERS

Plate Three: **The site of the 17th century Court House**

Plate Four: **The Bill Ring and High Street**

THE TOWN

Plate Five: **The site of the House of Correction**
(The Morgage Shop is the approximate position of this old prison)

Plate Six: **Applemarket Street, formerly Yate Street, at the junction with High Street.** (Note the narrowness of the street)

Plate Seven: **The site of the 17th century Swan Inn**
(This was an important hostelry where, in addition to hospitality, important meetings were held)

THE TOWN

Plate Eight: **The site of the Leadsmithy**
(The location is on the corner of High Street and Market Street, formerly Backhouse Street. It was here that the lead pans were cast)

OWNERS, OCCUPIERS AND OTHERS

Plate Nine: **The site of the 'Gripyard' at the rear of the Leadsmithy**
(Just around the corner on the right was the site of the bakehouse)

Plate Ten: **The open yard between High Street and Market Street**
(This open area is a feature of the 17th century town plan)

3

THE PEOPLE OF NORTHWICH

Population

How many people lived in Northwich and Witton? Any assessment of population size before the census of 1801 is difficult and relies on sources not intended for such a purpose. One would normally turn to the parish registers to estimate population size. Northwich lay within the ancient and extensive parish of Great Budworth, but the place of worship for its residents was the chapel of St Helen in Witton. Unfortunately the chapel's registers are of limited value for such an exercise as the townships of Lostock, Rudheath, Castle, Winnington and Hartford also lay in this large chapelry of Witton, and until the 1670s the registers hardly ever give place of residence. Some of the residents of these townships may from time to time have travelled to the parish church at Great Budworth for the celebration of baptism, marriage and burial. Added to these problems there are gaps in the Witton registers and according to one entry for 1645 the registers were not kept for three or four years 'throw civil wars, flying of ministers and Clarks, feares distractions and troubles of the tymes'. However, we can detect trends in population growth for the chapelry as a whole and reasonable estimates can be made as other contemporary sources seem to suggest that about 33% of the chapelry lived in Northwich and 20% in Witton.

Before looking at the 17th century population figures it is perhaps worth referring back to the mid- and late-16th century to establish a baseline. The muster roll of 1548 for Northwich lists 29 men, that for Witton 32, and for the rest of the chapelry 109 (see *Appendix One*). Using a multiplier of six or seven, as suggested by one authority,[1] we have figures of between 174 and 203 for Northwich, 192-224 for Witton and 654-763 for the remainder: a total for the parish of around 1100. The Witton registers, which commence in 1561, are somewhat difficult to interpret for many of the early years, but they do show that between 1580 and the end of the century, baptisms annually averaged 43 and were generally in excess of burials which suggests a steady increase in population. Using the standard annual figure of 33.3 baptisms per 1000 population, the average population in the last two decades of the 16th century in the Witton registers would be about 1,300. These indicators, the muster rolls and the parish registers, are not incompatible and would seem to suggests a steady rise throughout the last half of the century. Using a ten-year moving average over the last 20 years of the century suggests that the population rose from around 1,270 to 1,500 – an increase of 230 or 18%. Baptisms on their own are perhaps not a particularly reliable indicator, for mortality will have a part to play. The cumulative natural increase (baptisms minus burials) over this 20-year period suggests an increase of only 114.

Whatever gains there had been in population during the last half of the 16th century were wiped out by a visitation of plague. The registers record that on 13 July 1604:

'this day that terrible and mournful plague followed which commencing in the house of a certain John Venables in the West Place of the town of Northwich through an unknown woman lodger from the plague stricken town of Nantwich... '.

Two weeks later John's son Robert died and was followed within the week by his brothers and sisters. In that year the whole parish was blighted and 247 people were buried: many of whom, like the Venables family, Robert Fox, a burgess, and Hugh Winnington, were Northwich residents.[2] Other parishioners of Witton were affected too: Humphrey Phitheon, clerk, curate of Witton, 'an honourable man', and Richard Holford, 'a man much beloved and mourned by all'. Unfortunately the registers for the next two years are missing so that it is not possible to assess the impact of the plague, though it would seem reasonable to suggest that the population of the parish fell back to that of c.1580: that is between 1,250-1,300 people.

The population of Witton chapelry seems to have risen to around 1,400 by the 1630s only to fall back again over the next 25 years by around 300. It is difficult to account for this as the registers from 1642 to 1657 are missing. During the remainder of the century the population of the parish seems to have risen again to around 1,800 or 1,900 souls. A recent study of population growth in North-West England between 1563 and 1664 has suggested that the chapelry grew by over 100% as compared to the whole of the Frodsham deanery estimated at 19% and the county's 56%.[3] This does not seem to be borne out by the baptismal registers which suggests an increase over the century of 28%. Taking the figure for the chapelry as a whole would suggest that the population of Northwich started the 17th century at around 500 and rose to about 650. Witton seems to have had between 300 and 400 residents.

Two invaluable sources that help us to answer questions of demography in the 17th century are the Poll Tax, 1660, and the Hearth Tax, 1664 (see *Appendices Four* and *Five*).[4] For Northwich the entries in the Poll Tax list 221 names, of which 11 are known to have lived elsewhere and had only a proprietary interest in the town.[5] Despite one or two problems with using these returns,[6] it seems that Northwich had a taxable adult population of at least 210 and their arrangement is such as would suggest 77 households of taxable residents. Of the total number of names, 59 were married women listed and assessed along with their husbands and two were women who had husbands living elsewhere. If we add about 66% for children (those under 16 years) this gives an estimated population of about 350. There were, of course, a number of people who were exempted on the grounds that they were in receipt of alms who do not feature in these returns: if these poor people are added this lifts the population significantly, perhaps by at least a further 150, suggesting a figure approaching 500. In Witton there were 113 names which includes 30 married women living with their husbands and a further five unnamed wives. This gives a taxable adult population of about 118 in 56 households; of these eight are headed by spinsters and one by a widow. A population estimate of around 280, inclusive of the poor, would seem reasonable. By using the figure obtained from the parish baptismal register of 1620 for the early 1660s and taking 33% and 20% for the proportion of those in Northwich and Witton, figures of 430 and 264 are deduced.

Coming only four years later, the Hearth Tax forms a suitable means of cross-checking the information given in the Poll Tax, especially since it records both those liable to tax and those exempt on the grounds of poverty.[7] The surviving returns for Northwich indicate that there were 128 residential premises in the town giving a population of about 512 using the commonly accepted multiplier of four. As for Witton we find that there were 76 houses giving an estimated population of 304. This is not wholly incompatible. In 1664 the total estimate for the parish is 1,333 giving 444 for Northwich and 266 for Witton.

A suit roll for the Northwich Borough Court dated 4 November 1702 affords some check on the figures given. Then there were 120 names recorded – 97 'inhabitants' and 23 'burgesses'.[8] As it is likely that all bar three of the burgesses lived elsewhere, the list suggests about 100 heads of household and therefore a population approaching 500. By the mid-1750s the number of households in the Borough was 200 giving a population of around 800 and by 1810 the population was 1,382; by this time Witton had exceeded the township of Northwich by having 1,966 residents. The foregoing estimates may be summarised in *Table Two*.

Year	Criteria used	Northwich	Witton	Chapelry
1548	Men in Muster Rolls	188	210	1100
c.1580	Baptisms @33/1000	430	260	1300
1600	Baptisms @33/1000	500	293	1468
1630	Baptisms @33/1000	487	286	1433
1660	Taxable population	450	250	1500
1664	Households	512	304	1500
1664	Baptisms @33/1000	444	266	1333
1699	Baptisms @33/1000	602	360	1800
1702	Names on court roll	500		
1750	Names on court roll	800		

Table Two: **Summary of Population Estimates**

THE PEOPLE OF NORTHWICH

From the contemporary records it seems that in the 1660s Northwich and Witton had a combined population of around 700-800. How then do they compare with other towns? Around the 1660s Chester had a population of around 7,800. Nantwich and Macclesfield were large towns with around 2,900 and 2,600 respectively and Congleton came next with about 1,700: nearby Middlewich, with its close neighbour Newton, had a population of around 900. So, in the words of Celia Fiennes, writing about 30 years later, Northwich was 'not very large'.[9]

Whilst the population of Northwich and Witton does not seem particularly great to us today or by comparison with other towns of the age, nevertheless when compared to the populations of neighbouring townships Northwich was populous. According to the Hearth Tax returns Castle had a population of around 70, Hartford about 150, Winnington 75, Leftwich 120, Lostock Gralam 120, Davenham 110 and Shurlach 55. Of course these were rural settlements and their populations were often spread somewhat thinner. In addition to the figure of 500 for the area of the Northwich Borough, those six or seven acres will have attracted a not inconsiderable number of visitors from time to time for the purposes of attending court, visiting the markets and fairs, conducting business or for social purposes. Businesses along the whole length of High Street will also have attracted many customers. These out-of-towners will have had their horses and carts to add to those of the residents, their swine and poultry: all-in-all a bustling and perhaps chaotic situation and far worse than anything we might experience on a pre-Christmas Saturday of today!

Poverty and Wealth

Numbers and statistics are all well and good, but what sorts of people lived in the 17th century town, who were they and what did they do for a living?

As already suggested there was a significant level of poverty in the town. So far as the Poll Tax is concerned we have an unknown number in receipt of alms or poor relief paid by the parish, but the Hearth Tax records show that of the 128 households in the township of Northwich, 82 were in the exempt class and in Witton 31 households out of a total of 76.[10] These figures of exempt families represent 64% and 40% of their respective totals. The proportion of poor for the township of Northwich is double the average for the whole Hundred and higher than most towns in the county.[11] A list of those in receipt of poor relief from the parish dated 1619 lists 76 people in Northwich (over half the total poor in Witton parish) and 53 in Witton. Another list, undated but perhaps a year or so earlier, records 74 and 37 names respectively.[12] On the whole these townsfolk seem to have been without families as in only two instances are there references to daughters and a son and they include many women who were either widows or spinsters, and one who is described as a 'strange woman'. How the poor were provided for will be dealt with at the end of Chapter Four.

The Hearth Tax returns tell us more as regards the wealth of the town's population (see *Table Three*). This was a tax of 1s imposed on each hearth or fireplace in a house. Of the total, in both townships, of 91 premises upon which tax was paid, 44 had just a single hearth and their occupants were probably just above the poverty line. As is to be expected, almost all the exempt properties had single hearths, the exceptions being four houses in Northwich with two hearths and occupied by a widow, two spinsters and an elderly man. Similarly, in Witton there were two such houses but one was the school-house and probably exempt on that fact. At the other end of the scale, however, there were three properties in Northwich each with seven hearths and one with six, thus indicating substantial houses. Clearly there was a significant division of wealth in the town with 157 households (77%) apparently either below or just above the poverty threshold, 41 households (20%) in a comfortable state and six families (3%) who might be described as well-off. In the main, the poor families would have lived in single-storey hovels, with one or two rooms, and would have had a few pieces of furniture and the clothes they stood up in.

Although the Poll Tax is not a good indicator of poverty it is a fairly good indicator of wealth. The 1660 Act and a number of amendments that came into force towards the end of that year provided a fairly sophisticated means of raising taxation based on rank and possession of property. A set charge was made on members of the nobility: e.g. £100

	Taxed		Exempt			
Hearths	North	Witton	North	Witton	Totals	Status
1	8	36	78	29	151	'Poor', or just above
2	23	5	4	2	34	poverty level
3	6	2			8	'Comfortable'
4	4	1			5	
5	1	1			2	
6	1				1	'Well-off'
7	3				3	
Totals	46	45	82	31	204	

Table Three: **Hearth Tax Returns, 1664**

for a duke, £40 for a baron and £10 for an esquire. Gentlemen, yeomen, tradesmen and others lower down the scale were taxed on the following basis: 'Every person that can dispend in Lands Leases Money Stocks or otherwise of his or her owne proper estate one hundred pounds per annum the sum of forty shillings and so proportionally for a greater or lesser estate provided it extend not to persons under five pounds yearely. Every person being a single person and above the age of sixteene yeares the sum of twelve pence. An every other person... not rated before in this present Act, nor receiving Alms, and being above sixteene yeares of age shall pay six pence.'[13] Thus, those holding land and tradesmen were taxed on the value of their holdings or goods at the rate of £2 for every £100 worth. The basic tax for the ordinary working people was 1s. The returns for Northwich and Witton make an inclusive charge on married couples of 1s, or more dependant on income and status. A further provision was that widows were to be charged on a third of their late husband's estate. Assessments were made by the township and therefore it is often the case that individuals who held property in more than one township will appear more than once: it is this that causes problems when trying to interpret demographic statistics from the Poll Tax returns.

So far as the township's residents are concerned, Dr William Bentley seems to be the wealthiest. He had property in the township worth £10 per annum on which he paid the appropriate 4s tax, with further properties worth at least £29 a year in Lach Dennis, Lostock Gralam, Hulse and Rudheath incurring a liability for a further 11s 8d. Next in order of wealth are William and Ralph Leftwich, gentlemen; George Dewsbury, draper; Ralph Nixon, butcher and John Broome, innkeeper, all of whom were charged 2s on £5 worth of property. A number of 'outsiders' had property interests in Northwich. Peter Tarbock, gentleman of Witton, and John Partington, draper of London, both had £10 worth; Robert Warburton, gentleman, £7 10s worth; and Richard Partington, draper of London, William Harcourt, gentleman of Wincham, William Rowe, yeoman of Hartford, Joshua Hodgkis of London and Robert Venables of Lostock Gralam were all charged 2s on £5 worth of property. A Mrs Ann Moseley, presumably a widow, also paid 2s on £5 worth suggesting that her husband had held three times that amount.

In Witton, Susanna Bromfield, widow, held £30 worth of property and paid 12s tax. Peter Tarbock and John Partington, yeoman, come next with property worth £15 a year, then Richard Hilton, husbandman, with £10, and Mr Ralph Horton with £7 10s, followed by Edward Mariott, gentleman, and Thomas Ackson, collar maker, with £5. Once again there are 'outsiders' with interests in the township: William Harcourt, gentleman of Wincham, £15, Jone Birchall, spinster, £7 10s and Lawrence Birchall, husbandman, £5.

Comparing the Poll Tax and Hearth Tax returns can produce some anomalies. Edward Mariott had property in Northwich and Witton, each worth £5 p.a. and as a consequence one would not suggest that he was poor, yet in the Hearth Tax returns he is assessed on only a single hearth house. Such an example would seem to suggest that some care needs to be taken in interpreting these lists even though such instances are few.

Lifestyles

The use of wills and inventories in assessing standards of living and wealth is well recognised by historians today. Unlike many other historical sources, wills are a personal document giving intimate details of a deceased's family and friends, their possessions, their religious beliefs, and of their aspirations for those they left. Once made and witnessed the will became a public document in the hands of the church officials and provide for us today direct evidence of the circumstances of those who lived all those years ago.

Few people made wills and fewer have survived the passage of time. Between 1600 and 1699, 44 wills survive for Northwich and 45 for Witton. Usually the will was made by dictation a short time before death and whilst 'being sick in body but of sound and perfect rememberance': a statement made no doubt to avoid any contest to the will on the grounds of insanity. In most cases this memory will not have been what it once was and the writer probably had access to family papers in order to include details of lands, leases and personal possessions. Whether rich or poor it was vital to ensure that there was a proper disposal of one's goods and chattels. Wills tend to follow a standard fashion and each invariably begins with the words 'In the name of God Amen' followed by the date of its making. What then follows is a pious statement of thanks for one's possessions and life and a desire for a life beyond the grave. It has been suggested that this can give some clue as to the deceased's religious persuasion. However, one has to be mindful that it is unlikely that the person so near death would have uttered what was written and that the words are more likely to reflect the thoughts of the writer. Often the scribe was the parish clerk and it is likely that he would have available 'model' statements to copy. Nevertheless, the phraseology is of interest and can be classified as follows. A tripartite dedication with references to the Virgin Mary and the Saints often indicates Catholicism; a simple bequest of the soul to God is a common neutral form; an expression of salvation through the merits of Jesus Christ is clearly Protestant; and, finally, a hope of being one of the chosen in God's Kingdom and a belief in predestination is Calvinistic Protestant. So far as Northwich and Witton are concerned I have yet to find any that one might term as being 'Catholic'. All seem to be Protestant and more than a few 'Calvinistic'. The religious preamble is then followed by a request that the body be buried in a Christian manner either at the discretion of the executors or else in some specified church or churchyard, such as Witton. Then, following a statement to the effect that all debts and funeral expenses were to be paid out of the whole estate, the will continues with personal bequests and the disposal of goods and chattels. Here the will has its great value in naming the individual members of the deceased's family (particularly grandchildren, which is a boon in reconstructing families when there are gaps in the parish registers), friends and servants.

Sometimes a will has an inventory attached to it, and sometimes the inventory survives without the will. The value of these probate inventories cannot be overstated in supplying details of the standards of living of ordinary people. Since the days of Henry VIII, the probate of wills was granted subject to there being an inventory of the deceased's belongings to safeguard the executors from excessive claims on the estate and fraud and because probate charges depended upon it. It was normally drawn up within a few days of the funeral by appraisers who consisted of the deceased's neighbours or friends. The majority of inventories contain a detailed list of all the deceased's personal estate with each item separately valued, whilst the best examples also give the name and contents of each room of the house. Despite the spelling, which was almost entirely phonetic, these lists of property provide a wealth of detailed information. Of the 78 testators in 17th century Northwich, 69 have a surviving inventory, and of 66 testators in Witton, 59 inventories survive – enough to give a good indication of living standards.[14]

A particular value of inventories is their capacity to indicate the number of rooms in a particular house and the uses to which those rooms were put. However there is a need to bear in mind that the appraisers were only interested in the decedent's goods and therefore it is likely that if a room contained nothing it would not be mentioned. As to the size of rooms or the layout of the house we are told nothing save for the fact that a room might be next to another or above. Forty Northwich inventories list the rooms in the building (see *Appendix Six*).

The basic building design of the Tudor and early Stuart periods consisted of a single storey divided into two parts – the 'house', sometimes referred to as the 'hall', and the parlour: in larger houses the main room seems to be termed the 'hall'. Whether 'hall' or 'house' this would be the principal room in which everyday living took place. Here there would have been a large fireplace which catered for both warmth and cooking, the table at which meals were taken, the main forms of seating, and the items of luxury, value and entertainment. The parlour was the room situated behind the fireplace which would be used as the main bedroom, taking its heat from the back wall of the fireplace. In some properties the ground floor was modified by extension or sub-division so as to create a kitchen, buttery or shop. Butteries, where food and drink were stored, were often next to the hall and sometimes a part of it, being divided off by a screen. Fifteen properties are listed as having a buttery. Nine properties had a kitchen but these were not necessarily used for cooking, rather for storage of cooking utensils and other household items. In older properties these rooms would all be open to the roof but eventually a first floor was added, consisting of one or more chambers again open to the rafters, unless further modified by boarding over to create loft space. Upstairs rooms, both chambers and lofts, were used as additional bedrooms and for storage. Access to upper rooms would often be by means of ladders; a staircase is only mentioned in one inventory (Bromfield, 1667) – 'the little chamber at the stair head'. Of course stairs and fixed ladders were integral to the building and need not therefore be mentioned by appraisers. Glass too might be a part of the house, but in some inventories glass is listed. Wainscoting or panelling to reduce draughts is sometimes referred to and often in connection with a particular item of furniture to which it was attached.

Of the 40 inventories to mention rooms there are only four that refer to the main room as 'the Hall' (Holford, 1605; Venables, 1631; Norcott, 1679; Bentley, 1680). In three cases there is no mention of either 'house' or 'hall', the main room seemingly becoming a shop (Johnson, 1637; Norcott, 1665; Birkenhead, 1677). Curiously one inventory (Broome, 1634) seems to mention only chambers – 'street' and 'garden' in which there were beds and 'upper' in which there was another bed along with tables, chairs, and other items found in living rooms.

As already said the 'hall' or 'house' was both a living room and a place for cooking in most dwellings: it was the hub of the household. Here was the fireplace, usually the only one in the house. Fireplace equipment and cooking utensils are often listed in inventories and consist of combinations of shovels, tongs, bellows, hooks, racks, spits, gridirons (an iron grate with short legs for boiling over an open fire), cobirons (long bars fitted with hooks to carry spits and leant back against the back wall of the fire), brandreths (a form of gridiron, sometimes described as 'hanging', being suspended by chains over the open fire), and other pieces of ironware. Andirons (large iron firedogs which supported spits in front of an open hearth) could be decorative and might be three feet or more in height, in one instance they were tipped with brass (Heyes, 1629). Most of the simpler ironware was probably made by local blacksmiths. Cooking utensils include frying pans, dripping pans, kettles, skillets (a long-handled pan with three short legs for setting in an open fire), with occasional reference to toasting irons. A few inventories mention chafing dishes which were used to keep food hot, often placed on a small brazier containing hot ashes. Brass pots and pans figure often in the wills and inventories and were often bequeathed as heirlooms. Pewter, cheaper than brass, was commonly found in inventories and consisted mostly of plates, saucers, porringers and basins. In a few instances the weight and quality of the pewter is referred to. There is little mention of table cutlery though spoons and knives were the usual eating utensils. Some of the wealthier families owned silver plate and silver objects such as salt cellars, bowls, jugs, cups and goblets. There are a few references to glass ware, including drinking glass. Furniture in 17th century homes was very basic and utilitarian. It is likely that much of the furniture was home-made, though there are examples of 'joined' items, that is furniture made by skilled joiners.

Beds and bedding were important features of any house and often a valuable piece of furniture to be bequeathed to sons and daughters. Sometimes, with the more wealthy, these could be large and elaborate pieces of furniture with heavy carved head and footboards, and posts at each corner to support the 'tester' or canopy. The sides of the beds might be furnished with curtains to provide privacy and a valance to hide whatever was kept underneath. More often beds of a much simpler form – a pair of bedsteads, or 'bedstocks', were overlaid by boards on which was placed a coarse mattress. Interesting variations are the 'truckle' bed, which was a low bed on castors which could be stored away under the main bed; the 'press' which was a bed that could be folded up into a cupboard; 'wainscoted', that is having panelled sides; 'half-headed', being a medium-sized four poster with no tester, and the 'field' bed which was an elaborate four poster with an arched tester in the shape of a tent with the framework being entirely covered with curtains and draperies. Often beds are itemised by their separate parts so that we find 'bed boards' and 'bed stocks'. The bedding too was listed. There are references to sheets, coverlets, caddows (a rough woollen covering), pillows, pillow 'beares' (cases), blankets and bolsters. Mattresses, sometimes confusingly referred to as a bed, would consist of feathers for the wealthy, flock (a mixture of wool and cloth strips) and 'chaffe' (straw). In one instance, that of William Leftwich (1641), the weight of the mattress or bolster is given, presumably an indication of quality:

2 feather bedds and 3 boulsters wayinge 151[l]
2 feather bedds, 2 boulsters and 1 pillowe wayinge 109[l]
8 pillowes wayinge 29[l]

An example of a bedding entry is provided by Ralph Cheney's inventory of 1626:

One standinge bed in the Chamber over the parler
one covereinge one blanket one fetherbed
two boulsters one matteris

Tables were the next important pieces of furniture. Boards laid on trestles were still very common, for such items of furniture were most suitable in cramped accommodation as they could easily be taken down and stored at the side of a room. There are some examples of joined tables and tables being described as 'round', 'square' or 'littell' and these are often referred to along with their frames. Tablecloths and napkins are regularly found in inventories. For seating, stools and benches are far more common than chairs. Here again there are varieties: joined chairs and stools, the couch bed (a form of chair rather than a bed), 'twygen' chairs (made of wicker work or twigs) and chairs covered with 'needle wrought covers' -- luxury items indeed.

Storage in 17th century houses was mainly provided by chests and coffers, though occasionally there is mention of cupboards and sideboards. The coffer was a chest with a domed top covered in leather or cloth. It was the most frequently listed item of furniture in Northwich inventories. Apart from the bed on which the testator lay, the coffer was sometimes the only item of furniture he or she had. The chest differed from the coffer in shape, usually having a flat top, and was generally larger. Chests often stood at the foot of a bed and held bed linen, and were usually found in the parlour or in an upper chamber. The chest of drawers, designed to give greater accessibility to its contents, had drawers fitted at the bottom. The cupboard at this time was usually a sort of side table on which were placed cups, pewter etc., hence the term. The dishboard was similar in function. Wooden and pewter plates are often mentioned along with the shelves on which they were stored. In fact most household equipment was made of wood and that includes tableware known as 'treen ware'. Wooden trenchers appear throughout the period studied, sometimes in large quantities such as three or even six dozen. Wooden ware covered a wide range of items, including pails, bowls, troughs, barrels, tubs, looms, churns, presses, and sieves.

Much furniture and equipment was handed on from one generation to the next; most of a deceased person's goods, regardless of condition or value, were considered worth keeping and there are numerous references to items being 'ould'. The main beneficiaries in a will, the spouse or eldest child, usually received the larger pieces of furniture and the better quality items and these seem to have been family heirlooms. Smaller items were often left to other children, relatives or friends. Thomas Sudlow of Witton (1625) left an unusually large number of items to his eldest son, also named Thomas, as 'heire loomess': a gold ring, a silver ring, best brass pot and mortar, all bedding, cupboards, press, table, joined chairs, books, the wainscotting in the house and stones in the garden.

Some inventories mention basic foodstuffs stored in the house. Bacon, beef, butter and cheese were staple items. Food was highly spiced and many inventories record pestles and mortars used for grinding. Brewing equipment, including vats, coppers, barrels, hogsheads and tun dishes, might be listed, and would be found in the brewhouse where one existed. Brewing was a common activity in most households and small beer was drunk by all the family, including the children, as it was safer than drinking the untreated water.

The majority of the references to clothing in the wills and inventories use the general term 'apparel'. The only complete list of clothing is that of Robert Fox (1605); his inventory lists the following items:

1 Cloake	10s
2 liverie Cloakes	10s
2 jerkins	5s
2 dublets	13s 4d
2 sherts	vs
4 shert bands	16d
one hat	2s
one peare of Stockings	3s 4d
one hat of the Wives	20d
4 mufflers	12d
one yard of flaxen	12d
1 semark shert	2d
3 peares of Breches	5s
4 partletts	20d

Surprisingly there is no mention of Fox's footwear. George Broome (1639) left a number of items of clothing to his brothers and these included a broadcloth 'ending' coat; a broadcloth suit; a grey hat, 'lined with greene taffeta'; a white hat; and a 'freeze' (coarse woollen cloth) suit, except for its 'silken buttons' which he gave to his mother. Richard Billington (1641) left his 'best dublet, breches and yerkin' to his son Richard. Some items of clothing were obviously valuable and prized and thus suitable bequests. Thomas Sudlow of Witton (1625) left his half brothers, Robert, Thomas and Ralph Nickson a brown cloak, best breeches, a doublet and a hat between them. Examples of such bequests suggests that the handing down of clothing from one generation to the next was a widespread feature of the time amongst the well-to-do as indeed among the poorer sorts as might be expected. How much of the material used in clothing was woven in the town itself is impossible to say.

Everything seems to have been of value, from furniture to firewood, old clothes, even heaps of 'muck' (manure). Surprisingly there are frequent references to looking glasses, clocks, candlesticks, warming pans, pictures and books: in one instance, that of Thomas Sudlow (1625), 96 books are recorded – more than most people have today. Some other signs of luxury and wealth appear: musical instruments – a virginal (a small harpsicord), a citterne (a lute) and a kit (a sort of violin); hanging

OWNERS, OCCUPIERS AND OTHERS

Groups	Status / Occupation	Northwich	Witton
Males			
Gentry	Gentleman[15]	10	4
Agricultural	Yeomen	2	2
	Husbandmen	3	17
Food & Drink Trades	Innkeeper	3	
	Butcher	12	
	Miller		1
Retailing	Draper	3	
	Mercer		1
	Grocer	3	
Textiles & Clothing	Tailor	6	3
	Feltmaker	2	
	Sherman	3	
	Collarmaker		2
Leather Trades	Shoemaker	6	4
	Glover	1	
	Saddler	1	
	Tanner		1
Specialist Services	Barrow Maker		5
	Blacksmith	3	3
	Wheelwright		1
	Cooper	1	
	Joiner		1
	Carpenter	1	2
	Glazier		2
	Barber	1	
Labourers/ Misc.	Labourers	37	8
	Carrier		1
	Tinker	1	
	Schoolmaster	1	1
Females			
	Wives (specifically listed)	62	29
	Widows (*2 are presumed to be)	9*	1
	Spinsters (some will be servants)[16]	41	28
	Female Servants	4	
TOTALS		221	112

Table Four: **Occupational Structure 1660**
(Taken from the entries given in the Poll Tax returns)

candlesticks (candelabrum); carpets (then thick fabrics used to cover beds and tables); leather stools; needlework cushions and tablecloths. The 17th century was a time when there was much interest in family pedigrees and heraldry so that it is perhaps not surprising to find four inventories which mention coats of arms being displayed. Richard Holford (1605) had 'coats of armes in frames' in his parlour; Ellen Heyes of Witton (1629) had a number of pictures and 'eschocheans of Armes' in her hall and her heir, Peter Tarbock (1641), had eight escutcheons in the hall, which were presumably the same ones; William Bentley (1680) had ten framed escutcheons in his parlour. A number of wills mention military equipment – swords, rapiers, bows and arrows, bills and armour.

The need for capital and the availability of goods on credit were a necessity of any commercial community. It is not surprising therefore to find a number of wills and inventories which refer to debts owed by, or owed to, the decedent. Often the names of the various debtors and creditors is given and occasionally the reason for the debt. The regular instruction to executors to settle debts before making any bequests was of particular relevance given that the economy of 17th century society relied so much on credit. Debts might be described as being 'desperate' meaning that there was little hope of recovery, or else as being 'bond' or 'specialty' both of which mean that a deed existed binding the borrower to repay. John Sumner (1616) was in the unfortunate position of having debts amounting to more than was owed him, albeit the difference was only 8s 8d – £13 10s 4d in credit and £13 19s in debt. Poor old Ralph Tench, tanner of Witton (1671), left goods and chattells worth £7 4s of which £6 was a 'desperate debt due by bond' – desperate indeed! Peter Pavor (1633) was owed £63 15s 5d 'as appeared in his book' – but part of the debt was denied. George Broome (1639) was owed a total of £114 13s 10d 'by specialty' and £3 2s 8d 'without specialty'. It may be that some of the richer men and women of the town regularly lent money in order to accrue interest. William Leftwich (1641) was owed £366 4s 4d of which nearly half was described as being 'desperate'. Whilst interest no doubt formed part of the money due and was detailed in the bond there are no details of what rate was being charged. George Bostock's will (1699) refers to a debt due by bond 'and all interest due thereon'.

Earning a Living

A feature of the Poll Tax returns is the indication of an individual's status or occupation (see *Table Five*). Surprisingly, there are few people listed as having a direct link with the salt trade: the five barrow makers certainly were for it is they who made the containers to hold the damp salt, and it is highly likely that the blacksmiths, coopers and the numerous labourers were involved in some way. Some of the single women may have been employed as 'wallers' (brine boilers) for it seems that they were almost always women.[17] Of course there were many people, of varying occupations, who had an interest in the salt trade either as owners, or as occupiers of the many wich-houses in which the salt was produced. Earning a living from engaging in the salt industry will be considered separately in a later chapter.

Gentlemen

Neither of the two townships had resident members of the peerage, baronetcy or the upper gentry. Those bearing the designation 'gentlemen' were the most senior members of local society. Gentlemen were defined as being able to live without manual labour, to 'bear the port, charge and countenance of a gentleman' and to be called 'Mister'. It was also expected that they would be educated, have a comfortable lifestyle, undertake leisurely pursuits, be charitable and to take on administrative and official duties at parish, hundred and county levels. So far as Northwich is concerned, the resident gentry in the 1660s were Dr William Bentley, William Leftwich, Thomas Norcott and Ralph Leftwich. In Witton there were the Bromfields (represented by widow Susanna Bromfield), Ralph Horton, Peter Tarbock and Edward Marriott. A number of gentlemen appear in the list of surviving wills and inventories: Robert Walton (1630), William Leftwich (1641), Thomas Norcott (1679), Ralph Leftwich (1686) and Richard Church (1687) all described as 'of Northwich', and Robert Bromfield (1602), Geoffrey Bromfield (1612), Robert Walton (1631), Peter Tarbock (1641) and Edward Mariott, all 'of Witton'.

William Leftwich of Northwich wrote his last will and testament on 10 July 1641, a few weeks before his death. He had three properties in the town: a house in which he lived, another leased to William Norcott, and a wich-house in Yate Street occupied by John Broome (106); he also had parcels of land in Leftwich known as Long Meadow, Near Meadow and Hall Orchard. All his estate passed to his son, another William, who occurs in the Poll Tax and Hearth Tax returns of the 1660s.[18] The inventory drawn up on 10 September 1641, lists goods and chattels worth £687 0s 7d. Of this total over half, £366 4s 4d, consisted of debts owed to him. His dwelling house consisted of a 'howse', 'parlor', chamber over the house, 'clossitt', little chamber, cock loft, malt loft, corn loft, cheese loft, 'storehowse chamber' and buttery. Mention is also made of the 'milne' (mill) which, in view of the few items it contained, may be a room within the house rather than a separate building. William, or his wife, or both, seem to have had an ear for musical entertainment for he owned a pair of virginals, a citterne and a kit.

The inventory of Thomas Norcott of Northwich, recorded on 11 February 1679, is perhaps the best illustration of a gentleman with a fairly substantial house. His 'messuage' in Northwich was known as 'the Hall' and in it there were at least eleven rooms. On the ground floor there was the hall, hall buttery, kitchen, kitchen buttery and another buttery. Above were the blue chamber, Samuel's chamber, boarded chamber, gallery, and cheese chamber, and finally, a cockloft. Outside, though not necessarily in the town, there were stables and barns. The total value of the inventory is £935 10s of which £600 was the valuation of Simcock's tenement (Broken Cross house), £60 the value of Sudlow's tenement in Rudheath and £40 from debts due to him. Amongst his personal possessions he had £60 worth of livestock, £36 in horses, £14 in hay, and £25 10s in wheat and barley. In addition to his house in Northwich, Norcott also had another messuage situated near 'the Hall', which he leased to Thomas Barlow, butcher, and Thomas Baker, carrier. During his lifetime he leased wich-houses and had in his possession two 'wich house pans', brass, planks, bearers and barrows. It is interesting to note that this gentleman paid tax on three hearths in 1664 and that in 1660 he paid the basic rate of tax of 1s for himself and his wife Marie, which would seem to suggest that he acquired his wealth somewhat later: at that time he seems to have employed two male labourers and two spinsters.

Peter Tarbock of Witton, who died on 7 July 1640, had personal possessions amounting to £291 11s 2d with £17 17s worth of property in St Clement Street, London, and two unaccounted debts. His home consisted of a hall, parlour, lower parlour, a chamber over the lower parlour, a kitchen chamber and a hall chamber; he also had some of his possessions, including three tables, a bed and his wearing apparel, at the 'New Swan' in Northwich. In the hall were a great inlayed chest, eight 'eschochions of Armes', a hanging candlestick, a 'Turkie' carpet, two pairs of virginals, stools, chairs, needlework cushions, wall hangings and curtains. In his parlour he had 16 pictures 'with frames'. Details of his estate are recorded in an *inquisition post mortem* that was held on 22 September 1640.[19] Firstly he was in possession of a burgage property called 'New Swanne' which lay partly in Northwich and partly in Winnington and was occupied by Margaret Dutton and Thomas Holford. Next he had two shops in Northwich leased to William Birkenhead, William Jeffery and Peter Tarbock along with half a wich-house in the tenure of Alice Dewsbury (108 or 109). These properties were all held directly from the King and were worth 40s. He then held from the Earl of Derby, 'in free burgage' and for a rent of 1s 0½d, properties worth 50s. These were half of a burgage known as 'Old Swanne', half of another burgage occupied by George Pavor, half shares in five wich-houses (24, 25, 27, 45, 46), a half share in two acres of meadow, and 12 acres of pasture in Witton. The *inquisition* finally records that he left a widow, Mary, and a son Peter who was aged six on 2 September. It seems that Peter inherited his possessions from his aunt, Ellen Heyes (née Tarbock), for her *inquisition post mortem* held in 1629 lists identical property.[20] Her will refers to Peter son of Peter Tarbock and also states that the shops were in Market Place, 'neer Bridge End'.[21] Interestingly, despite a span of twenty-one years, the inventories attached to both her will and that of Peter have a great deal of similarity. Geoffrey Bromfield of Witton who died in 1612 left a total of £414 16s 11d and had a home consisting of hall or house, kitchen, great parlour, little parlour and buttery on the ground floor, with chambers over the great parlour and the house; his home is the only one known to list a 'sellar'. It seems that Bromfield made cheese for market as there was £56 worth in his little parlour.

The wealthiest resident of the town for much of the century seems to have been Dr William Bentley. Born into a local family in 1601, he received a good education and attended Balliol College, Oxford, where he matriculated in July 1623 and obtained his Bachelor of Arts that October.[22] Throughout his adult life he was a licensed 'Doctor of Physic'[23] but exactly how he made his fortune is not clear: he may have benefited from his three wives, although the marriage portion of the last of these had not been paid in full by the time Bentley made his will in 1680 as part was still owed by Mr Joseph Burgess of the East Indies.[24] Bentley lived in a large 'ancient mansion', rated at seven hearths which was situated at the entrance to the town below Winnington Hill. For some time Bentley, along with fellow townsmen William Leftwich and Thomas Robinson, was a member of the Commission of Sequestration for the Northwich Hundred and one of the principal feoffees of Sir John Deane's Grammar School.[25] He died in 1680 and was buried in a vault at the top of the terraced gardens at the rear of his home on 16 September. The inscription mentioned that he had at least 50 years experience in medicine and was 'pie, perite and benigne' and was the 'best'. In his will Dr Bentley bequeathed his 'mansion house', his wich-houses, and lands in Winnington, Leftwich, Witton, Hulse, Lach Dennis and Rudheath to his wife Dorothy and these eventually passed to his daughters. The inventory of his possessions lists items totalling £1,415 1s 10d, of which debts owing to him amounted to £1,100 14s – then an enormous sum. His house contained 14 rooms, all well furnished with beds, tables, chairs, cupboards, chests, curtains and wall hangings. Perhaps indicative of his wealth and status were the '3 picture with silk curtains and ten scutcheons in frames' that hung in the parlour, his 13 leather covered chairs and a leather covered couch, his library of books worth £40, silver plate vessels worth £40, and £45 in ready cash. Incidentally, Bentley was not the only person to be buried in his garden – John Warburton was buried in his garden on 30 November 1635.

Clearly, gentlemen such as Bentley, Tarbock, Norcott and Leftwich were well-to-do, but there were those described as 'gentlemen' who seem to possess little. Edward Mariott, who in the 1660s lived in a one-hearth house and had lands in Northwich and Witton worth £10 p.a., was only able to leave his three sons 12d each when he died in 1688 and his inventory, recorded on 26 April that year, lists possessions worth only £13 9s 10d. According to the poll tax returns his son John was a tradesman – a shoemaker. Similarly, Richard Church, who was classed as a 'gentleman' when he died in 1687, was listed as a labourer in 1660, exempt from paying the Hearth Tax, and left only £29 14 10d in goods and chattels. His designation may have something to do with his relationship to the wealthy Nantwich gentry family of the same name.

Yeomen and Husbandmen

Northwich's rural setting and links with the surrounding agricultural community is suggested by those styled as yeomen and husbandmen who lived in Northwich. Yeomen were those who held freehold land worth 40s or more a year and in agricultural terms such an individual was just below the gentry rank. During the 17th century a number of yeomen were involved in trade or business and seem to have held the distinction by virtue of the fact that their fathers were classed as such. By holding such a title there were responsibilities of performing jury service, minor public offices and military service. Thomas Pickmere of Northwich, who died in 1597 would seem to have been ready for armed service as his inventory lists armour, bows and arrows, sword, dagger, boots, spurs and a saddle. Although there are only two yeomen listed in the Poll Tax returns for Northwich, both non-resident, there are 12 men styled as 'yeoman of Northwich' amongst the list of 17th century wills and inventories preserved at the Cheshire Record Office. Among them was Thomas Skelhorne, who died in 1605 leaving goods valued at £107 17s 2d, which included cattle, a 'nag' and crops of rye and barley. Although not named as a yeoman Richard Holford of Northwich certainly earned his living from agriculture and seems to have had the wherewithal to warrant the designation. He leased lands in 'Twenbrooks' (Witton) and when he died in 1605 he was in possession of a six-roomed house, outbuildings, a cart, a plough and items of husbandry, a store of rye, barley, oats, malt and hay, along with livestock consisting of three oxen, seven cows, two 'heffers', seven calves, two horses and a mare, seven pigs, five hens and a cock – a valuable inventory amounting to

Figure Seven: **The Carpenter and the Cooper**

over £278. Others include Thomas Sumner (1616) who had a messuage and a cottage in Northwich but worked fields in Winnington and Castle; Lawrence Birchall (1623) who had lands in Twembrook, and Ralph Cheney (1626) who probably had property in Leftwich. When Cheney died he had 10 cows, 3 'heffers', 4 calves, 2 horses, 4 'styrkes', 4 rearing swine, 3 pigs, items of husbandry and quantities of peas, beans, barley, oats, malt and hay. Peter Pavor (1680) certainly farmed lands in Leftwich and in the Poll Tax returns he is classed as a husbandman; interestingly though, by the time of his death his appraisers, who record goods worth £193 19s 8d, use the term 'yeoman'. William Houghton (1665) is listed as a yeoman, a style employed by his appraisers, however in his will he is said to be a carpenter – an example of a yeoman-tradesman.

Witton had two yeomen listed in the Poll Tax – John Partington (though elsewhere he is styled as a woollen draper) and Thomas Sudlow, and a further 16 amongst the wills and inventories.

The term 'husbandman' is more numerous in both townships. This referred to a man who was engaged in agriculture and generally refers to a tenant farmer, though some husbandmen might hold a small number of freehold acres. In Northwich in 1660 there were three husbandmen who worked land in neighbouring townships. For example, Geoffrey Harrison, who prior to his death in 1615 leased a tenement in Hartford as well as the horsemill in Northwich. In Witton there were not surprisingly, seventeen husbandmen in 1660.

Food and Drink Trades

Food and drink trades were well represented in Northwich and Witton. In the 1660s three men described themselves as innkeepers, 12 as butchers and one, in Witton, as a miller. As a market town, with good communications in all directions and frequented by people from all around, it is perhaps hardly surprising to find three innkeepers. Mentioned in the wills and inventories are a cook, an innkeeper, a miller and a butcher.

John Broome was an innkeeper with an income of at least £5 p.a. and he employed six servants in his seven-hearth house. This was one of the three largest buildings in the whole of Northwich and as an inn, perhaps a coaching house, must have made an impressive sight. In addition to this he was in possession of a number of properties, one of which he converted into a kitchen (no. 47 on the town plan). With a slightly smaller business, Robert Barlow and his wife employed two female servants, including one Ann Broome (perhaps some relation to John), in their four-hearth home. Was this, I wonder another coaching house with a stable attached, for their son John Barlow who lived with them was a blacksmith. On a smaller scale there was the inn run by Henry Smith and his wife with one female employee. Robert Nixon was, according to his will and inventory (1679), both a yeoman and an innkeeper. He seems to be the same man listed in the Poll Tax as a butcher living with his wife Elizabeth and his father Ralph Nixon, also a butcher: Robert's will refers to his wife Elizabeth and their children Ralph Thomas and Katherine. According to the inventory Robert had a home with 13 rooms and a cellar in which there was ale and brewing tackle. He also held leases of lands in Gadbrook (Rudheath) and Holford. Apparently Robert Nixon also owned a wich-house called 'the Barne Wich-house' and a house which, at the time he wrote his will, was occupied by John Jackson, the glover.[26]

Butchering employed a good many people as no fewer than twelve men are recorded in the Poll Tax lists for Northwich as following this trade: Edward Geffery and his son of the same name; Samuel Geffery and his son John; William Geffery, James Geffery, John Geffery, Mathew Helsby, Ralph Nixon and his son Robert (see above); Samuel Broome, and William Percival. Despite these large numbers we have only one will, that of Richard Fryer of Witton (1612). Of all these Ralph Nixon seems to have been the most wealthy with an income of at least £5 p.a. and a six-hearth house. As to the others they seem to have experienced mixed fortunes. The Gefferies were all related, but whilst Samuel lived in a house taxed on two hearths, John was exempt from paying the tax on his one hearth. Mathew Helsby and William Percival were also in the exempt class. It is perhaps likely that these butchers who were living under modest conditions were actually in the employ of the more well-to-do such as Nixon or Samuel Geffery.

The presence of a cook in Northwich is interesting and unusual. Robert Singleton is not listed in any of the taxation returns for the

OWNERS, OCCUPIERS AND OTHERS

Northwich Hundred and, therefore, may not have been living in the town for very long before his death in 1673. His possessions although valued at only £32 2s 4d suggest that he had a comfortable lifestyle. The inventory lists a 'silkworke' chair and glassware in his six-room house, and it seems he had young children for there is reference to a cradle, a 'high stoole' and a 'childs chaire'. What we do not know is whether he was self employed and provided a 'café' type establishment, or whether he was a cook employed by a gentleman, or, perhaps more likely, by John Broome in his kitchen (47).

Witton certainly had a mill and its miller. The mill on the banks of the Witton Brook was regularly in service throughout the 17th century, but the only known individuals who had a lease of it are Richard Cranage whose inventory is dated 1611, and John Stubbs who occurs in the Poll Tax. As early as 1558 there is evidence of the lord of the manor (Venables) leasing the mill to the Bromfields and of them subletting to a William Partington and John Crowfoot in the 1570s, but the names of other millers are not known.[27]

In Northwich the horse-mill seems to have been owned by the Huxley family of Castle and then leased to a variety of individuals. The Pavor family occupied the premises at the turn of the century and then Geoffrey Harrison, husbandman (1615), had a lease of this mill from Mr Ralph Huxley, but other tenants are not easy to trace.

Retailing

According to the Poll Tax there were there were three grocers, three drapers and one mercer conducting business in Northwich. Of the drapers, brothers John and Richard Partington resided in London in 1660 and only had business or property interests in the town. It is possible that the third draper, George Dewsbury, was in some way linked with the Partingtons, perhaps at the Northwich end of the business. Dewsbury and the Partingtons were certainly well-off with incomes in excess of £5 p.a. and George Dewsbury lived in a two-hearth house with his wife and a young woman – Isabell Heath, who may have been in his employ. It seems that John Partington moved back to Northwich as he left a will dated 1667 in which he describes himself as a woollen draper of

74

THE PEOPLE OF NORTHWICH

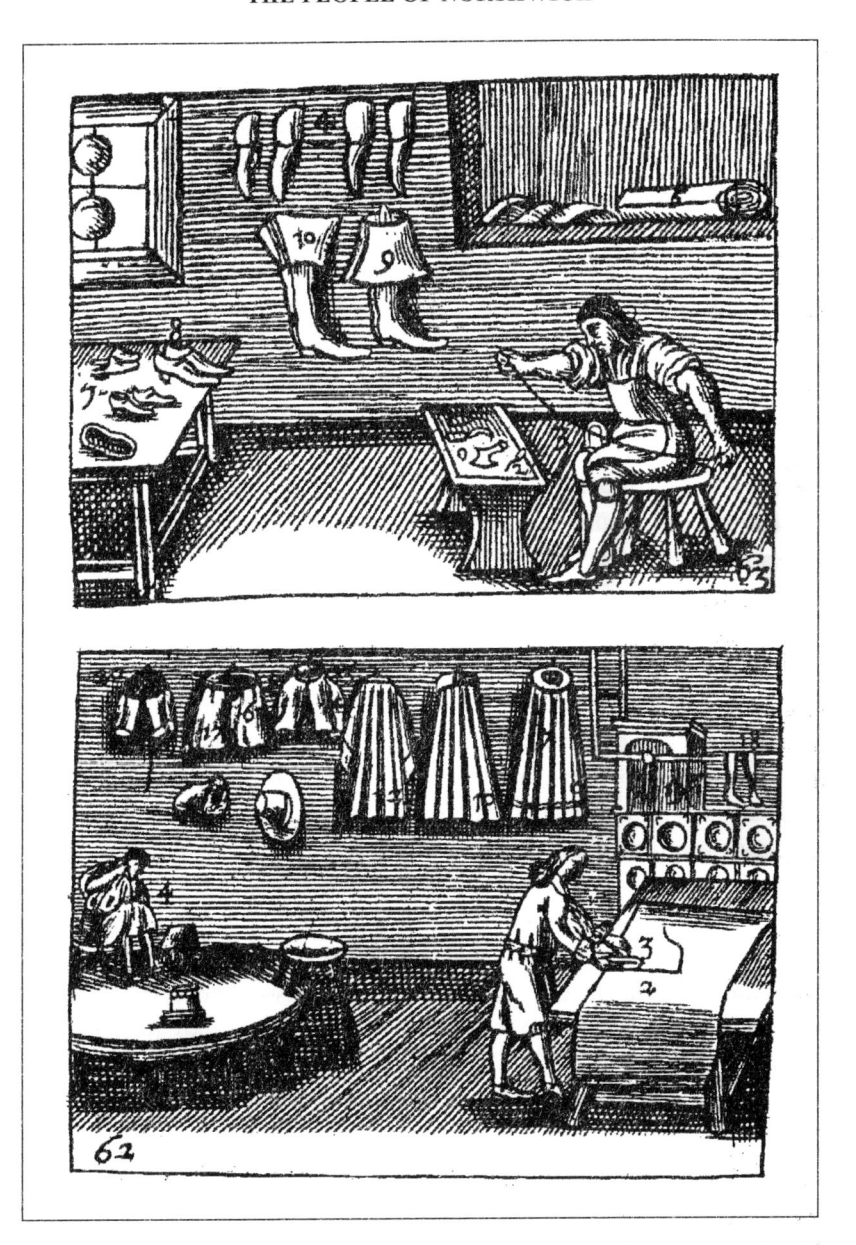

Figure Eight: **The Shoemaker and the Tailor**

Northwich: George Dewsbury's will was dated 1683. The grocers, all resident in Northwich were: Daniel Radford (later called a mercer), William Swinton and John Wrench. Other retailers whose names appear amongst the list of wills and inventories were: John Johnson, mercer of Northwich (1637); Daniel Radford, mercer of Northwich (1675); William Hewitt, mercer of Witton (1679); Samuel Higginson, ironmonger of Northwich (1672); John Cawley, grocer of Northwich (1680), and Ralph Cheney, ironmonger of Northwich (1691).

John Johnson was probably the only mercer in Northwich until his death in 1637. His shop is indicated on the town plan as being the last premises along the Market Place, or High Street (74). The inventory of his goods drawn up in March that year is particularly well detailed and the 383 entries list an amazing array of goods in his shop, his household possessions and numerous debts owing to him. In all his inventory shows his estate to be worth £195 9s 8d.

The interesting feature of the inventory is the large variety of different fabrics of varying qualities that Johnson offered for sale. Hard wearing fustian cloth, sack-cloth, worsted, canvas, buckram, grogram and serge are found amongst the more delicate lengths of calico, taffeta and 'paragan' (a cloth of mixed fibres) which were all stocked in large quantities. A cloth known as 'holland' was stocked by the ell (45 inches) along with 'phillip and cheyney' – a glossy cloth of wool and silk. To have such a variety of materials in stock seems to suggest a high level of demand. In addition the seamstresses and tailors could obtain accessories in the form of different types of lace – crew, parchment and loop – along with gartering, edging, buttons, various threads, hooks and eyes and many types of ribbon. Strangely, whilst thimbles are listed, needles are not. Normally, in the days before a customer could buy ready-made clothes these materials would be bought and handed to a tailor to make up the required garments. Having said that Johnson did stock some items of clothing. He had a number of 'belly pieces', girdles, woollen stockings and hose as well as nine hats. It would seem that up-to-date styles were important as the appraisers noted a quantity of hatbands that were 'out of fashion'. Groceries too might be purchased from Mr Johnson. He stocked a good deal of honey, prunes, currants, raisins, hops, nutmeg, pepper, cloves, cinnamon, tumeric, rice, licorice, almonds and 'sallett oyle'. Medicinal items too were stocked – 'orpiment' and 'verdigriss'. A little hardware in the form of barrels, chests, weights and scales was available, as was soap and starch. Anyone with a gun could buy shot and those with a crossbow could buy the necessary string. The presence of the grammar school at Witton and a number of gentleman's residences required Johnson to stock books and writing materials. The inventory lists 29 'grammars and psalters' at 9d each, 17 primers at 2½d each, 30 horn books, which young children used to learn to read, and 'divers' other books – in all nearly 150 books were in stock. He also had spectacle cases, parchment, ink and ink horns. As a result of owning a well-stocked shop Johnson had many customers and many of these owed him money on the day he died. One hundred and fifty-seven customers owed a total of £48 3s 7d, or just over 6s each. Besides many people who were from the immediate vicinity of Northwich, there were some from as far as Middlewich, Kelsall and Swanlow Lane, Over.

The goods in Johnson's shop, which account for half the items listed, are shown to have totalled £76 2s 1d. However it seems there are some mistakes in the calculations and a price of around £85 is more likely. It appears that he had run out of space in his shop for a number of extra items are found listed amongst his furniture in the living accommodation. Here there was half hundredweight of hops, a bundle and eight bales of flax and a barrel containing a remnant of vinegar amounting to a further £8 18s 3d. These living quarters were small and modestly furnished. In a room over the shop Johnson had a 'joined' table and three stools: for the table he had a tablecloth and two napkins. Here he had a copy of the Bible and Catechism. Above this room, in the cockloft, was the bedroom. There were two beds with their furnishings, a close stool, a 'joined' chair, a broken chest and two cushions. To warm his bed on those cold nights he had a warming pan. His other domestic utensils amounted to three pairs of sheets, pewter, brass, three old silver spoons, ironware about the fireplace, dishes, pots, a milk pail and two vessels for small beer. In all his domestic possessions came to £18 10s 9d.

In addition to his activities as a shopkeeper, Johnson also had interests in the salt business for he had £15 worth of wood for firing the pans, a right to boil eight leads, and a number of barrows in which to dry the damp salt. He also had husbandry interests with tenements in Witton and Twambrook, farming equipment and hay in his barns. These salt-making and agricultural pursuits were worth £43 15s.

Daniel Radford made his will on 24 April 1663 which was proved in May, 12 years later. He originated from Chester where his father, Robert Radford, was a linen draper, and where, in St John's Church, he was buried. According to his will he had property on Bridge Street in Chester (near to 'The Swan') and in Lichfield. All his brothers were engaged in the retail business or similar trades: Samuel and Robert were linen drapers in Chester, John was a spectacle maker in London, and Nathaniel was a shoemaker in Chester. Daniel's inventory totals a fabulous £1,321 3s 7d of which nearly half was in monies owed to him.

Susanna Bromfield seems also to have been a successful shopkeeper. She is listed in the Poll Tax as a widow residing in Witton with an income of £30 a year. She made her will on 15 February 1667 and died a few days later. The inventory of her goods made on 20 February by William Leftwich, Peter Pavor and William Green lists items totalling £71 14s 3d. The premises she occupied were in Northwich and consisted of 'the dwelling house', street chamber over the shop', 'the little chamber at the stair head', 'the little chamber next the shop' and the shop itself. It seems that her bedroom was in the room over the shop for here stood the main items of bed furniture, the 'joined bed stead with tester' along with its curtains and 'vallence'. The goods in the shop are, as with Johnson and Radford, an interesting assortment of necessities for the local people. Edible items included brandy, wine, hops, treacle, honey, brown and white sugar, carroway seeds, pepper, nutmeg, ginger and salad oil. Smokers could buy their cut and rolled tobacco and pipes. Dressmakers might purchase flax, linen and rough cloth, fustian, buckram, fine threads and silks, lace, buttons and other odds and ends. Workmen might obtain pitch, nails, lime, glue, turpentine, and brimstone. She also stored gunpowder and shot. Like Johnson she also had a wich-house and in it were stored iron pans and bars, a coal rake, and barrows; interestingly she had both wood and coal stored for fuel. Susanna also had a cow and two pigs. The last few items of the inventory are list-

THE PEOPLE OF NORTHWICH

Figure Nine: **The Husbandman and the Blacksmith**

ed under what is termed 'the ould hall'. This might refer to the family's property in Witton.

Ralph Cheney, ironmonger, was the son of Ralph Cheney, blacksmith. Of the total inventory value of £284 5s 2d, shop goods accounted for £22, debts recorded in his book amounted to £88 8s 3d, and 'desperate' debts amounted to £102 2s 5d. No doubt his debts were due to his allowing customers to have goods on credit of which less than half were recorded. Like other businessmen of his time Ralph also engaged in husbandry, having livestock worth £21 6s 8d, two horses worth £4 and crops worth £9. He also had £10 worth of cheese which was no doubt intended for market.

One man who was also a retailer but is not listed as such is William Eaton whose inventory was drawn up in July 1697. This records that in his shop he had hundreds of yards of kersey, linsey, holland, serge and broadcloth, both dyed and plain. He also stocked 'parragon', crepe (a light cotton silk), tape, ribbon, thread, laces, buttons, pins (3,000 of them), combs, ink, spectacle cases, spectacles and horn books. Eaton lived in a building which consisted of a house, dining room, shop, kitchen, buttery, best room, passage room, room over the shop, and red chamber. His personal possessions included books, pictures, a glass case and an old watch. Considering the large quantities of linen, was he related to the William Eaton, webster of Newton, Middlewich, who occurs in the Poll Tax, 1660?[28]

The Cloth Industry

The cloth industry is well represented in the town and provided employment for at least seven men, their wives and in some cases their children; two felt makers, three shermen and two collar makers. Wills and inventories include that of a silk weaver and a cloth worker.

Clothmaking went through a number of processes. Wool would have been combed or carded to make it ready for spinning and then the spun wool would be woven into raw cloth. This cloth would then be washed and fulled to thicken, de-grease and felt it, a process often carried out in a walk-mill or by some mechanical means of beating the cloth. Following this the product was then re-washed, dried and then had the nap teased before being sheared to produce a smooth fabric. The last stage was to stretch the cloth on tenter hooks before dyeing it. Exactly how the cloth industry was organised and for how long it had been carried out in the town is hard to say. There is every likelihood that the drapers had some influence over the business and also it seems they had trading links with London.

The two felt makers resided together: William Tanner and his wife seem to have employed Phillip Low who lived with them.

The three shermen are also found in one business. John Norcott and his son Samuel seem to have employed John Vernon as an apprentice. When he died in 1664, John was described as a cloth worker. He had a workshop in Northwich which was equipped with looms, reeds, presses, sheares, tenters and a variety of tools all of which he left to his son Samuel. Above the shop there was a lodging chamber in which perhaps the apprentices John Vernon and lived. Norcott also had a three-hearth dwelling house on Witton Heath and his wife had a house in Wincham. Judging by Norcott's possessions it would seem that as a sherman he was responsible not only for shearing the cloth but for weaving and stretching it too; did he also dye the cloth, for there is no mention of such an occupation? His designation 'cloth worker' would seem to be more apt than that of sherman.

The Leather Industry

A town in the centre of grazing country naturally became involved in the leather trades. One glover, one saddler and ten shoemakers were recorded in the Poll Tax; in addition Thomas Ackson, saddle maker of Witton, had a will and inventory proved in 1661; William Tench, tanner of Northwich, left a will dated 1671; Ralph Birkenhead, saddler of Northwich, had a will proved in February 1677/8; and Robert Brough, tanner of Witton, 1699.

John Cooper and his wife seem to have employed two other shoemakers – Ralph Kilshall and Henry Frodsham – together with a young woman Marie Chow. In addition to Cooper there was also Roger Phithean and his wife; and John Horten and his wife with their tailoring son and two daughters. John Jackson was the only glover and William Birkenhead was the saddler. Cooper, Horten and Birkenhead lived in two-hearth houses, whereas Jackson and Phithean had single hearths and the latter was exempt from paying the tax on the grounds of poverty.

Ralph Birkenhead's modest inventory was appraised in August 1677. Of the total sum of £12, £5 consisted of goods in his shop and £2 10s were debts listed in his book. However, his will gives a different picture of the man and his possessions. He left to his sister, Elizabeth Baguley, a gold ring, and to his other sister, Mary Jefferies all his household goods, 20 yards of flaxen sheets, two shifts of 'Osinbrigg' (meaning 'Osnabruck', a town in Germany where a coarse plain-woven fabric used for sacks, furnishings, etc. was originally made), sheets and a white 'flannell cote' for her child. Cousin John Baguley received a black saddle worked with green silk, a white bridle and snaffle, a pair of girths and a pair of gloves. Cousin William Baguley had the bed in the shop, Ralph's new serge clothes, shoes, stockings, shirts, cravats, handkerchiefs, a pair of gloves and all the working tools. Cousin Randle Baguley had a pair of gloves and cousin Elizabeth 'the press which standes in my shop'. Brother Edward Baguley received Ralph's new hat and brother Peter Baguley all the rest of Ralph's goods. Two gentlemen also benefited from the will: Peter Tarbock was bequeathed a new saddle and Ralph Leftwich, a new tan bridle and saddle. The items left in his shop consisted of leather worth 4s, buckles worth 6d, five saddle trees and five collar rings worth 5s 4d, and his tools worth 1s.

The other saddler, Thomas Ackson, provides something of a comparison. Though he is not listed in the poll tax he resided in Witton in a home which consisted of a house with a chamber over it, a little room and a shop. His inventory, dated August 1661, totalled £7 17s 7d. According to Ackson's will the family business was entrusted to brother John for the bringing up of the children and then handing over to Thomas's son, or else another brother Moses; likewise brother John was also granted a field of corn near the church called 'Chappell Croft' and a piece of ground called the 'Backside'. Thomas's horses were to be sold to pay off debts: £3 to his mother-in-law; 5s to William Hignett, 5s to William Swinton; 6s to George Barker of Newchurch (Whitegate) and £7 6s 8d to brother John.

Other Specialist Services

Amongst the list of wills and inventories there are, in both Northwich and Witton, instances of various occupations providing specialist services: tailoring, silk weaving, smithery, candle making and carpentry.

The Northwich tailors were John Newall and his wife and son William; Thomas Alexander and his wife; Mathew Moores and his wife; William Rogerson who lodged with Ralph Leftwich, gentleman; and Thomas Horton who lived with his father, a shoemaker, and mother. Two other tailors are revealed by the witnesses to a disputed will in 1668: Richard Fisher and Richard Travis. The Witton tailors were Thomas Alexander, Thomas Worsley and William Sudlow. A more specialised form of tailoring – collar making – was provided by Thomas and John Ackson of Witton (presumably a father and son).

Hugh Winnington, the silk weaver, died in May 1605 as a result of the plague that affected so many in Northwich. The inventory drawn up a few days later is very modest, listing a few household possessions amounting to a mere £1 9s 6d. The house in which he lived he left to his wife Ellen and their two daughters Elizabeth and Ellen: should they die he named his nephew Robert, son of his brother John Winnington. Hugh's will was contested by his brother and in evidence given to the Consistory Court, William Robinson and Robert Winnington of Leftwich, a cousin, stated that when he was called upon to write Hugh's will he advised him to nominate his brother John as an executor, but Hugh would not hear of it and wished that his brother have nothing to do with his family or his possessions – one can only wonder why.

Candle makers are not often found in the records, but at Witton there lived Richard Wright who followed just such an occupation, though he seems also to have done some paving work in Leftwich for which he was owed 6s by Joseph Royle. His inventory (1641) is interesting in that it sheds some light on the business of pawning and that a man of modest means could be involved in advancing cash loans. He had in pawn a pillow from Adam Heywood and his wife for 8s, a pillow from Frances Burgess for 2s 8d and from Thomas Royle, 'one fether bed and a litle Brasse pan which if he pay me 7s and all his muck then hee is to have thym againe'. When he died he was owed the sum of £49 12s 5d:

amongst his debtors are a number of people who owed money for candles, including John Bostock who owed 9s 3d and John's father, another John, for a further dozen costing 5s.

In any community there would be blacksmiths. John Sworton's inventory dated 4 December 1616 is particularly fine and lists amongst his possessions the tools and implements of his trade: two 'stiddies' and two pairs of bellows, hammers, spits, 'gobberts', axes, wires, files, pincers and tongs in all worth over £6. In addition to his smithy John also farmed a small amount of land and had livestock worth £12 10s and crops worth another £12. Overall John left only a little for whilst he was owed £8 5s he had debts amounting to £29 9s and a list of possession amounting to £70 11s. He did however manage to provide for his wife Elizabeth, son John, daughters Elizabeth and Margaret and his mother Katherine. She was to receive twenty half hoops of corn a year for so long as his lease with Sir Edward Bushell remained in force and every two weeks a further half hoop; also 12s a year for so long as she 'remain absent from my house' but if she lived in the house this payment was to cease. William Leigh and fellow blacksmith and brother-in-law Ralph Cheney were appointed executors. William Swettenham's goods were appraised by William Leftwich, Peter Pavor, Ralph Cheney and Jeffery Houghton on 8 July 1671. Inside the smithy he had two anvils, five hammers, a vice, two pairs of bellows, scales, weights, tongues, a nail tool, a hammer mould and other odds and ends. In addition to the smithy he had a house on 'Crumbhill' and a dwelling house. In total his inventory comes to £86 8s 4d, of which £42 was owed in debts, £15 came from salt-making equipment in Rachel Sudlow's wich-house (96), and just under £6 was accounted for by equipment in the smithy. John Birkenhead was another blacksmith: he left a will proved in 1674.

Other men who followed specialist trades can be found in the Poll Tax returns for Northwich: George Barker, barber; Ralph Cheney, blacksmith; James Gerrard, tinker; Robert Ditchfield, his son Robert and Francis Trevis and Thomas Hilton, barrow makers. In Witton were the following: Peter Weedall, carrier; George Ellams, glazier; John Sworton, Peter Leigh and John Sunderland, blacksmiths.

A Case Study – The Houghton Family

It is perhaps appropriate to look at a particular family, their possessions and lifestyles – that of William and Margaret Houghton of Northwich.

Where the family originated is not known though the family name, sometimes spelt Horton or Horten, is not unknown in Northwich from the medieval period. An inventory of a Roger Horton of Northwich was appraised in 1616 and there were Hortens in the 1660s. William's recorded family begins with Jeffery Houghton, a husbandman, who had two sons: Thomas (born in 1621), a husbandman, and William (born 1624), a carpenter, who both lived and worked in Northwich. Jeffery seems to have leased a dwelling house from William Leycester and premises in Yate Street (95) and in Swine Market Street (122).[29] In the 1660s the two brothers leased a number of properties: William, one from John Swinton of Knutsford (144), and three from Richard Bradford of Shipbrook (56, 117 & 119); and Thomas who had one from the Pavors of Northwich (28) and one from Dr Bentley (88).[30] In the Poll Tax returns Jeffery is described as a labourer living with his wife Margery and their daughter Elizabeth; William is described as a labourer living with his wife Margery; and Thomas, also a labourer, living with his wife Ann. The three men also appear in the Hearth Tax returns: Jeffery and Thomas with a single-hearthed houses and William with a two-hearth house. Both the brothers engaged in salt-making activities as occupiers of wich-houses, which will be referred to in Chapter Six.

William married a local girl, Margaret Baguley (in some instances she is called Margery), some time in the 1640s and had at least one son, another William, and a daughter, Margery. William's will, dated 26 February 1664, mentions his daughter who was to receive the benefit from £40 invested for her benefit over the following six years which suggests that she was 15 at this time. Son William was similarly provided for until he attained the age of 21: his portion was invested over seven years suggesting that he was 14 years old. William also instructed that his wife should provide 'meat drinke clothes and all other necessaries fit and convenient' for their son over the same period and that his executors should set him to apprenticeship in order that William might

```
                    Jeffrey Houghton  =  Margery
                    (living in 1664)
    ┌───────────────────┬──────────────────┬──────────────────┬─────────────┐
    Thomas = Ann        William    =      Margaret (? Margery)  Elizabeth =   Mary =
    (living in          c.1620 –          Baguley               Richard Travis Richard
    1664)               1665              died 1668                            Fryer
                             │
                        ┌────┴──────────────────────┐
                        William                     Margery = William Swettenham
```

The Houghton Family

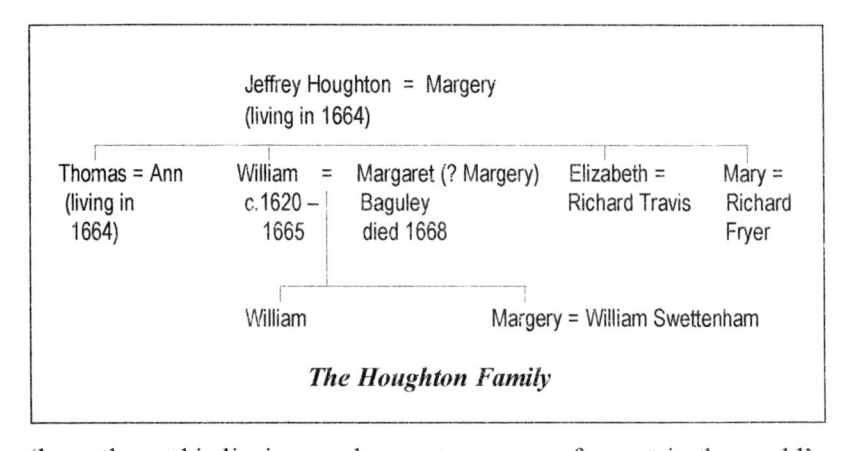

'honestly get his liveinge and come to some preferment in the world'. Following these provisions the will then lists a number of bequests. Father Jeffery was to receive the best suit of clothes and best hat; brother Thomas, 5s; brother-in-law John Ratcliffe the carpentry tools; brother-in-law Richard Fryer some old clothes; niece Margery Hunter 5s; aunt Ellen Leigh the sum of 30s to be spent on a new suit of clothes, and finally, Randle Lamb a 'blue medley' suit of clothes. The executors were William's wife, Margaret, and his father Jeffrey. William was buried at Witton on 5 September 1665 and four days later William Leftwich, Richard Bradford and Peter Pavor made the inventory of his goods. This records that in the main room of his dwelling house he had two cupboards, one long joined table and one coffer, a number of chairs, stools and forms, cushions, brass, copper and earthen wares, and an iron fire grate. In the chamber over the house he had a joined bed and a truckle bed, curtains and bedding; three coffers and a little table; a 'turnell' (a large oval tub used for salting meat or scalding pigs – though he could have used it to have a bath!), a 'flaskett', four little boxes, one little form and two shelves; his carpentry tools, nappery ware; a lawn sieve ('lawn' being a fine cotton material) and a 'racker'; a twig basket and a lantern. These household possessions amounted to £10 12s 8d. In addition he had a further £141 18s 8d in relation to his salt workings.

Following her husband's death in 1665 it seems that Margaret did well for herself and her children by increasing the family's interest in salt-making and securing a marriage for Margery with the local blacksmith – William Swettenham. Unfortunately Margaret died on 31 August 1668.[31] Being extremely ill and expecting to die, Margaret sent her sister Mary Fryer to fetch William Leftwich and request that he record her will. He attended about 8am on Sunday, 30 August and made notes of her intentions on a scrap of paper which she agreed to and made her mark, but before he could write the will in its proper form she died. At a hearing before the Consistory Court at Chester, William Leftwich gave evidence of what had happened and the details of her will. It seems that Margery and her husband, William Swettenham, challenged the will which in essence left the bulk of the estate to the infant son William. In addition to Leftwich there were a number of witnesses including her brother-in-law Thomas Houghton, who was described as being a salt worker aged 47 years. He stated that he had visited Margaret on that Sunday between 9 and 10 in the morning and found her with Mr Leftwich, Richard Cawley (whom he describes as a Quaker), and her sister Mary. Leftwich and Cawley were whispering together and so he went straight to her bedside but found that he could not understand Margaret and considered her 'unsensible'. He then departed and went to church but left just before the minister went into the pulpit. After lunch he again visited his sister-in-law and found her to be raving saying "I must have it in lease, I must have it in lease or else I cannot wall it". Other evidence of what went on in the room was given by Richard Walton of Witton, an innkeeper, aged 28; Elizabeth Lee of Northwich, aged 25; Margaret's sister Mary, aged 45, wife of Richard Fryer, a tailor; and finally, Elizabeth, aged 36, wife of Richard Travis another tailor. Interestingly Elizabeth gave evidence that she had been asked to attend court by Peter Pavor who had offered her more money than she would normally have received in wages for 'walling' for 48 hours.

Leftwich's version of Margaret's will was that she had entrusted to Richard Cawley of Witton, a mercer, and his son John, her estate for the 'use, profit and best advantage' of her son. Peter Pavor and John Cawley were nominated as her executors. Bequests were made to her relatives: sister Mary received £25 and her children a total of £20; unmarried sisters Elizabeth and Alice Baguley each received £6 and half-sister Ellen Baguley had just 20s; father-in-law Jeffrey Houghton had £10 and brother-in-law Thomas had 20s. Others receiving the same small sum were: sister-in-law Elizabeth, wife of Samuel Hunter a shoemaker; Jeffrey's children; the children of brother-in-law John Ratcliffe; aunt, Ellen Leigh, and William Leftwich. She did not forget the Cawley family for John received £10 and his sister Mary had £5. Any surplus was to be divided between her two children – the infant son and Margery Swettenham. The value of Margaret's estate was nearly £400 and included valuable salt-making rights, so there can be little doubt about why Margery and William Swettenham challenged her mother's intentions. The inventory of all her 'goods, Cattells and Chattells' was appraised on 11 November that year by William Leftwich of Northwich, gentleman; Thomas Nield of Mershton, yeoman; Jeffrey Houghton of Northwich, husbandman; and Ottiwell Broome, of Northwich, blacksmith. Margaret's house consisted of four rooms – 'the house', 'the buttery', 'the chamber over the house', and 'the little chamber'. It was a two-up and two-down house which in the Hearth Tax returns of 1664 was rated as having two hearths. This is presumably the same house that her husband lived in, which had either been extended or else her husband's appraisers ignored the 'buttery' and the 'little chamber' as having nothing in worth recording.

 The main pieces of furniture in the main room of her home were her 'great joint table', four chairs and four stools. For comfort she had six embroidered cushions and seven others. She also had a small table and a form. For eating and drinking she possessed a number of pewter utensils: 12 dishes, nine large 'sawcer dishes', nine small 'sawcers', two old flaggons, and one dozen spoons. Some of these were no doubt stored in the two cupboards, or the presse, or even the 'great old chest'. Cooking will have been done over iron grate and she had a number of pots and pans for the purpose: two tin dripping pans, a tin pan, a saucepan, two large brass pans, two small brass pans, two brass potts, a posnett (a large round cooking pot with a handle and standing on three feet) and two skelletts (pans with three feet and having a long handle). She also had a twig basket and another brass pan which was said to be in a furnace. The fireplace was equipped with fire shovel, a pair of bellows, a pair of tongs and a 'hanging brandreth'. Foodstuffs would have been stored in the buttery, but none is mentioned though here she had a milk tub and a beef tub, a small 'Coumpe', a 'Turnell' (a large oval tub used for salting pigs) and a small piggon (a copper can). In this same room she also had some earthenware and some old iron.

Above the buttery stood 'the little chamber' in which there was a bedstead, a 'chaffe' bed (or mattress), two feather bolsters, two 'chaff' bolsters, a coverlet and a 'caddow' (a rough woollen bedcover). In the main bedroom, 'the chamber over the house' stood a 'joynt bed' with a featherbed (a feather mattress), a 'chaff' bed, three feather bolsters, a white rug (meaning a coarse woollen bedcover), two white blankets, curtains and valance. In addition there was another featherbed, a 'chaff' bed, a feather bolster, two feather pillows and three white blankets. Perhaps these additional items made up a separate bed on the floor as there is no mention of another bedstead. Other items of furniture were a chair, two stools and two chests. A number of items of linen were to be found in this room: seven round sheets, a pair of scotchcloths (a coarse fabric said to be made from nettle fibres), a pair of flaxen sheets, a pair of new linen cloths, a dozen napkins and a table cloth: presumably the linen was kept in one of the chests. In this room there was another firegrate (the second hearth on which tax was paid). Other items were four door locks, a 'lawne sieve' and two little baskets. Some of these items are the same as those referred to in her husband's inventory.

In one of her chests Margaret had £23 1s 8d in ready money – no doubt the chest was lockable. She was owed £114 10s in bonded debts and a further £62 1s 8d according to her debt book, but these were without any bond. Her wearing apparel was valued at £5. In addition to these domestic items Margaret had possessions in a number of wich-houses in the town and reference to these will be made in Chapter Six. She also had a lease on three cottages for several years worth £8; these were presumably in Northwich.

---

[1] W.G. Hoskins, *Local History in England* (1972), p. 172.
[2] Par Reg; CRO: WC Winnington, 1607.
[3] C.B. Phillips & J.H. Smith, *Lancashire and Cheshire from AD 1540* (1994) p. 8.

OWNERS, OCCUPIERS AND OTHERS

[4] All the information that follows is taken from G.O. Lawton, (ed.) *Northwich Hundred: Poll Tax 1660 and Hearth Tax 1664*, Lancashire & Cheshire Record Society, cxix (1979).

[5] External residents in Poll Tax: Peter Tarbucke, Edward Meritt, Richard Bradford, John Partington, Richard Partington, Robert Warburton, William Harcourt, William Row, Mrs Ann Moseley, Joshua Hodgkis, and Peter Venables.

[6] Firstly, a person may not have actually been resident in the town but simply have had a property interest there: for example, Richard Bradford, yeoman, is listed as having an income of £5 p.a. from his interests in Northwich but he is also listed under the townships of Witton and Shipbrook and is known to have lived in the latter place. But the number of such people seems small enough as to not affect the estimated population. Another problem is that we cannot tell where the houses were sited though there does seem to be a particular order in which they were listed starting at one end of the town, below Castle Hill, and this may give some clue as to locations.

[7] The Hearth Tax has a drawback in that it does not tell us where each house was situated or exactly who lived under each roof, though invariably, as with the Poll Tax, the listing starting at one end of a town follows a particular path.

[8] CRO: DSS/1/4/6.

[9] J. Howard Hodson, *Cheshire, 1660 – 1780: Restoration to Industrial Revolution*, (1978) p. 93.

[10] I have used a slightly smaller multiplier for the exempt class as many will have been lone parents or else widows and single women without children.

[11] See Introduction to *PT & HT*.

[12] CRO: DSS/1/4/6.

[13] *PT & HT*, p. 2.

[14] Extracts made from wills and inventories that follow are all CRO, the reference being the WS followed by surname and date, e.g. WS/ Holford, 1605; Venables, 1631; Norcott, 1679; Bentley, 1680.

[15] These include Joshua Hodgkis, Peter Venables and George Leftwich who are presumed to be gentry.

[16] In many cases the lists of households end with a spinster or spinsters of a different name to the family head and these may be presumed to be female servants, and even where they have the same family name this may still be the case.

[17] Calvert, p. 1046, rule 17 mentions wallers as female.

[18] *PT & HT*, pp. 143, 238.

[19] 'Inquisitions Post Mortem 1603-1660', *LCRS*, vol 91 (1938), p.103.

[20] *ibid.*

[21] CRO: WS 1629.

[22] *Oxon.,* 1500-1714, vol 1, p. 111.

[23] He was licensed as a doctor as early as 1630, since when he was accused by the churchwardens of Witton of practising of 'physick' without a licence he was in fact able to produce one.

[24] CRO: WS 1680.

[25] Cox, p. 76.

[26] See also *PT & HT*, p. 148, 239, which list John Jackson.

[27] CRO: DLT/D241/3, 4.

[28] *PT & HT*, p 139.

[29] CRO: DLT/A2/51, 56.

[30] CRO: DLT/A/2/56.

[31] CRO: WC 1668 & WS 1669.

4

NORTHWICH TOWN GOVERNMENT

The Lord of the Manor and the Burgesses
Since 1484 the lordship of Northwich had been in the hands of the powerful Stanley family. Richard III had granted the town to Sir Thomas Stanley as a reward for his support and then at the beginning of the following reign Stanley was created Earl of Derby by Henry VII. Stanley and his successors exercised particularly strong influence in political, military, economic and religious affairs in both the region of north-west England and the kingdom as a whole. In fact for much of the 16th and 17th centuries successive members of the family were hereditary Lords Lieutenant of both Cheshire and Lancashire. In Northwich this great lord's authority was exercised through his courts which were presided over by his steward or a deputy steward.[1]

Northwich had been regarded as a borough throughout the medieval period though the exact nature of its status is not known as no charter survives.[2] It was a manor and seigneurial borough which meant that the governance of the town was under manorial control and although it had a more complex organisation than most towns, it was not as free as incorporated boroughs for the lord of the manor retained control over the governmental affairs: not then a *liber burgus* with a fixed rent and a measure of incorporation. What independence the burgesses had was purely in relation to trade, perhaps in return for their service on the jury of the town courts and in other offices. However, as a group the burgesses of Northwich held a position of not inconsiderable importance in the organisation and control of the borough and its salt-trade, for it was they who, with the lord's consent, drafted the laws and customs and elected the various officials who policed the town and its business activities. In these respects the burgesses had much in common with the members of the merchant guilds of the larger towns and cities.

Who then were the burgesses? In essence they were the townspeople who had been given freedom from the normal manorial constraints in order to allow and encourage trade. Non-residents who had links with the town could also be appointed as burgesses: in Northwich they were known as 'foreign' burgesses. Burgess-ship was hereditary: sons, during their fathers' lifetime as well as afterwards, unmarried daughters and unmarried widows could inherit the freedoms, rights and privileges. That said, I have yet to find a female burgess in the few extant lists. New burgesses were created from time to time by the lord of the manor and could be elected and presented by the burgesses themselves with the lord's consent – if his consent was not forthcoming the election was void.[3] William Hyde of Frodsham, who occurs as a burgess for the first time in 1671, seems to be the only known case of an appointment in the 17th century. It is difficult to estimate the number of burgesses and it may be that their numbers varied from time to time. In 1569 it is said that there were 13 living in the town and over 40 living elsewhere suggesting a significant number. A similar proportion of resident to non-resident burgesses is likely to have been always the case.[4]

The only known full list of burgesses is that contained in the court roll for 4 November 1702; for any other time all that we have are occasional listings of those present at a particular court session and these are set out in *Table Five*.[5] The fullest of these is from December and January 1672 when 27 names are recorded. Of these there are only 12 different family names of which ten feature regularly in other 17th century listings – one name was new in 1671 (Hyde) and the other was new in 1663 (Fox), though this person is likely to have a direct family connection with a burgess of the same name from the previous century. The kinship qualification is certainly born out by the figures given in *Table Five*.

The names of the burgesses which appear from time to time do not necessarily represent those engaged in the salt trade: conversely many families who were, such as the Bostocks, Wilbrahams, Broomes and Tarbocks, are not listed as burgesses. Another fact is that of the 1656 list only three men were resident within the town: the others lived in Witton, Lostock Gralam, Comberbach, Plumley, Shipbrook, Rudheath, Tarvin, Kelsall and Middlewich. Similarly, of the 27 names listed in 1671 only six were townsmen and the others resided in Witton, Antrobus, Lostock Gralam, Rudheath, Hartford, Shurlach, Shipbrook, Plumley and Tarvin. These low figures for resident burgesses seem consistent with the ratio given in 1569.

In addition to their 'rule' of the town the burgesses' privileges included freedom from paying the 'lead fine' for the houses they occupied, though this only applied to those who were resident in the town, and freedom from all fair and market tolls throughout the county and the city of Chester. They were also exempt from taking the office of constable and any other post excepting those associated with salt-making, and even then having been appointed as a 'lead-looker' they were not to take any inferior office. They also had a power to arrest offenders and their goods in the absence of the lord's bailiffs. Like any other resident, burgesses were required to assist the lord's officials if called upon to do so and if they refused they could forfeit their 'burgesseship'. One rather quaint privilege was their right to have an oven 'to heat pies in', whereas others were not permitted to have an oven at all and had to use the lord of the manor's bakehouse.[6]

Local Rivalries

The appointment of new burgesses to serve on juries did not always work well as local rivalries, jealousies and town politics surfaced to give the lord's steward a few problems. Hyde's appointment as a burgess caused some aggravation. At the court leet held on 20 August 1671 there were 12 'reputed Ancient Burgesses and one a new Burgese', but when they retired into the jury room to consider their verdict the 'ancient' 12 refused to sit down with the new member, William Hyde. Then the 12 could not agree a verdict as one of them, Peter Venables of Brownslane, refused to agree with the others and failed to attend. The steward,

NORTHWICH TOWN GOVERNMENT

| Family Name | Occurrences ||||||||||
	1595	1637	1638	1641	1656	1663	1666	1672	1702
Bromfield		2	1	1					1
Fox	1					1	1	1	1
Frodsham		2		1		1	2	3	2
Hyde							1		
Johnson	1								
Leftwich	1	1	2	3	2	2	2	2	2
Litler	1	1	1		2	1	2	4	3
Robinson		2	3	4	1	1	1	1	2
Shaw	3			1	2			1	1
Sudlow	1	1	2	1	3	3	1	4	4
Taylor	1								
Venables		2	1	2	1	1	2	4	2
Walton	1								
Winnington	5	4	4	2	2		2	3	4
Wright	2		1	3	1	1	3	4	
Totals	**19**	**14**	**15**	**14**	**17**	**12**	**15**	**27**	**23**

Table Five: **Burgess Families**

95

Thomas Robinson, adjourned the jury until 26 September, but due to sickness this was further adjourned to 10 October. Then on this day, two of the jury failed to appear and were both fined 40s, and another adjournment was made. Finally, on 7 November all 13 members of the jury attended but, once again, Venables was obstructive and so the steward asked Hyde to separately view the decision made by the others and to sign it in order that a full jury of 12 were in agreement. Hyde duly signed the verdict and the court was discharged. The foreman, Robert Litler, expressed his displeasure and considered that Robinson had acted illegally in requesting Hyde to sign the verdict and correspondence concerning this was exchanged between the two men.[7]

The steward also faced problems on 19 December that year. Seventeen burgesses assembled for business of whom Robinson listed nine, including the same Robert Litler and Peter Venables, whom he 'durst not entrust with the Lords concernes' considering them to be enemies of the lord's interests. He further suggested that one of these nine, Ralph Leftwich of Northwich, 'doublely fell within exceptions against, first as an Enemy to the Lord.... and 2dly as a Leadlooker by order not to be upon the Jury'. He presumably trusted the other eight but they were not sufficient in number to form a jury. Robinson then adjourned the court until 2 January whilst other 'trusted' burgesses might be summoned. On the appointed day 17 burgesses appeared and a jury of 12 was appointed. The nine 'enemies' did not appear and neither did William Hyde. The steward seems to have been acting lawfully in selecting what he considered to be an appropriate jury. It was a town custom that when summoning a jury from the list of names supplied by the bailiff, the steward could determine how many to call – 12, 13 or 14 or more. He could also refuse to impanel anyone he disliked and to replace them with either a resident or foreign burgess.[8]

Courts

As already said, the normal legal, administrative and commercial business of the town was conducted through the manorial court with its jury of burgesses. There can be little doubt that the way in which the Northwich courts operated during the 17th century in the same way as those operated during the medieval period when, according to the few available extant court rolls, it would seem they were held every other Tuesday throughout the year. On a regular basis local people were presented to the court for licences to occupy wich-houses and to boil salt; for the payment of taxes and various dues especially as regards the markets; for brewing ale without licence; for pleas of debt and trespass; for offences of battery, affray and breaches of the peace; and of obstructing the roads and the channels through which the brine ran. The perquisites Cof the courts and the collection of tolls and dues provided a modest trickle of funds into the coffers of the lord of the manor. Weighty legal issues and serious criminal offences could not be dealt with in this court of summary jurisdiction; rather they were sent on to the county's court of quarter sessions, which occasionally met in Northwich, or to the court of assize at Chester. Matters of an ecclesiastical or moral nature would be referred to the Bishop's Consistory Court at Chester.

A summary of fines and payments from a court session of the late 16th century gives a little insight into court business at the beginning of our period. Breach of the assize of ale, encroachments, carrying wood, failing to make pavements in front of wich-houses, not removing a standing and not shutting up the swine-cote door are all referred to along with the payments of lead fines.[9]

In essence the Northwich court consisted of two courts rolled into a single session: the Court Leet and Court Baron. The Leet would hear evidence and consider any offence that occurred within its jurisdiction in order to ensure good governance, prevention of public nuisance and maintenance of the Peace, and would appoint officials. The Court Baron would record transfers of land; receive heriots, duties and customs; hear and determine matters that could only be decided by the lord of the manor or his steward; and take cognizance of trespasses, debts, slanders and other minor matters where the damage did not exceed 40 shillings. Twice a year – a fortnight after the feasts of St John the Baptist (24 June) and Michaelmas (29 September) – the court sittings were known as 'the Great Courts', when matters pertaining to the lord of the manor's affairs were tried.[10] Ordinarily, matters affecting the town and its business were dealt with in the fortnightly sessions throughout the year and in addition there were three fair courts, held immediately after each of the fairs in April, July and December.[11] The place of meeting during the Tudor and Stuart periods was the 'Court House' situated on the southern side of the Market Place and close by the Town Bridge. During the medieval period the 'house of pleas of the court', in which people could be detained, was described as being on the bridge of the town. Was this lock-up actually on the bridge? If so it might have been similar to that at St. Ives, Huntingdonshire, where the surviving medieval bridge has a small building, a chapel, halfway across, or else similar to that at Warrington where there was a lock-up in the central pier.[12]

The manor courts of Northwich, both leet and baron, were commonly referred to as the 'Burgess Court with View of Frankpledge'. The first part of this rather quaint title refers to the composition of the jury and the term 'view of frankpledge' refers to a town's mutual responsibility for good order and of the community meeting together to determine who had transgressed. Unfortunately the actual affairs of the courts are lost to us save for a few scraps and what seems to be a complete roll dated 4 November 1702: interestingly a Saturday, instead of the traditional Tuesday which had been the case throughout the 17th century and earlier.[13]

The surviving court record for 4 November 1702 begins with a list of 120 names of the men and women who had a duty to attend court: the clerk recorded 23 burgesses and 97 inhabitants of the town. Of the burgesses, the name of Peter Venables 'senior' is crossed through as is the appellation 'junior' given to his son, as the clerk realised at the last minute that old Peter had passed away. He likewise made amendments to the list of residents by crossing out the name of Thomas Baker and deleting the first name and status of Mary Robinson, widow, and inserting the name of her son James as a replacement. From this it seems that the practice was to simply copy the list of suitors from one session to another and then to make the amendments on the day of the court as the names were called. About half of those listed failed to appear and of them the majority seem to have no reasonable excuse. A fine of 1s was imposed on each of the 'inhabitants' who failed to appear or offer an excuse. The burgesses were exempt from this normal penalty but could have a larger fine of 40s imposed if having been summonsed to appear they then wilfully refused to attend. Once the court had assembled a jury of 12 burgesses was selected. On this occasion the names of the jurors were Nathaniel Leftwich, Wareing Robinson, Richard Shaw, Samuel, Thomas and Joseph Sudlow, Peter, Robert and Thomas Winnington, Peter Venables, Robert Fox and John Deane. This jury would then hear the business of the court which consisted of a number of presentments made by the town's officials. The cases heard may be divided into matters of anti-social behaviour, nuisance, trading irregularities and disobedience of the court.

Constables William Moores and Thomas Edgar named several people for breaching the 'Queen's Peace' and causing an affray for which they were fined the standard 3s 4d – Thomas Knight of Castle and Robert Lindsey, upon each other; Josiah Lowe, George Barlow and James Gorst, on each other; Richard Dobson on Samuel Peacock; and William Gandy on Richard Sutton. Tantalisingly we are not told the stories behind these minor assault cases. A more serious assault, one which drew blood on both parties and therefore attracted a penalty of 6s 8d, was committed by Raph Bassmith and Josiah Kennerly. On a more mundane matter, 13 people were presented by Daniel Barker and fined 10s each for allowing their swine to roam in the streets of the town. The town baker, Thomas Smith, presented John Malbon, the miller, John Malbon a carrier, William Burroughs, Phillip Morris, Jonathon Roberts and John Hunt, all inhabitants of the town, for breaking the rule that required everyone to use the lord's oven for baking bread and pastry: each man was fined 6d. It is interesting to note that it was men who did the baking.

The overseers of the market seem to have been busy: John Wood was accused of selling pork that was unfit in open market and was fined 1s and Edward Kennerly of Middlewich and Josiah Williamson of Weaverham were each fined 2s for offering sub-standard shoes for sale.

A number of matters appearing before the court were for disobeying an order made at a previous hearing or of failing to perform a particular duty and the fines for residents who did not attend court. John Walton and Peter Young were on this occasion fined 6s 8d each for not 'rectifying their abuses' – whatever they were; Mr John Hewitt, Peter Cook and William Baguley were each fined 20s for not observing the orders of the last court; Mr Thomas Asshall had not taken down his 'house of office' (his privy!) as ordered and was fined 20s; and likewise Thomas Barlow senior was required to remove his house of office before the next court on pain of 10s as it was causing annoyance. Sometimes officials neglected to do their duty: John Broome and James Antrobus 'Supervisors of the Township' failed to keep the common leads in good repair and were each fined 40s and Joseph Twemlow neglected his office of scavenger and was fined 3s 4d. An amusing entry is the instruction to Constable Moores to find the culprit who had taken a leaf of the table of the 'further court house chamber' and to make presentation at the next court hearing or else pay 2s. Obviously someone had decided to make use of a nice piece of board and had the cheek to steal it from the courthouse! Moores failed, for this matter came up again on 30 December. Mathew and William Moores, Jeffrey Houghton and William Jenkinson, 'for want of the Cort Table Leafe' were presented and ordered 'to make & discover of it before next Court in 3s 4d a piece'.

Town Officials

It was the Michaelmas session of the Leet – the Great Court – that appointed the town officials for the following year. Each was required to swear an oath of office and could be punished if he failed in his duty.[14] The first of these, and arguably the most important, were the constables. It was they who were required to detect offences, arrest offenders, maintain public order and to present matters to the courts; they also had the right to punish 'Rogues and Vagabonds and Sturdy Beggars'. The 'Affeerers' were also of some importance as it was they who attended court hearings to impartially assess the level of amercement (fine) paid by a defaulter according to the facts of the case. The other town officials may be separated into two categories – those whose duties related to the salt industry, and those whose responsibilities were linked to commerce or were of a more general nature.

The lead-lookers, or 'Rulers of Walling', were required to keep and maintain the 'Ancient Customs Orders and Liberties of the Towne' and to select which of the wich-house occupiers could 'wall' at any particular time and to allow walling in the early part of the year. They were required to keep a record of all walling activities and give an account when required to do so by the steward or his deputy. Originally there were two such officials chosen from the burgesses and both had to be resident in the town, but later the rule was amended so that there was one resident and one 'forren' (non-resident) burgess. The 'Overseers' or 'Surveiors' were required to record what 'Peecings' (rights to boil and make salt) the lead-lookers had set, as well as themselves setting the 'Ordinary Peecings of Walling' to the best advantage of occupiers and the town, and the customary 'Extra-ordinary Peecings' which covered the costs of officers' fees and taxes. Other officials were required to ensure that occupiers made salt of a good and sufficient standard (the salt-viewer); to broker fairly between the buyers and sellers of salt and to ensure a proper price was charged (the killers of salt); to check the channels through which the brine flowed and order defects to be repaired (the gutter-viewers); to check that pans were of the correct size (the pan-cutters); and to watch for people carrying wood (the wood-tender). Wood was such a valuable commodity that the theft of it was regarded as a serious offence and offenders were fined 6s 8d, one shilling of which was paid to the wood-tender who informed.

Various officials were appointed to supervise the markets, check for bad meat and ale, inspect leather goods to ensure they were properly tanned and dressed, test the weights and measures in use and ensure that the streets were left clean and tidy. These officials probably ranked quite low in the town's hierarchy for they were not elected from the burgess class but from the ordinary residents.[15]

Amongst the few papers that exist for the court hearing of 30 December 1702 are nominations for office holders for the 'ensuing year'. The 'market-lookers', John Hunt and William Jeffrey, nominated Roger Lindsey and Samuel Dorton. 'Ale-tasters' Samuel Lathom and Robert Helsby nominated Thomas Parsefull and Joseph Twemlow (then the 'scavenger') to be their replacements. The 'sealers of leather', William Miller and George Ditchfield, do not seem to have made any nominations and continued in office. For the onerous post of constable, John Hunt, Phillip Moriss, Robert Littler and Richard Smith were nominated by William Moore and Thomas Edgar, but only Hunt and one

Stephen Waterworth were selected. Twemlow's replacement as 'scavenger' was Peter Yanning and the office of 'burleyman' (a court official who collected various dues) was performed by Ottiwell Broome. Each man was required to swear his oath of office before 10 January or else pay a fine of 40s 11d: they took the oath – naturally.[16]

The Customs

Each of these officials was charged with keeping the customs of the town and ensuring that the community abided by the various rules and regulations. The court and its jury of burgesses acted as the town's legislature. The decisions they made were set down in the town's 'Book of Customs' and kept in a chest in the Court House.[17] Once entered, these customs were effectively the town's bye-laws. The most comprehensive record of the customs of the town and of salt-making was that collected by Peter Warburton, when steward of Northwich, and confirmed by the jury in 1638 and again in 1641.[18] 'The Ancient Customs of the Burrow and Town of Northwich... concerning the Liberties and Priviledges of Burgesses, As also concerning the making of Salt and well ordering and government of the said Towne' is the preamble to Warburton's book which lists over one hundred orders. These orders, rules, or customs, seem to have been developed over time as and when particular problems came before the court. Sometimes over a lengthy period of time they were repeated or reinforced. Though not listed in any particular order, the customs covered a number of categories: trade and the markets; the conduct of the townspeople and officials; safety of the town; free passage along the streets; 'foreigners'; and last, but by no means least, the salt trade itself. With so many officials and regulations there can be little doubt that the courts were kept busy and so it is even more disappointing that the records do not survive.

It would perhaps be tedious to quote all of the customs of the town, so I have selected some which seem to be important and interesting as regards 'good order & government'.[19] Those concerning salt-making will be dealt with in the next chapter.

First those which refer to trade and the markets.

That noe Ale house keeper or Innkeeper shall suffer any person or persons (but travellers) to bee drinking or typling in their houses upon any Sunday in the aforenoone at the tyme of divine service that is to say betweene nine of the clock and eleven in the aforenoone upon paine to forfeite for every offence 12d.

Quite right too, some might suggest! And shopping for the best cut of meat on a Sunday was prohibited too.

That noe butcher shall set any flesh to sale either in shop or shambles or elsewhere in the sayd towne betweene the sayd houres upon paine to forfeit for every offence 1s.

Two clauses refer to the quality of meat sold in the town. There was concern that some butchers adulterated their meat to make it appear softer or redder.

If any Butcher abuse his flesh in beateing or pricking the same for every such offence to forfeite 6s 8d, and the flesh to bee forfeited and distributed to the poore by the discretion of the market lookers & constables of the towne.

The next two clauses refer to the sale of corn. It would seem that this commodity was sold in that part of the Market Place near to the Court House.

That the Baylffe or Tolltaker of Corne shall not take above a pint of Corne at the Bushell, and soe after that rate, and shall keepe just measures, and make cleane places for corne to stand upon, and make cleane the streets adjoyning to the Court house upon payne to fyne to the Lord for every default 3s 4d.

It is ordered by this Jury that the Towletaker of Corne shall every Markett day Ring the Markett bell within half an houre after xii of the Clock at the furthest and if the Seller of Corne after warninge given them, the next markett day do not come with their Corne in time shall either be debarred from selling their Corne that day or else pay double Towle, and the Towletaker for every his default to fyne, to the Lord 20s.

The time restriction on the sale of corn was a serious matter and designed to give all traders an equal opportunity to sell their wares and to prevent illicit trading. There were three ways in which a trader might make an unfair profit: first, there was 'forestalling' which occurred when traders waited outside the market town and bought up the goods as they arrived in order to corner the market; the second was 'regrating' by which a trader might buy up goods in order to sell them on again towards the end of the day when there was less competition; and thirdly, the practice of arriving at a market late in the day when many goods had been sold and thus avoiding competition.[20] On market days shoemakers were similarly restricted in order to allow all-comers to have a reasonable chance to sell their wares: shoes, boots and other leather goods could not be displayed for sale until after 12 noon.

It would seem that millers and carriers had been buying corn at Northwich market and then selling it on elsewhere for a profit and thus depriving the lord of any tax – that certainly had to stop.

> *That noe Milner nor Carrier shall buy any graine in the market of the sayd towne, but onely for his or their owne proper uses upon paine to forfeite for every such offence 1s.*

Carriers also bought malt into the town for sale but any money they made had to spent in buying salt, thus restricting their profit and benefiting the town.

> *None shall buy malt of any Carrier except the Carrier will bestow the money or most part thereof upon salt upon paine of 20s & to be imprisoned at the discretion of the Steward or his Deputye.*

The townspeople were only allowed to bake their bread in the oven belonging to the lord of the manor, which was situated near the Leach Eye. Burgesses were excepted and could have their own ovens in which to bake small pies.

> *All the Inhabitants of the sayd towne by ancient custome ought to bake at the Lords Oven in the sayd Towne (except such as by privilege are excused) upon paine to bee amerced for every default according to the quallitye of their offence. And the Baxter ought to have the value of a penny in Dough at a hoop & not above upon paine for every offence 12d.*

The use by all of a common oven necessitated a need for regulation about when and how the oven could be used and to prevent people causing a nuisance by congregating there presumably to warm themselves.

> *To the intent to establish & set some good rules & orders as well for the Baxter as the Bakers It is ordered and presented that the Baxter shall warne or streyne the Bakers to come with their dowe to the Bakehouse at a due hower and the Bakers shall bring for every houpe of Dowe a good kid & a halfe of wood, and all their sayd ffuel to be brought to the Bakehouse one whole hower before they bring*

their dowe and for every default either in the Baxter or them that bring bread to bee baked... ... ...6d and alsoe the Baxter shall not bake or suffer to be baked any horse bread in the Lords Oven after the inhabitants of the towne have baked, but shall for the bake-ing of horse bread heate the oven againe because the moistnesse of the horse bread doth coole the oven and putteth the towne to greater charge in fewell and moreover the Baxter shall restraine all such idle persons as use the sayd bakehouse and have nothing to doe there upon paine of a penny for every such person, or else to bee punished at the discretion of the Steward or his Deputy and if any person inhabiting in the sayd towne doe bake away from the sayd Bakehouse they shall forfeite for every such default & offence.

Inside the bakehouse there were a number of moulding boards on which the dough could be kneaded into shape.

It is ordered and presented that the moulding boards in the Lords Bakehouse and the oven are to bee sufficiently amended & repaired for the moulding & bakeing of the Inhabitants bread ... . upon paine for every default to fofeite 3s and the defaults to bee present-ed at every single Court.

The court was particularly concerned with the safety of the town, its population and its industry. With the dual threat of flood and conflagra-tion there was a need for contingency planning and supporting orders. Flood defences were formed by waste tips along the banks of the River Dane. These, known as Crum Hills, were ancient tracts of common land on which the townspeople could lay their earth, ashes or 'crum', and as such it was forbidden for any person to make use of these areas for their own purposes.

The tipping of waste from the wich-houses was confined to the Crum Hills and the depositing of it anywhere else in the town, especially another man's vacant wich-house site, could render an offender to a fine of 5s. Tipping was encouraged between the Brine Pit and the bank of the River Dane and along the river towards the Dane Bridge in order to pro-tect both and the town itself from 'hurts and inconveniences' caused by the 'great floods'.

Additional flood barriers in the form of splash boards and fences were erected along the river banks:

It is ordered and presented that all they which have lands by the syde of the Rivers Dane and Weever doe plash and make their fence before the next Court upon paine for every one not soe doing to forfeite 6s 8d.

Of course the rivers were the natural means of providing the wherewith-all to fight fires in the town so it was necessary to ensure that access to them was not impeded. Therefore, it was an offence to obstruct any of the ways leading to the river:

If any person doe cast any crum or rubbish in any highway that leadeth to the water and soe stoppeth the same way shall bee presented by the Coroner at every single Court and forfeite for every such fault 1s.

Specific mention is made of access at the 'Lodstone' (on the west bank of the Weaver); alongside the Court House; between the properties of Messrs Yate and Downes; between Wilbraham's and Pickmere's properties, and alongside the 'Kiln Orchard'. With the ever-present danger of fire from the salt processing further dangers had to be minimised and so the making of a fire in the wich-house streets at night was prohibited. In case of an emergency the town had ladders kept in particular places and it was an offence for anyone who had used them not to return them, as the following ordinance, dated 2 October 1593, states:

It is ordered and presented that what person doth take away any of the towne ladders from the places where they are usually hanged and kept, not making them privye thereto who keepeth the sayd ladders and doe not bring them thither againe the same night shall forfeit to the Lord's use 5s to bee presented and estreated at every single Court.

It is probable that irresponsible behaviour by a townsman had prompted this, but we cannot be sure.

The leadsmithy was a place of particular risk. Consequently there needed to be space in front of it and access to water nearby.

It is ordered that ye Leech Eye shall bee from tyme to tyme kept open and purged.

It is ordered that the Lord of the Leadsmithy shall make a lawful gripyard at the end of the Leadsmithye towards the backhouse streete without incroachment upon the sayd streete and keepe clean the lake at the sayd end of the said Leadsmithie upon warning given by the Coroner upon paine to forfeit 6s 8d.

Cleanliness and tidiness of the streets was important to the town, not so much in the interests of public health, though there was a requirement for the place where corn stood to be kept clean, but rather in the interests of the staple business and the convenience of those involved. Once a fortnight occupiers of wich-houses were to sweep the streets in front of their doors and wood stacks. And also

> That every Inhabitant of the sayd towne shall weekly every Saturday make cleane the streetes before their dwelling houses and at all other tymes when the Scavenger shall give warning upon paine to forfeite for every default 6d.

Dung hills, swine cotes and troughs were not to be kept in the street, neither were logs and timber, nor empty carts at night. Pavements had to be repaired each year before the Easter court session or repaired at any time after being given due notice by the Coroner. Of course it was particularly important to keep access to the wich-houses free and the streets along which the brine channels ran unimpeded and clean, and we will return to this later.

What about anti-social behaviour?

> Scoulds chiders & misdemeaned persons being soe duely proved or presented shall abyde a day & a night in imprisonment in the Court house in the sayd towne or else to pay immediately to the Bayliffe to the Lords use for the first offence 3s 4d at the election of the party offending and for the second offence two dayes and two nights or else 5s & that every such offences bee presented at any Court viz either at single Court or any Great Court Leete by the bayliffe or any other officer of the sayd towne, upon every such presentment the Steward or his Deputy shall presently proceed to the punishment thereof: And that every party so offending & will not come to the Court house before the Steward or his Deputy being commanded by the Bayliffe shall be published in the Church openly upon the Sabboth day and there if all and if they doe not then yeild themselves then their punishment and fyne to be doubled.

Those who might interfere in the prosecution of this custom would also suffer.

> If any doe wilfully withstand the officer in bringing such disordered persons to the Lords Gaole to bee punished as aforesayd they shall pay fyne to the Lord 6s 8d or to bee punished at the discretion of the

OWNERS, OCCUPIERS AND OTHERS

Steward.

If in the process one of the lord's officers was assaulted this was regarded as a serious offence and could lead to a £5 fine and imprisonment. Failing to assist an officer was also an offence.

That every Burgesse all Inhabitants and occupyers of this towne doe ayde and assist lawfully every Officer of the towne in executing their office upon paine every Burgesse that offendeth to bee grievously punished and every other to bee fyned for every offence 10s.

If the officer happened to be the steward, his deputy, chamberlain, bailiffs or toll gatherers the penalty could be as much as 39s 11d.

Fighting was not tolerated. Causing a 'fraye' was categorised and penalised depending on whether or not blood was drawn: an offender guilty of 'bloodwipe' was fined 6s 8d and for a 'dryewipe' 3s 4d. 'Bragg and puglement', that is using threatening language and using one's fists, were fined at 1s, and causing trouble in the wich-house streets at night to the disturbance of those making salt could land the offender in jail for 24 hours. It seems that those employed to draw the salt water from the brine pit were rather prone to fighting and brawling as they are the subject of a specific rule.

It is ordered that if any of the Bryne drawers shall not be obedient to their Ruler for the tyme being called the Lord of the Seath as well when to take rest and when to cease and give over as alsoe if any fighting braweleing or other disorder shall happen amongst them at the Seath, if hee shall command them to give over and bee quiet, if any bryne drawer shall disobey him therein that then upon notice given thereof by the Lord of the Seath unto the Steward or in his absence to the Constables and the Lords Bayliffe every such offender shall suffer imprissonment in the Court house by the space of two dayes and two nights or else shall pay fyne to the Lord of the Towne for every offence 3s 4d.

Besides imprisonment there were stocks in which to confine miscreants. Presumably when the custom of the town referred to punishment at the discretion of the lord's steward this was an option.

It is ordered that the farmer of this Towne shall make a paire of stock for the punishment of Offenders punishable by the Lord of the sayd Towne for offences committed against the good orders of the sayd towne.

Combating Poverty

Several of the town's customs dealt with combating poverty and providing for poor people. Statutory provision for dealing with the poor had been in existence since 1563, prior to which the church, through the monastic institutions, had been responsible for them. Following the dissolution of the monasteries and the consequent problems of the sick, lame and destitute, each parish was expected to provide for its own unfortunate flock by collecting and distributing alms. Nine years later the initial act for the relief of the poor was reinforced by the imposition of a compulsory poor rate. In 1597 it was enacted that the churchwardens of each parish and four 'substantial householders' were to be appointed annually as 'Overseers of the Poor'. It was they who were to put the poor to work, to organise materials for them to work with, to provide cottages, and to dispense money to provide for the relief of the sick, lame and those others unable to work. The children of poor families could, if necessary, be bound as apprentices. These measures were to be paid for by the levying of a poor rate amongst the parishoners; refusal could mean the distraint of their goods and even imprisonment until their obligation was met. A further act of 1601 again strengthened these provisions. Much later, in 1662, it was ordered that every person had to have a place of settlement – a parish of origin where he or she was entitled to poor relief and to which the individual could be forcibly removed if he or she became dependant upon alms. Such a place of settlement was normally the parish of birth, or, in the case of a married woman, her husband's parish. It could be acquired by completing apprenticeship or being hired for at least a year within a particular parish.

It was ordered by the burgesses of Northwich that some of the profits from the salt workings be applied to the poor.

That the peeceings which shall be given to the poore shall bee agreed upon yearely by the greater number of the Occupyers assembled in the Court house by the Tolle of the Common bel before the later Faire and shall be set and walled before the Feast of St Thomas the apostle yearely & the money payed upon St Thomas day to foure honest men to bee by them distributed to the poore inhabitants chieefly of the Northwich and others adjoyneing by their discretions, and no other guift peeceing or peeceings to bee set or given upon paine of 20s for every offence.

The agreement about the allocation of salt boilings for the poor had to be made at some time before the last fair of the year – 6 December – and then to take place before 21 December – St Thomas's Day. Presumably the number of boilings agreed by the majority of occupiers was dependant upon the number of poor people then resident. It is interesting to note that four men were made responsible for distribution: are these the same four who would have been appointed by the parish as Overseers of the Poor, or are they additional men? Perhaps the former suggestion is correct in view of the fact that the money raised could be distributed to the poor of surrounding townships, i.e. the parish.

Unfortunately the customs do not shed any light on providing employment or housing for the poor people. The Acts of 1597 and 1601 allow for the erection of cottages for the poor families on common or waste land but this would have been somewhat difficult in Northwich due to a lack of space and the fact that Crum Hill was to be kept free from such improvements. It is likely therefore that some provision would have been made in neighbouring Witton. Primarily it was the parish authorities who were responsible for the poor, but unfortunately the records are unrevealing. Only two lists of those in receipt of benefit exist – one dated 1619 and the other, undated, but apparently within a year or so of the other. In 1619 a total of 30s 2d was distributed to 76 Northwich people and 21s to 53 Witton residents.[21] The undated list accounts for 74 Northwich people receiving a total of 24s 8d and 37 from Witton having 10s 8d.

Increasing population in Cheshire and the consequential lack of employment opportunities in the rural areas attracted many to the towns, and Northwich with its salt industry will have been no exception. But the towns could not necessarily satisfy the needs of these immigrants and neither did they welcome them because of the threat of overcrowding, vagrancy, crime and disease. Little surprise then to read of provisions against newcomers – the 'foreigners' or 'outsiders' – amongst the town's customs. There was a real danger of such people becoming a burden on the community and therefore a need to try to avoid having a destitute population in need of support.

If any person receive Inmates or make more households than one to forfeite, for every week that any such inmate or new household shall remaine there after warning given by the Bayliffe, 5s and every such Inmate and new householder 4d.

So taking in lodgers and sub-letting a part of one's house to newcomers were prohibited. Further, in 1632 it was ordered that should any person have in his dwelling any 'tenant, inmate or stranger', then, within one month of their arrival, the houseolder was to give sufficient security to the churchwardens and overseers of the poor in order to absolve the parish of any 'charge, damage or hinderence'. The alternative to this was to evict the newcomers within the month.[22]

It seems that individual cases of genuine charity were permitted. Householders or tradesmen might take in and employ poor children and keep them at their own expense, but this had to be on a permanent basis.

If any person doe take into his house any poore children not borne in the Towne & suffer them to beg at mens doors or else turne them out at winter to forfeit for every such offence 3s 4d.

This clause expressly prohibits taking in and employing poor children on a temporary basis when there was a need to do so and then allowing them to fend for themselves thereafter.

Illegitimate children born in the town were a particular problem and a potential burden on the parish. Townspeople were discouraged from taking in unfortunate pregnant women.

If any person doe keepe any woeman in their house within the sayd towne being gotten with child in fornication to forfeit for every weeke that she shall be kept after warning given to the contrary by the bayliffe 2s.

Thus a warning would be given for the woman to leave the town.

That every woman being with child in adulterye or fornication that doth lodge or remaine in the Northwich as a dweller or sojournere there, shall avoyd the towne upon warning given by the Bayliffe upon paine to forfeite for every week that they shall tarry there after warning given 2s or else to bee punished by discretion of the Steward or his deputie.

The authorities were keen to avoid a birth out of wedlock in the town, for the mother would be able to make a legal claim for assistance on behalf of her child.

OWNERS, OCCUPIERS AND OTHERS

If any such woman be brought to bed in the house of any person hee, in whose house she is soe brought to bed, to forfeite 6s 8d.

Whilst we do not have detailed court rolls for Northwich, the customs were not dissimilar to those found in manors in other parts of Cheshire. For example, in the nearby manors of Over and Tarporley the court rolls frequently mention fines imposed on those who had lodgers, or 'inmates', and instructions, on behalf of the churchwardens, that certain individuals remove 'inmates' from their homes. Whilst all of this might seem harsh today, one needs to remember that in the 17th century when money and opportunity was hard to come by, charity began at home. There was a need to look after one's own, so that any reluctance to pay the poor rate was more intense when the recipient was an 'outsider', or someone who was seen to have loose morals or had caused their own misfortune.

---

[1] It has not been possible to compile a complete list of stewards, but they include men such as Thomas Venables (1570), Peter Warburton (1637), Thomas Berrington (1638/9), Thomas Robinson (1656 and 1702) and William Worrall (1663).

[2] It is first recorded as such in the Inquest of Service, 1288, when there was a requirement for the town to provide 12 foot-soldiers for war in Wales.

[3] CRO: DLT/A/2/60, p. 45.

[4] *ibid*, p. 35.

[5] The listings come from Calvert, pp. 1039-1063; CRO: DCH/M/37/60; and Wirral Archives, MA/T/1/124.

[6] DLT/A/2/60, p. 36.

[7] DCH/M/37/60.

[8] CRO: DLT/A/2/60, p. 36, rule 15.

[9] CRO: DSS1/4/9.

[10] CRO: DLT/A/2/60, p. 37.

[11] *ibid.*

[12] I am grateful to Alan Crosby for mentioning the bridge at Warrington.

[13] Wirral Archives, MA/T/1/123, 124, 125.

[14] The oaths of office are in Calvert pp. 1063-67; CRO: DLT/A/2/60 and D4360/2.

NORTHWICH TOWN GOVERNMENT

[15] Nantwich and Middlewich do not seem to have the same number of officials. At the former we hear of Constables, 'Rulers of Walling', 'Leave-lookers' (Market-lookers), 'Ale-tasters', 'Fire-lookers' (who reported defective chimneys and acted as fire prevention officers), 'Channel-lookers' (Scavengers), and 'Heath-keepers' (an official who reported concerning the ancient common land at Beam Heath). At Middlewich there were 'Rulers of Walling' and 'Seath Dealers' (men who shared out the brine, perhaps akin to the Lead-lookers at Northwich).

[16] Wirral Archives, MA/T/1/123.

[17] CRO: DLT/A/2/60, p. 367, rule 18.

[18] Calvert, pp. 1039-63. CRO: D4362/2 and DLT/A/2/60.

[19] All the following extracts are taken from DLT/A/2/60, with some additions from Calvert pp. 1036 –1062.

[20] I am endebted to Alan Crosby for these comments about market practices.

[21] CRO: DSS/1/4/6.

[22] This clause only appears in Calvert, p. 1055.

5

THE WICH-HOUSES

The Wich-houses

Leland's rather unflattering picture of 16th century Northwich was no doubt influenced by the large volumes of smoke emanating from the numerous wich-houses crammed into the town's six-acre site. To a man of his time an industrial town was a rarity and something to be remarked upon. Conditions had not changed a century and a half later when Celia Fiennes commented that the town was 'full of smoke from the salterns on all sides'.[1] Thus we have a gloomy picture of 17th century Northwich caused by the numerous wich-houses, but a picture that may be somewhat exaggerated as it implies that all of the wich-houses were belching out smoke 24 hours a day, seven days a week throughout the year – this was not the case for the number of houses making salt, and the times during which they might be at work, was controlled by the town's officials.

Of the 170 plots shown on the early town plan, 108 were the wich-houses in which brine might be boiled to produce salt.[2] Sixteenth and 17th century documents which refer to lists of wich-houses invariably contain the following statement: *There is and tyme out of mynd hath been wthin the Towne of Northwich 112 four leads and one odde lead and now more; and four leads called the Running Wich-house. Soe the totall is 113 foure leads and one odd lead.*[3] From this assessment, it is apparent that wich-houses were rated on the basis of having four lead-pans, so that the total assessment for the town was 453 leads, including the 'Horsemill' which had a single lead. However, ten houses are known to have contained six leads, and the Earl of Derby's 'Running House' of four leads was an allocation of 'walling' rather than an actual house, so it would seem that the total number of wich-houses was in fact 108. These can be placed in Seath Street, High Street, Yate Street, the Leach Eye and Horsemill Street (see *Fig. Ten*). One source, a copy of a court entry for 18 April 1570, is curiously at slight variance.[4] This states that there were '106 wich-houses and 3 odd leades', that is 427 leads, and of these, eleven houses had six leads and the remainder four, which suggests a total of ninety houses and one odd lead. This is certainly at odds with the usual descriptions found as early as 1565, again in 1595 and at other dates too. It may be that for some reason in 1570 several houses were out of production and therefore not counted, even though they were still wich-house sites and should have been just as they were on other occasions. Either that or the copyist was wrong.

In Nantwich each wich-house had six leads giving a total of 1,296 leads, and in Middlewich, whilst anciently there may have been between four and eight leads per house, this was fixed in the late 15th century at six, with a total of about 500 leads.[5] Six leads to a wich-house is not common in Northwich in the 16th and 17th centuries and applies to only ten houses, but it may have been at an earlier date for there are a number of references to individuals having shares of a third part of wich-houses with four leads suggesting houses originally of six leads. Also, during the 17th century restrictions on the occupancy of wich-houses was traditionally based on six: Northwich residents were allowed to occupy an annual maximum of 'three six-leades' of walling, and non-residents were limited to 12 leads. Such a rule is similar to that in Nantwich where occupation was limited to 18 leads. This limit does not seem to have existed in the mid-16th century when some occupants were using between 22 and 28 leads (see *Appendix Two*) and, judging by other lists of occupiers, may have been relaxed from time to time during the 17th century.[6] The reasons for the restriction are not clear but it may be due to a need for tighter rationing of the brine, or a need to conserve fuel, but more on this later.

So what did the wich-houses look like and what did they contain?

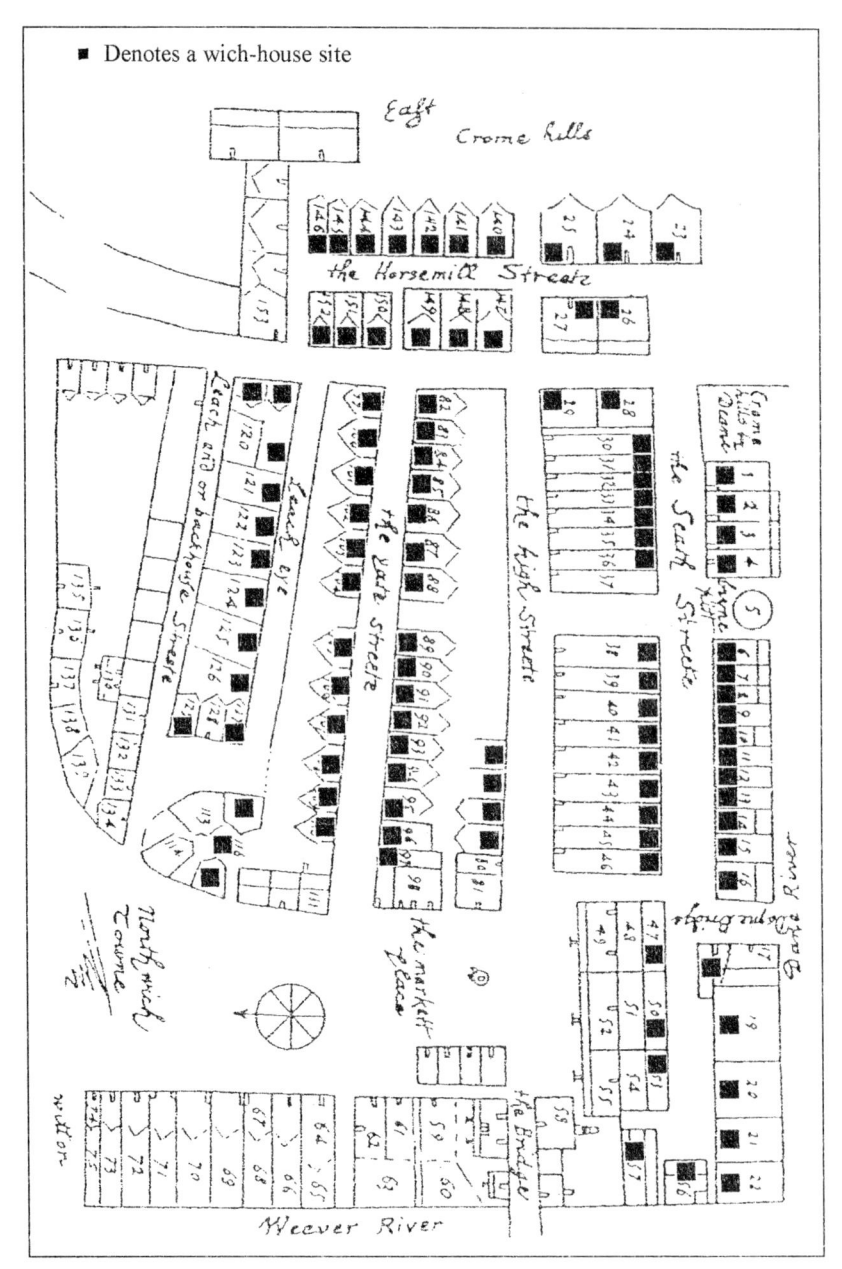

Figure Ten: **17th Century Wich-houses**

According to excavations that were carried out in Nantwich, wich-houses there were long narrow open-ended sheds, some twelve yards by eight, of simple construction with timber frames and wattle walls; it is likely that Northwich houses were similar.[7] Whilst such a size would certainly fit some of the wich-house sites in Northwich, for many this was perhaps a little large. A six-yard frontage was the norm for the plots of land on which they were sited, and the layout of the streets was such that the length of some would be somewhat shorter than twelve yards.[8] Whether or not the wich-house covered the full extent of the building plot is not known. We do not know whether the buildings were against one another as in a row of terraced houses or whether there was an alley way between them. It may be they were 'terraced' as in most cases the building plots ran through from one street to another allowing access to both front and back, and in the few cases where this was not so the plan suggests a dividing back street (nos. 76-79 and 93-97). There seems to be little doubt that wich-house buildings were simple single-storey structures 'like barns open up to the thatch with a cover-hole, or two to vent the steam'.[9] In the early years of the 17th century, judging by an account for the repair of wich-houses owned by the Cholmondeley family, they were certainly constructed of wattle and daub with thatched roofs.[10] This account, dated 1615, records work done by thatchers, carpenters, daubers and renderers, the purchase of building materials, and work done on the ovens and 'ships' (storage pits). Clearly such a construction was a significant fire hazard and it is little wonder that conflagration was a constant threat.

The term 'wich-house' did not simply apply to the building, rather it referred to a parcel of land upon which the right to produce salt, or to 'wall', might be carried out. Within the confines of the site there would have to been room for not only the wich-house, but also a yard where fuel, the 'great stakkes of smaul clovyn wood' described by Leland, and other commodities might be stored. The boundaries of wich-houses were often described in relation to adjacent houses and streets. Thomas Holford issued a grant dated 2 June 1546 conveying a wich-house (4) in Seath Street to Ralph Hanmere of Plumley and this was described as being between the 'sethe or bryne pytt' to the south and the 'kyngs hey strete' to the north, and between Thomas Heyes' wich-house (3) to the east and the street to the west.[11] In 1556, when Maria Fovell of Middlewich granted a wich-house to Richard Walton, its boundaries were given as the houses of Roger Horton of Coole and Lawrence Winnington of Hermitage, Yate Street and Little Street (104): these same bounds are given again in 1630.[12] In 1560 Thomas Dutton sold to Edward Golbourne a wich-house (37) in High Street which stood between the highway to the north and Thomas Holford's (4) wich-house to the south (on the other side of Seath Street) and between the 'streate descending to the bryne pitt' to the west and Thomas Leftwich's wich-house (36) to the east.[13] By the end of the century this site was no longer used for making salt as it does not appear in the lists of wich-houses and by c.1610 it seems to have been owned by Thomas Bromfield.[14] During the late 16th and 17th centuries a number of sites became derelict and were used for purposes other than salt manufacture. In 1593 one of Peter Leycester's wich-houses had already been converted into a cow-house and a barn (41), one of the Earl of Derby's had been converted into shops (98), and of the 107 properties then listed 19 were described as 'not standing'.[15] Later, in the 1620s a wich-house alongside the Leach Eye became a 'new shop' (115) and another in the same place became a barn and then a dwelling house (126); another on the High Street was also converted into a dwelling, and yet another in Seath Street became a kitchen (47).[16] In 1637 approval was given for a wich-house to be converted 'to the best use and advantage' as there was reduction in trade due to the erection of new salt works in the area.[17] As the century progressed new sources of salt were found, competition increased, and the use of the town's brine pit diminished. Consequently some wich-house sites were permanently converted to other uses, though the designation 'wich-house' continued to be employed in describing such properties. The use of sites for other purposes was perhaps not as great as it was in Middlewich and Nantwich. It has been suggested in the case of Middlewich that the wich-house sites were regularly used for other purposes or left waste due to the fact that only 36 houses were allowed to be in production at any one time and that salt production could only take place in the weeks between Ascension Day (six weeks after Easter) and

Martinmas (11 November).[18] It would seem to make sense therefore to do just that, and perhaps lease the use of another owner's wich-house when the time came to produce salt. It would make even more sense at Nantwich, where 'walling' was limited to 12 houses at any time and for 12 days a year: six days set in what was termed 'Baron's Week' and the other six at 'New Year'.

What then of the interior of the wich-houses? It is likely that there would have been two or three rooms. The main working area would have consisted of two brick lined hearths or ovens over which were placed iron bars to support the lead pans – two to each hearth. These were probably placed in the centre against an internal wall so that warm air could pass into the drying room behind. Another feature of the main room was the 'ship' in which the brine was stored prior to boiling. In Nantwich archaeologists discovered that these were narrow troughs along the length of the wich-house and this accords with a description given in 1675, but in Northwich it seems that the 'ship' was set in a clay-lined pit.[19] The term 'ship' seems somewhat curious but may refer to the way in which the barrel-like container was caulked in much as the planks of boats were sealed to render them water-tight. Along one of the walls of the main room there would be a series of hooks from which hung the conical baskets, known as 'barrows', to hold the wet salt. Below these was placed the 'leach tub' to collect the brine residue for recycling. Wooden implements would have been found lying around the wich-house: paddles to stir up the brine mixture and rakes for bringing the salt crystals to the side of the pan; in some instances these tools are mentioned in inventories. More will be said about these features later in the description of the salt-making process.

Much of what has been said about salt-making and the equipment used can be seen in two 16th century German prints (see *Figs Eleven and Twelve*). The method of conveying the brine to the wich-houses was different in that the brine is being carried in casks. The houses are of simple construction, have thatched roofs with holes to allow the smoke to escape, and have three rooms. Interestingly on the front wall of the houses there is a painted sign which probably denotes the owner or occupier – did Northwich houses have similar signage? The stacks of fuel outside

ANCIENT SALT WORKS

A. Sheds. B. Painted Signs. C. First Room. D. Second Room. E. Third Room. F. Windows. G. Window in Roof. H and I. Wells. K. Casks. L. Pole. M. Forked Resting Sticks

From an Old Print   Published in 1556

Figure Eleven: **A 16th Century Salt Town**

each house are clearly evident. The master, his wife and an assistant are shown making salt surrounded by implements. The furnace, the boiling pan, the 'ship' for holding the brine and the barrows hung on the wall are all illustrated. Making salt was thirsty work so it not surprising to see mention of a beer tankard, but beer had another use too and this will be mentioned later. How similar these pictures are to the scene in Northwich we cannot say, but they are extremely useful in understanding salt-making at this time.

The salt-making Process

Contemporary topographical descriptive sources explain something of the way in which salt was produced. Fundamental was the existence of a brine pit which according to Leland was 'hard by the Brinke of Dane river' and a 'a good butt shot' from the junction with the River Weaver.[20] The general location of the pit is without doubt and is clearly shown on the 17th century town plan. From this pit the high quality brine was drawn in abundance on a regular basis. Camden reports that it was '...deep and plentiful with stairs about it by which, when they have drawn the water in their leather buckets, they ascend, half naked to their troughs and fill them, from whence it is conveyed to the wich-houses'.[21] How deep the pit was we do not know but something may be gleaned from the descriptions of salt-making given by Doctor William Jackson of Nantwich to the Royal Society in 1669.[22] He stated that the depth of the salt springs was generally 'not above three or four yards' but at Nantwich the pit was seven yards deep. At Droitwich, Staffordshire, where there were similar salt workings, the pit was 10 yards deep. Whatever the depth, the evidence suggests a fair degree of manual labour in carrying the buckets up to ground level, but it is far more likely that the brine drawers descended to fill the buckets and that they were then hoisted up either by human or mechanical effort. As early as 1636 Nantwich had mechanical pumps for this purpose and at Middlewich the pit was 'four square, very broad and deep, boarded up on each side and with great cross beams in the middest' which would seem to suggest some form of hoisting arrangement.[23] The relationships between Northwich and Middlewich were fairly close, with a number of salt proprietors, such as the Venables family, having interests in both towns, therefore it would therefore be surprising if similar arrangements were not present. That being the case we can assume that the Northwich pit would have been set with boarded sides and cross beams. The contemporary German print (see *Fig. Eleven*) shows two pits, one with a simple well with a cantilever drawing arm and the other with a more sophisticated system of wheels and cogs to draw the brine up, but it seems unlikely that arrangements in Northwich were anything like these.[24] Unfortunately the customs of the town are silent as to the drawing processes beyond stating that the brine drawers were prone to brawling and that they were supervised by an official known as the 'Lord of the Seath'. Such an official might be represented by the rather imposing gentleman with the staff shown in the German print.

Having arrived at the surface the brine was poured from the leather buckets into a container which was linked to the wich-house by a wooden trough. Leland says that the pit was 'set aboute with Canals that the salt water is easily derived to every Mannes House' and Smith adds 'the brine runneth on the ground in Troughes of Wood, covered over with boards until it commeth to the wich houses, where they make the salt.' This system of canals had existed for some time as it is mentioned in the 14th century. Nantwich had a similar system but in Middlewich instead of the channels being at ground level they were ingeniously 'over men's heads'.

Reference to the Northwich town plan suggests the course of these troughs. From the brine pit there is a regular gap between the wich-houses running due north. At right angles to this it is likely that troughs would run along the streets to service each house. If this is so then it is equally likely that there was some method of diverting the brine to run to an appropriate area or quarter of the town as and when required. When wich-houses were leased specific reference was made in the deed to these channels or 'gutters'. In January 1582 Sir Hugh Cholmondeley leased to Thomas Venables for £10 a year the wich-house he had built on an 'ancient site' together with 'woodroomes, easements, bryne or Sawce, wallings, buylings and making of salt and all bryne courses, gutters and gutter places.[25]

THE WICH-HOUSES

ANCIENT SALT WORKS
A. Wooden Ladle. *B.* Cask. *C.* Tub. *D.* The Master. *E.* Assistant. *F.* The Master's Wife. *G.* Wooden Spade. *H.* Boards. *I.* Salt-baskets. *K.* Hoe. *L.* Rake. *M.* Straw. *N.* Bowls. *O.* Bucket for Blood. *P.* Beer Tankard.
From an Old Print   Published in 1556.

Figure Twelve: **A 16th Century Wich-house**

123

The importance of this system of transference of the brine was expressed in the book of customs.

> *That there shall bee sufficient Roome left at every Course of bryne where it runneth that men may follow their bryne upon paine of 1s.*[26]

It seems that when a man was due to receive an allocation of brine he would see it drawn at the pit and then follow the flow to his house. In order to facilitate this sufficient room had to kept alongside the wooden channel by other townspeople. The quality of the salt that was to be produced was much dependent on the cleanliness of the brine as it travelled along the streets and as there was every likelihood of contamination there was a pressing need for board coverings and side screens.

> *That Occupyers shall make low pales where any Course of brine goeth betweene Wich-houses to keepe the brine cleane upon paine of 6d and to bee presented at every single Court.*[27]

Having arrived at the appropriate wich-house the brine was then transferred into the storage 'ships' set in the floor of the wich-house where it remained until the time came to boil it in the lead pans. The wich house leased to Thomas Venables had two 'bryne ships' and the fact that it was mentioned might suggest that one was the norm. The pans were made locally at the leadsmithy (114) to a specific size in order that each man boiled the same amount – about 24 gallons of brine: a pan found in the town measured 3ft 6ins x 2ft 6ins x 6ins deep and the rules of the town stated that leads were to weigh 10 stones before being cast. The possibility of favouritism or corruption by those employed in the smithy was catered for.

> *If any Leadcaster doe show any partialitye or receive any rewards to defraud any person of their right Course or turne in casting of their Leades for every default vid.*[28]

The smithy was kept busy not only because the pans did not withstand prolonged use but also because it was customary for the two 'foremost' pans of every wich-house to be 'taken down' and renewed when the permitted period for 'walling' came to an end.[29] Failure to comply rendered both the occupier of the house and the 'waller' liable to a fine of 12 pence. From around the middle part of the 17th century iron replaced lead for making pans, though confusingly the pans were still referred to as 'leads'.

At the allotted time, 'when the bell ringeth', fires were lit beneath the pans and so, by evaporation, the salt was produced. This process was performed by women who were known as 'wallers' and they were obliged to 'wall' and to stop walling, when notified by the Leadlookers who would ring the town bell.

> That every waller that either walleth before the ringe of the bell, or ceaseth not at or after the ringing of the stinting bell ought not onely to pay the Leadlookers the usual fee of 1s, but alsoe if they shall not obey them in walling, kinding, stinting or otherwise scould with them, to fyne for every such offence to the Lord 6s 8d to be presented at every single Court.[30]

The fuel used was predominantly locally grown wood, though later in the century coal was introduced. The fuel stock was often listed in inventories as one of the most valuable items – a distinction being made between the wood stacked at the wich-house and that still in the 'country' awaiting delivery. Thomas Skelhorne in 1604 had wood 'standing in the toune' worth £53 6s 8d with a further £4 worth 'out of toune', and Lawrence Birchall in 1628 had £8 worth at his 'wichouse door' and a further £20 worth 'in the Cunterie'.[31] Ralph Pownall's inventory refers to piles of wood stacked in Northwich to the value of '19 Peecings & a night & a daye' (wood for 39 days boiling) worth £26, as well as wood stored in Witton, Marbury and 'Reddiche' worth £86 5s.[32] It is not surprising that wood was specially protected by the town's customs.

> That if the servants or children shall pyke or steale wood unlawfully in the wich-house streets, by colour of pykeing of sticks or otherwise, that then every such person keepeing and such children or servants shall for every offence of their sayd children or servants bee imprisoned at the discretion of the sayd steward and alsoe anyone that shall receive such wood knowing thereof bee imprisoned in like manner.[33]

> Noe manner of Waller shall deliver or carry or cause to bee delivered or carryed any of her Masters wood without licence or privitye either in the night or in the day, except such as shall bee spent for the casting of their leads, and if any such offence bee duly presented at any Court the offender to pay for a fyne 12d.

> That if any person or persons receive into their houses any wood by night or by day by the way of exchange for candles, meat or drink,

> *every such person as well ye changer as the receiver shall pay fine to the Lord 2s or bee punished by ye Steward.*

The stacks of fuel had to be kept tidily and not too close to the street in order to allow carts to pass.

> *That there shall be left at every pyle made at the end of any wichhouse a yard and a halfe between ye sayd pyle & the crist of the payment to thentent that waines may have better passage.*[34]

The quantity of wood required by the salt industry was certainly considerable. Correspondence from 1605 concerning the costs of fuel in producing salt states that at Northwich nine 'quarters of wood' were required for every house of four leads at a cost of 40s a quarter, amounting to £2,056 10s 0d per year.[35] In comparison Middlewich spent an average of £13 6s 8d on a six-lead house, but only an annual total of £1,435 4s 0d and, similarly, Nantwich, spent £8 per house and a total of only £1,728 a year. Fourteen years later a quarter of wood cost £3 so that the cost of fuel that year for Northwich was £3,561.[36] The reason for Northwich's large expenditure in wood fuel was due to the fact that their season for 'walling' was about nine months, whereas at Middlewich and Nantwich there were strict restrictions on the number of houses allowed to 'wall' at any one time and on the salt-making season as I shall explain shortly.

The salt-making process involved applying a particular recipe of blood, egg whites and ale. In Cheshire both blood and beer were added to the brine during the boiling process to improve clarification and the egg whites would improve whiteness by carrying away the impurities as they formed a scum that rose to the surface. One contemporary observer describes the method thus:

> *Saltwater taken out of the brine pit in two hours and a quarter boiling, will be evaporated and boil'd up into salt. When the liquor is more than lukewarm, they take strong ale, bullock's blood and whites of egg mixt together with brine in this proportion: of blood one egg-shell full, the white of one egg and a pint of ale, and put it into a pan of twenty four gallons or thereabouts...*[37]

Dr William Jackson of Nantwich corroborated this when, in 1669, he informed the Royal Society that at the first boiling of the brine, half a gallon of a pre-mixed solution made from brine and blood, in the proportion of 40:1, was added to the pan and then boiled rapidly.[38] This caused a scum to form that was then raked off. Boiling continued until half the quantity had evaporated. The pan was then topped up with more brine from the 'ship' and to this was added half a gallon of another mixture of brine and egg whites, mixed in the same proportions. Once the scum from this had been raked off, and half of the pan had again evaporated, 'a quarter of a pint of the best and strongest ale' was added and the solution was then allowed to simmer. It was during this third stage that the salt crystals began to form. The contemporary print showing the interior of a wich-house (see *Fig. Twelve*) shows the ale tankard, the bucket for blood and other vessels in which the various mixtures could be made. There seems to be little doubt that such techniques were well known as other contemporary writers also mention the same recipe. So who followed whom in using these techniques? Is the German illustrator depicting local salt-making, or somewhere else such as Cheshire?

After boiling the 'wallers', using a tool known as a 'loot', would rake the wet salt, or 'corne', to the side of the pan and place it into the 'barrows' which were then hung along the wall of the wich-house to drain before being removed to a hot room behind the furnace to dry off.[39]

Besides producing salt, the 'wallers' were also responsible for selling the salt on behalf of their employers.

> *That every Waller shall sell the salt she maketh by the Walme or Cranock and not by the load or sack at the price which the officers set downe to bee Common price of the towne upon paine of every default 5s and alsoe to make full price to her Mr upon her wages.*[40]

The references to 'walme' and 'crannock' need explanation. These were measures of salt regularly used for trading purposes. A 'crannock', which in the early years of the century was valued at 18s, consisted of 24 'walmes'.[41] Their capacity in relation to the standard dry measures of pecks and bushels is not known for sure but a crannock was probably about 10 bushels (¼ ton). A 'walme' is a term that might derive from the word 'wall' – to boil – and mean the amount of salt produced at a boiling session. The officers referred to in the passage were the 'Killers of Salt' who were appointed annually and sworn to deal fairly with the buyers and sellers of salt, to ensure that a price was agreed which was not less than the town rate and not to favour any particular person's salt. On that point it was also an offence for 'wallers' to entice salt merchants, the 'salters', away from other wich-houses.

As regards the wallers' wages, we know that in the middle of the century the rate was 1d per hour, for when Elizabeth Travis was asked to attend court to give evidence over a contested will she was told that she would be paid more than her usual 4s for 48 hours of walling.[42] Payment to the wallers had to be in cash rather than in kind.

> It is ordered and agreed from henceforth noe waller shall take any manner of walme or white salt from their Masters nor shall take any harding salt but bee contented with their wages agreed upon paine that every one soe offending to be punished at the discretion of the Steward. [43]

As suggested earlier in this chapter, the production of salt was not a continuous process but was confined to a season that lasted from Palm Sunday until Christmas Eve – between thirty-six and forty weeks. For special purposes extra periods could be allowed between New Year and Palm Sunday. Production was also limited in Middlewich and Nantwich. In the first of these, production took place in the weeks between Ascension Day (six weeks after Easter) and Martinmas (11 November) and the number of houses able to work at any time was limited to thirty-six.[44] In Nantwich 'walling' was limited to 12 houses at any time and for 12 days a year: six days set in what was termed 'Baron's Week' and the other six at 'New Year'. Confusingly these weeks were 'moveable feasts' for in 1573 the first period began on 17 June and the other on 11th October, and two years later the dates were 9 February and 24 June respectively.[45] At Droitwich too salt-making was only permitted from June to December.

Anyone wishing to make salt would be allocated a set number of 'pee-ceinges', each of two days and two nights for every four leads, during which he or she was permitted to 'wall'. Each year, before the fourth Sunday of Lent (i.e. two weeks before the season began) those who wished to 'wall' were required to inform the Lead-lookers of the number of leads they intended to use and, if not their own, from whom they were leased and to which house they belonged.[46] Those who made application to boil more than their entitlement, or made a false declaration, or boiled outside the permitted times, could be fined quite heavily. The officials would then inform the applicants of the number of 'Peecings' they were to be allowed and the dates on which they would be allowed to 'wall'. Then on the allocated day or days they would have to wait until the 'common bell' was rung before he or she might commence boiling. A list of 'Peecings' from an unknown year of the first quarter of the century lists 29 dates on which a total of 48 'Peecings' were commenced.[47] This begins in April with a statement 'walled at the ringe of bell 21st' and continues until 23 December. On 17 occasions eight leads were 'walled', on another the person 'walled' 12 leads, and on the remaining dates used the basic four leads. On 11 December, when working eight leads, a note records that one 'peeceinge' was for the benefit of Lord Robert Cholmondeley.

How much salt was produced? This is not an easy question to answer as much depended on the strength of the brine solution at any particular time and place. Sea-water contains only 3% salt, whereas the Northwich brine spring contained 25.3% – eight times stronger and close to a maximum saturation level – and those at Nantwich and Middlewich are believed to be somewhat weaker. Clues in relation to this matter only refer to Nantwich. We are informed by one writer that a standard pan of brine containing 24 gallons would produce 3½ pecks of salt in two hours boiling.[48] Dr Jackson gives two equations: that a single pound weight of salt could be produced from six pounds weight of brine, and that a quart measure of brine produced between five and six ounces of salt.[49] Unfortunately these three equations do not seem to equate exactly. Using the Nantwich evidence that 3½ pecks could be produced in two hours from a single pan, this would mean that in Northwich for every two-day 'Peecing' a wich-house would produce 336 pecks of salt, the equivalent of just over two tons. Further, using this fact, the unknown occupier whose salt-making activities are referred to above, would have produced a total of 16,128 pecks or about 100 tons in that year.[50] However, Northwich brine was somewhat stronger, so that up to 150 tons might well have been produced by the occupier. Using the other Nantwich formula based on the number of ounces of salt per quart of brine, a figure of 1½ tons for a two-day period is arrived at, suggesting that the unknown occupier would have made at least 72 tons in the year. To gain a total annual production figure the number of occupiers and the number of 'peecings' each occupier was allotted is needed: a reasonable estimate might be 30 occupiers having a single 'peecing' a week throughout any given year. Such an estimate would give a total figure of around 4,500 to 5,000 tons. This is not unreasonable given that the Staffordshire town of Droitwich produced 3,000 tons in the mid-17th century.[51]

The amounts of salt produced are recorded in 1675 by William, Lord Brereton who made a number of observations concerning fuel consumption. He calculated that 12,214 bushels (305.35 tons) of salt were produced in a week at Northwich using 1,488 loads of coal (186 tons) at a cost of £81. By comparison the figures for Middlewich and Nantwich were, respectively, 4,300 and 4,200 bushels (107.5 and 105 tons), using 79 and 152 tons of coal costing £31 12s and £60 16s. In other words, at Northwich it took only twelve cwt. of coal to produce one ton of salt, whereas at Middlewich it took 15 cwt. and at Nantwich, 29 cwt.[52] The weekly figures of 300 tons indicates a very considerable quantity of salt produced annually.

Throughout the century Northwich seems to have been a leader in the production of salt and yet it had fewer houses and leads in operation than the other two wiches. For much of the century Northwich had a total of 453 leads, Middlewich had 646 (107 houses of six leads and one of four leads), and Nantwich had 1,296 (216 houses of six leads). Whilst there is a significant difference in the numbers of pans in the three towns with Nantwich seemingly the largest producer, what is more crucial than numbers of leads is the frequency of use and the strength of the brine, and in those respects Northwich was certainly ahead of the other two. Collins, who seems to have been in no doubt that in the 1680s Northwich was the leading salt producing town, remarks that Nantwich's brine was much weaker than that found in the other two towns. So, not only did Northwich produce much more salt, it produced better quality salt more economically.

During the 17th century there were three changes to the traditional methods of working: the use of pumps to raise the brine, the use of coal as a fuel, and the change from lead to iron for making the pans. These changes meant that the older traditional style wich-houses needed modification. Viscount Cholmondeley entered into an agreement with John Broome in March 1652 to re-build a wich-house 'of three bays' with 'iron pan complete to wall with coals'.[53] This agreement cost Broome £50 and £10 a year for 21 years. Whilst the change to iron pans and coal-fired furnaces may have been seen as improvements, salt production in Northwich actually diminished as the century progressed due to the irregular supply of brine from the town's pit and the successful quest for other sources in neighbouring townships. Lord Brereton's observations suggest that in 1675 there were only 23 pans in the Northwich area – four owned by Earl Rivers, four by the Baron of Kinderton, six by Mr Brook, two by Mr Marbury and seven described as being 'Town Works'.[54] The salt works owned by the four men were established outside the town boundaries in neighbouring townships, where new sources of brine had been found, but why only seven in Northwich? That seems rather curious when one considers the fact that there were over 450 for much of the century and that seven does not correspond to the ancient customs based on four pans. Does Brereton really mean 'salt pans' or does he mean salt-houses? If he does mean pans, then it is likely that he is referring to the 'new' large iron pans rather than the smaller traditional standard 'leads'. The same is true of Middlewich, where we are told there were only 12 'pans' in the town, though 40 might be used, with the Baron of Kinderton having a further seven, and Messrs. Oldfield, Cotton and Mainwaring having one each...but one 'pan' or 'one' house? At Nantwich it is said that there were 24 'pans' with a further three on Sir Thomas Delves land. To add to the confusion Celia Fiennes wrote that in 1698 there were '12 salterns together at Northwich'.[55] Here it seems that the writer is referring to the number of wich-houses or salt works. It is impossible to say how reliable any of these figures are or indeed what is meant by them. Whatever the actual reasons for these dramatic reductions it is known for certain that there was a gradual decline in the industry and wich-houses were increasingly and regularly being put to other uses in all three towns. It may also be the case that as fewer wich-house sites were engaged in salt production, those that continued were using iron to make much larger pans.

It seems that the brine pit in Northwich was drying up for in 1691

Samuel Starkey wrote to his employer Mrs Dobson to report that he had heard that the 'Inhabitancy of Northwich have found brine lately and intend to revive their walling'.[56] That same year an agreement made between the Lord of the Manor and the proprietors of walling rights, including Thomas Cholmondeley and Leftwich Oldfield, refers to the 'Ancient Brinesheath or Saltspring' having been for several years 'in decay and of noe advantage to the owners'.[57] It seems that in order to improve the town's salt workings, several of these owners paid 10s for each lead they held but several more refused to pay so that the improvement scheme was then incomplete. The proprietors then had the idea of transferring a bequest of £100, left by Richard Chrymes for the upkeep of the town bridge and brine pit, to their use in making the repairs they required, especially since the costs of bridge repairs were a charge on the County. Accordingly, on 30 April, the agreement was drawn up to secure the money.

Whilst the diminishing supply from the town's brine pit was certainly a problem it is also clear that the additional salt works that had sprung up in Leftwich and other townships posed a threat as they experienced more profitable trade through being free from the town regulations. As early as 1637 there is reference to 'the decay of trading of Salt in this Town', due to the many 'new Salt-Workes lately found out and erected about us' with a consequent reduction in the value of salt being produced in the ancient wich-houses. In November 1675 Earl Rivers let five acres of land along the banks of the Weaver in Leftwich to Peter Tarbock with the right to 'search for, sink to, and dispose of brine' and to erect buildings for the purpose: the lease was for 99 years during the lives of Peter Tarbock, his son Peter and Anne, daughter of Robert Venables of Wincham.[58] The agreement of 1691 mentioned above refers to the fact that the town's regulations and customs made by the burgesses to control the salt industry were inconvenient considering the establishment of the new salt works nearby: by 1681 there had been five salt pits sunk outside the limits of the Borough. The result was that those proprietors who had made a contribution towards the improvement of the town's salt workings, or who were prepared to pay by 29 September that year, were freed from the regulations so that their trade might 'stand and forever bee upon an equal foote and bottom with the Outworks'. They were also permitted to farm out their entitlements to whom ever they might choose or to appoint on their behalf an agent to manage all their saltworkings to their benefit – they chose this latter option and appointed Thomas Nixon as their first manager.

The discovery of rock salt in the area gave impetus to a new form of salt production. In March 1670, whilst searching for seams of coal to supply the wich-houses, John Jackson discovered rock salt in Marbury on the land owned by William Marbury. However this important find did not have any significant effect on the traditional methods of salt production until the end of the century. In 1689 comment was made that rock salt had been found in Cheshire and that men 'digged out the rock and carried it by sea to all parts of England and Ireland, and melted with sea water, and boiled it up into a strong salt'.[59] Once again the writings of Celia Fiennes refer to the new methods: 'they have within these few yeares found in their brine pits, a hard rocky salt that looks cleer like sugar candy, and its taste shows it to be salt; they call this rock salt; it will make very good brine with fresh water to use quickly, this they carry to the water's side into Wales and by those rivers that are low'd with the tyde's in, which produces a strong and good salt as the others.' In 1693, Sir Thomas Warburton also found a seam of rock salt on his estates and it is during this decade that the exploitation of rock salt led to disputes and a bitter struggle for dominance in the salt trade between the traditional brine men and the new rock salt men. Transport of rock salt to those areas where coal could be produced cheaply naturally meant that Northwich proprietors were at a disadvantage and consequently they sought to have a prohibitive rate of tax placed on rock salt, but were unsuccessful.[60] In the 1690s salt refineries were set up along the Mersey at Frodsham, Dungeon, Liverpool and Sankey near Warrington. The problems associated with sending salt out of the Northwich area and bringing in coal were arguments in support of making the River Weaver navigable: a scheme first mooted in 1663 but not implemented until 1721.

With the sinking of new brine pits outside the limits of Northwich, the use of iron pans, the burning of coal and the discovery of rock salt, the ancient methods of producing salt and the associated customs in Northwich and the other 'wiches' were now lost to the past, and salt-making in Cheshire was now to change forever.

---

[1] C. Morris (ed.), *The Journeys of Celia Fiennes*, (1947) p.224.

[2] 112 wich-houses is normally given and an explanation of this figure is given later.

[3] CRO: D4360/2; DCH/M/37/60; Calvert, p. 1089.

[4] CRO: DLT/A/2/60, p. 47.

[5] *A Middlewich Chartulary*, LCRS, (1944), pp. 38, 63.

[6] CRO: DLT/A/2/60.

[7] R. McNeil, *Two medieval wich-houses excavated in Wood Street, Nantwich – 1980;* Salt Museum Publications. *1980.*

[8] For dimensions of plots see for example: CRO: D4048/3; LuNo 11/2 and 60.

[9] J. Collins, *Salt and Fisheries* (1682), p. 32. From a photocopy in possession of the Salt Museum, Northwich.

[10] CRO: DSS/1/4/3/2.

[11] CRO: DCH/J/134.

[12] CRO: DSS/1/1/50/10.

[13] CRO: DCH/J/135.

[14] The boundaries given by many of the extant grants from the 16th century and earlier coincide with the map of c.1610. However it does seem that there is an anomaly here for Golbourne's wich-house is said to border Leftwich's house, which accords with the wich-houses listings, whereas according to the schedule to the plan Venables' wich-house was next door with Leftwich next door to that. It seems that the schedule is in error.

[15] Calvert, pp. 1111-1118.

[16] Calvert, pp. 1089-99; CRO: D4360/2.

[17] Calvert, p. 1057.

[18] *A Middlewich Chartulary*, p. 37.

[19] The description is given by Thomas Branker, a Macclesfield schoolmaster who described the salt-making process in Northwich. See Hall, J., *History of the Town and Parish of Nantwich*, (1883), p. 259.

[20] John Leland's *Itinery* (c. 1540) and Camden's *Brittania* (1607).

[21] Camden.

THE WICH-HOUSES

[22] Dr Jackson's observations are taken from the Royal Society's *Philosophical Transactions*, iv, no. 53. November 15, 1669.

[23] Camden.

[24] The illustrations are by Georgius Agricola of salt-houses in Saxony.

[25] CRO: DCH/J/135.

[26] CRO:DLT/A/2/60, p. 17, rule 25.

[27] *ibid*, rule 26.

[28] CRO: DLT/A/2/60, p. 33, rule 23.

[29] *ibid*, p. 15, rule 19.

[30] *ibid*, p. 15, rule 18.

[31] CRO:WS 1604 & 1624.

[32] CRO: WS 1606

[33] *ibid.*

[34] CRO: DLT/A/20, p. 18.

[35] Calvert, pp. 75,76.

[36] Calvert, p. 1081.

[37] The words of John Ray from his *A Collection of English Words not Generally Used*, (1674) and quoted in Chaloner, W.H., 'Salt in Cheshire', *TLCHS*. Another contemporary commentator is Thomas Brancker, headmaster of Macclesfield School, whose observations are recorded in Hall's *History of Nantwich*, p. 260.

[38] *Philosophical Transactions*, IV, no. 53, 1669, pp. 1063-4.

[39] Leland describes the process thus; 'They seethe the Salt in Furnesses of Lede, and lade out the salt, some in cases of wicker, through the wich, the water voydith, and the salt remaynith'. The fuel used to light the fires was wood and each wich-house had piles of wich-wood outside which prompted Leland to remark 'by the Salters Houses be great stakkes of smaul clovyn woode, to seethe the salt water that thei make white salt of'.

[40] CRO: DLT/A/20, p. 19, rule 36.

[41] CRO: DSS/1/4/3/2; DSS/1/4/33.

[42] CRO: WC 1688 – Margaret Houghton.

[43] CRO: DLT/A/20, p. 19, rule 37.

[44] *A Middlewich Chartulary*, p. 37.

[45] Hall, p. 256.

[46] The records call the fourth Sunday in Lent 'Care Sunday', if this is supposed to be 'Carle Sunday' then it should be the fifth Sunday in Lent, i.e a week before Palm Sunday.

[47] CRO: DSS/1/4/33.

[48] W.H. Chaloner, 'Salt in Cheshire, 1600-1870', *TLCHS*, p. 63.
[49] *Philosophical Transactions*.
[50] A bushel of salt was reckoned at 56 pounds weight (Calvert, p. 282) There were four pecks to the bushel.
[51] J.D. Hurst, *Savouring the Past: The Droitwich Salt Industry* (1992), p. 26.
[52] Chaloner, p. 65.
[53] CRO: DCH/J/135.
[54] Calvert, p. 282.
[55] C. Morris (ed.), *The Journeys of Celia Fiennes*, p. 225.
[56] CRO: DSS/1/4/66.
[57] CRO: DLT/A/2/58.
[58] CRO: DLT/J/135.
[59] Chaloner, p. 67, quoting from *The Autobiography of William Stout*, ed. J. Harland (1851).
[60] ibid.

6

OWNERS, OCCUPIERS & OTHERS

The Owners

Who were the proprietors and the entrepreneurs engaged in the salt industry? Wich-houses were owned by a number of local land-owning families, the sovereign and the Earl of Derby. Both Witton School (later and now known as Sir John Deane's) and the parish church had interests in the salt business too. In 1565 there were 53 proprietors and by the end of the century there were 49 (see *Appendices Two* and *Seven*). During much of the 17th century the number seems to have been either 46 or 47.[1] The largest share was held by the Sutton family who during the period under discussion held 12 houses containing 48 leads: about 11% of the total. The Warburtons of Arley came next holding a total of 30 leads in seven houses, and they were closely followed by the Earl of Derby, along with the families of Leftwich, Dutton, Winnington, Leycester, Pavor and Marbury who all held 20 or more leads in five or six houses. Together these nine families owned over half of the wich-houses in Northwich. Whilst the crown had a more modest two houses containing ten leads in all, and one or two individuals had a similar number, the majority of wich-house owners had just one house of four leads.

Wich-houses, like any other property, could be bought, sold, leased or exchanged. Judge Peter Warburton purchased one from William Robinson of Northwich according to a 1589 entry, and in 1619 Sir Thomas Ireland sold a wich-house to Margaret Shakerley.[2] In the main it seems that in the early decades of the century, they remained part of family inheritances, being passed to sons or conveyed by marriage. James Pavor had a large number of houses that became the property of his heirs and Sir Hugh Cholmondeley held salt rights through marriage to Mary, daughter and sole heir of Christopher Holford.[3] Women also occur as wich-house owners: Lady Julian Holcroft, widow, Mrs Margaret Shakerley and Margaret Foxley are all listed in 1619. Later in the century there was much buying and selling of wich-houses and their associated rights. John Partington, woollen draper of Witton, purchased a number of houses from William Oldfield, William Leycester, Hugh Crosby and James Wright, and also leased a further three.

Some wich-house owners paid a small chief rent to the lord of the manor depending upon the status of the house. Even if a wich-house was 'downe' (i.e. no longer used for walling) and the right of walling was transferred to another house, the chief rent was still due and had to be paid before walling could take place in the other house. Furthermore, a payment known as a 'lead fine' of 8s was paid on most houses when occupied by an 'unfree' man (i.e. a non-burgess) or else nothing if the house was of free occupation. The lead fine was reduced to 2s if the house was classed as a 'Judger's House'. There were 23 such houses, each taking the name of a local township, and so called due to an ancient legal obligation imposed upon the township to find a judger to attend the Earl's court to give advice and arbitrate on matters of difficulty[4] (see *Chapter 1*).

All wich-house owners were responsible for the upkeep of their houses and could be fined continuously whilst their house remained in disrepair. If it were the case that a wich-house was 'downe' the owner was allowed to transfer the salt-making rights to another house and have an appropriate number of 'peecings' there. However an owner required permission of the town's officials before this could take place and this might not always be granted. Jeffery Shakerley of Hulme Hall had some difficulties in this respect.[5] He held two wich-houses, a total of eight leads, but reported in 1655 that they had been ruined both by fire and flood and he had been told that he might not benefit from his rights until the houses were repaired. Due to the high costs of repairing his houses he wrote to William Leftwich, a burgess, to seek permission to 'wall' twelve leads in another man's house on the basis that the customs of the town allowed for 'downe' houses to be compensated with two 'peecings' a year. Replying immediately, in very harsh tones, on 18 March 1655/6, Leftwich challenged Shakerley's rights of inheritance in the town, suggested he had no right to 12 leads and accused him of the deliberate destruction of one of the houses. Shakerley then wrote to Sir George Booth accusing Leftwich and Peter Venables of debarring him from his rights for their own advantages, and requesting that justice be done where 'others (whether by advantage, pryde or malice I know not) deny me'. In his support he had the backing of the influential Dr Bentley. Correspondence passed between him, Booth, Peter Leycester of Tabley and Roger Wilbraham of Dorfold during 1656. Unfortunately the records are silent as to the outcome of this matter but they do indicate a degree of partisanship, jealousies and perhaps snobbish behaviour amongst the wich-house owners, occupiers and burgesses of the town. Leftwich may have had a point, for it seems that Shakerley's aunt, Margaret, held only two houses each of four leads, and in the 1660s he is listed as holding the same and not the 12 as claimed.

The Suttons

The Sutton family was not of local origin but based at Sutton, near Macclesfield. They seem to have become involved in the town during the reign of Henry VIII. The 12 houses owned by them were located in Seath Street, Yate Street, along Leach Eye and in what was known as Horsemill Street or Little Street.[6] Exactly how they became possessed of so many wich-houses is not clear. Some may have been acquired through the marriage of Richard Sutton (1521-1582) to a daughter of George Booth of Dunham Massey, as one of the houses (92) was designated as belonging to the 'Judger of Dunham Massey'. Two more (107 & 108?) may have been purchased following the Dissolution as they had previously been the property of the abbot and convent of Whalley. In addition to being major property owners in the town they may well have been benefactors of St Helen's, for there was once a chapel dedicated to their family name.

Due to the premature death of the last male heir of the Suttons in 1601, the ownership of these 12 houses is often seen listed as 'the heirs of Sutton of Sutton'. These heirs were the spouses of Richard Sutton's three sisters, Margaret, Mary and Anne (who respectively married Sir Philip Monckton, Sir Humphrey Davenport and Rowland Moseley). Despite an equal sharing, Sir Humphrey Davenport, Chief Baron of the Exchequer (1631-41) seems to have been in sole possession in the 1630s. This was perhaps in part due to the minority of his nephew Francis Monckton. Thereafter the 'heirs' are listed as Sir Francis Monckton, Lady Davenport and Mrs Moseley. By the late 17th century, Monckton's share had been sold: 14 leads were bought by Earl Rivers and the remaining two by Mistress Heyes; following her death in the 1620s these were passed her nephew Peter Tarbock.

The Warburtons

The Warburtons of Arley came next, holding 30 leads in seven houses: one of these (90) was a six-lead house.[7] Being a local gentry family it is highly likely that these houses had been with the family for many generations, and indeed they remained so throughout the 17th century. The family were also represented by Justice Warburton during the early decades of the century: as Sir Peter Warburton, a Judge of Common Pleas since 1601, he purchased a wich-house (118) from William Robinson of Northwich and another three from the Leghs of Adlington (7, 18, 30). All these passed to his grandson Sir Thomas Stanley of Alderley following his death in 1612.

The Earls of Derby

Since 1485 the Earls of Derby had been lords of the manor of Northwich and as one might expect had four wich-houses containing 16 leads in their own hands.[8] By tradition the Earls also had the profits of what was called 'the running house'. This was not a wich-house as such, but rather was an allocation of walling allowed for the Earl's benefit by the burgesses and townspeople. Following the seizing of the assets of the 7th Earl by Parliament during the Civil War, these walling rights were eventually purchased by Joshua Hodgkis, a London furrier.[9]

The Leftwich Family

In 1527/8 this family had eight houses, 18 years later they had seven and by 1595 they owned six houses comprising 26 leads – five of four leads and one with six leads.[10] As a local family there is little doubt that they had held these for many generations: in 1478, according to an *inquisition post mortem*, the family had five wich-houses. In March 1506 Richard Leftwich of Leftwich granted his son, Richard, the use of a wich-house that stood next to the bake-house (127).[11] At the Dissolution they acquired a six-lead house (36) once held by the order of St John of Jerusalem. One of their houses (39) had the designation 'Judger of Eaton', named from the township in Davenham parish which was part of the manor of Leftwich. For a time they held half a wich-house (13) once held by the nuns of Chester, but they soon sold this to a Harcourt of Wincham. With the failure of the main line the wich-houses were inherited by the Oldfield family, via a marriage to an heiress (127 & 150), a minor branch of the Leftwich family (79) and a kinsman Raphe Harcourt of Wincham (36). Two were purchased by the Partington family (39 & 115).

Duttons of Dutton

This family held a great deal of land along the River Weaver to the north-west of Northwich. They had three wich-houses, each of which was associated with one of their manors – Bartington, Little Legh and Dutton: the latter (89) contained six leads.[12] Up to the last decade of the 16th century the family seem to have held five houses, four of four leads and two of six, including one which was the house of the Judger of Acton (37), but that one seems to have passed to the Cholmondeley family by the end of the century.

Thomas Dutton, who was Sheriff of Cheshire in 1611, died in 1614 leaving an only daughter Eleanor, who passed her father's wich-houses to her husband Sir Gilbert Gerard, later Lord Gerard. By the 1660s these same wich-houses were in the hands of Lord Cholmondeley (11, 12) and Thomas Rossendale of Aston Grange (89).

The Winningtons

So far as this family is concerned there were two closely related families – those of Northwich, who later settled at 'the Hermitage' in Cranage, and those of Birches. Both descended from the family that resided at Winnington who, since at least the time of Richard II, had five wich-houses, one of these was the house of the Judger of Leftwich: originally the Winnington family held Leftwich and a junior line settled there and assumed the name. Following the Dissolution the Winningtons acquired a wich-house that had been the property of Whalley Abbey (106). The Winningtons of Hermitage eventually (c.1650) had to sell off their estate.[13] The purchasers of the six wich-houses were Ralph Nickson (8, 10, 106), George Leftwich (142), Peter Venables (143) and John Read (103). The Winningtons of Birches had just one house (91), originally 'Judger of Tatton', and this passed with the marriage of Paul Winnington's daughter to Raphe Starkey.

The Leycesters

Like the Winningtons there were two branches of this family: those of Tabley and Toft. The main line of the family based at Tabley may have had property in Northwich for many generations. Peter Leycester's *inquisition post mortem* of 1577 records that he held five wich-houses, two shops with a chamber above the shops, a stable with another chamber and a further wich-house of eight leads. By 1593 the family had six wich-houses – presumably the so-called eight-lead house had been divided into two (40 & 41).[14] Of these one was previously the property of Vale Royal Abbey (40); two others (44 & 95) were owned by the Starkeys of Darley; one (44) being Judger of Tattenhall; and another was previously owned by Venables of Kinderton (32) and was the house of the Judger of Little Witton. As regards the Leycesters of Toft they had two houses (85 and 122) one of which (85) was Judger of Lostock Gralam. The Tabley wich-houses were eventually shared with William Leycester of Newcastle who had two (32, 44) and a half of another (41).

The Marbury Family

The Marburys had five wich-houses, one of which was an ancient holding, being the Judger of Marbury's house (29).[15] These were all purchased in the mid-17th century by Sir Thomas Cholmondeley.

OWNERS, OCCUPIERS AND OTHERS

The Wilbrahams

The Wilbrahams of Radnor and later Woodhey had had interests in Northwich since the time of Edward I when Sir Richard Wilbraham married an heiress of the Vernon family. During Richard II's reign the family had two houses and in the 17th century they had the same two houses (21, 22). A branch of the family who lived at Witton had a single house (20) which was originally the property of Sir John Done of Utkinton.

The Pavor Family

The Pavor family can be traced in the surviving medieval court rolls of Northwich back to the early 14th century.[16] In the parish registers at Witton they appear first with the baptism of Ellen, daughter of John Pavor, on 10 September 1561,[17] and during the later 16th century there seem to have been a number of families, headed by John, Peter, William, Ralph and Roger who were brothers or cousins. It is likely that the family were freeholding husbandmen or tradesmen, but there are intriguing references to a Mr James Pavor of Watford, Hertfordshire, who was one of the major wich-house owners of the mid-16th century.

James Pavor of Watford seems to have been of gentry status and had five wich-houses (in Horsemill Street and Seath Street) and a part of the salt-house held by the feoffees of Sir John Deane's school (124), together with a property in the Market Place (65). In 1565 he leased all 21 leads to local occupiers.[18] He was dead by 1589 when his properties were said to be in the hands of his heirs. Exactly how he fitted into the Pavor family tree is not clear. He seems to have been related to Dame Dorothy Pavor who, in 1543, was living in the precincts of the former priory of St Bartholomew, Smithfield, London, where Sir John Deane, the founder of Witton Grammar School, was the incumbent from 1539. The old priory close was also the home to royal courtiers including Sir Richard Rich, Chancellor of the Court of Augmentations.[19] In her will (1548) Dorothy left Sir John a 'gilt pece', the lease of her house, and 20s for his work as her executor. It seems that she had connections with Watford where James Pavor later lived. Her will also makes bequests to another John Deane, Margaret Bradford, Anne Deane and her 'servant' Agnes Deane (later Bradford) who was a co-executor of Sir John's will.[20] When

Sir John founded the grammar school he appointed a Peter Pavor as one of his two attorneys responsible for conveying property to the trustees, a matter which was concluded on 6 November 1557 in front of a number of local witnesses amongst whom was a Roger Pavor.

Peter Pavor, like James, had interests in salt production but on a more modest scale: he had one wich-house of four pans, located next door to James' on the north side of Seath Street. In 1565 he leased two of his salt pans to a local entrepreneur. In this same year mention is made of a John Pavor leasing salt pans. In the muster rolls for 1548, Peter Pavor is listed for the town as a man able to serve in the army but lacking equipment.[21] An Ellen, daughter of a Peter Pavor of Northwich, married Edward Golborne of Overton, Malpas, and after his death in 1567, married again to Richard Davenport of Weltrogh, Siddington.[22] This Peter seems to have lived between the years 1520 and 1585, in which year he was buried at Witton on 17 May.

In the late 16th century a memorial window (which no longer survives) was placed in Witton church mentioning members of the family: *"Pray for the souls of Roger Pavor, Jonet his wife, Roger the younger, and Emme his wife, and for the good health of Rafe Pavor and Jone his wife, Peter Pavor and Ellen his wife."*[23] Clearly the two Rogers, father and son, were dead: the memorial was presumably commissioned by Rafe, Peter and their wives. Some further information comes to light through an agreement, dated 22 March 1591, between Hugh Winnington of Birches and Richard Wood. The Crown had granted Winnington the wardship and marriage of Peter Pavor, along with a lease of all of the boy's property, on 25 March 1579. In 1591, he agreed to sell the wardship and lease to a Richard Wood for the sum of £70. The agreement was that, should they be willing, Peter and Richard's daughter Ellen were to be married.[24] They did agree and the union was solemnized at Witton on 28 March 1592. In another document Hugh Winnington records some domestic details. He states that Roger Pavor had died on 9 August 1575 and that Roger's wife, Hugh's sister, had died in 1578. Peter was sent to school at Nantwich for two years and £4 a year was spent on his 'tabling' to Mr Wickstead, and 10s a year was paid to the schoolmaster, Mr Kent: Hugh queried how much had been spent on books.[25] It seems then that

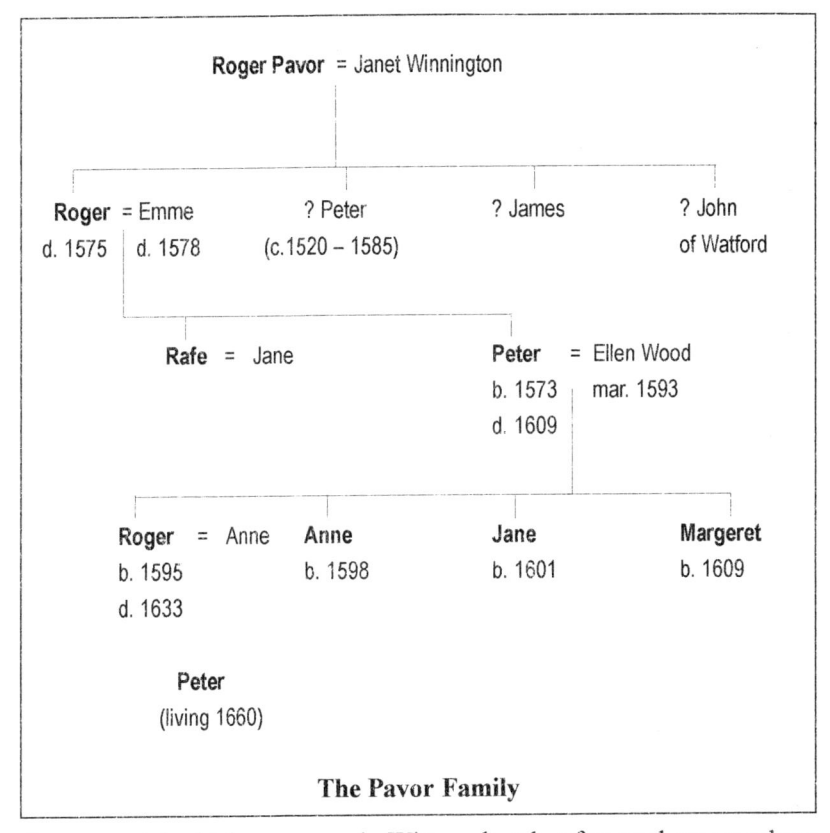

```
                    Roger Pavor = Janet Winnington
                                │
       ┌────────────────┬───────┴────────┬────────────────┐
   Roger = Emme       ? Peter         ? James          ? John
   d. 1575 │ d. 1578  (c.1520 – 1585)                  of Watford
           │                             │
           │                             │
       Rafe = Jane                   Peter   = Ellen Wood
                                     b. 1573   mar. 1593
                                     d. 1609
                                        │
                ┌──────────┬────────────┼────────────┐
            Roger = Anne   Anne        Jane       Margeret
            b. 1595        b. 1598     b. 1601    b. 1609
            d. 1633

            Peter
            (living 1660)
```

The Pavor Family

the memorial which was once in Witton church refers to these members of the family and that Roger, 'the younger', Rafe and Peter were brothers and that their mother Janet was a member of the Winnington family.

Peter Pavor (1573-1610) is referred to in the parish registers and other contemporary records as a 'gentleman'. According to his *inquisition post mortem* taken on 21 January 1609/10, he held a messuage situated in Stanthorne and Bostock, then occupied by William and Hugh Farrington; a wich-house containing four leads, occupied by Robert Aynsworth; and a messuage and horsemill, then in the tenure of Helen Pavor, his late wife.[26] His son and heir was declared to be Roger, who had his 15th birthday on the previous 2 October: in fact Roger's christening took place at Witton on 11 October 1595. The messuage in which Peter and his family lived was situated on High Street (136) and both this property and the wich-house in Seath Street are later listed as being owned by Roger Pavor.

An inventory of Peter's goods and chattels was made on 26 January 1609/10.[27] This records that he had a house with the following rooms: the 'house' (or hall – the main living room), parlour, chamber over the parlour, miller's chamber, new chamber over the stairs, buttery and the little buttery. There are references to goods in the mill, presumably the horsemill, and to two wich-houses and eight leads. Presumably, at the time of his death Peter had a lease on another wich-house besides his own. He also had a barn which contained corn and hay, and five cows (one of which was to pay heriot). In all his possessions amounted to £42 1s 8d.

The younger Roger Pavor's inventory was appraised on 20 February 1632/3. It makes mention of the following rooms: hall, parlour, chamber over the parlour and the man's chamber and also refers to old mill ware and a wich-house. This description of the mill ware being 'old' is because the family no longer had possession of the town's horsemill. The inventory lists corn, rye, oats, malt and yarn in the house, hay and corn in the barn, and some livestock – five cows in calf, three calves and two young swine. In all his goods totalled £69 2s 4d. Roger kept a book of debts owed to him and these amounted to £63 15s 5d and included 15s 3d owed by Joan Pavor and £1 11s 6d owed by Margaret Pavor and her mother. After debts he owed and other expenses were allowed for, £29 18s 6d remained.

By 1660 Peter Pavor and his wife Elizabeth were the only members of this family resident in the town. He is shown in the Poll Tax returns as having lands worth £10 a year in Leftwich and £25 a year in Stanthorne. Four years later he paid tax on a two-hearth house in Northwich.[28]

The Crown

Since the earliest times the reigning monarch had an interest in the salt industry. From the mid-16th century the direct interest was limited to two wich-houses – one of six leads (34) and one of four (36). As one might expect the walling rights were let on a regular basis: in 1565 the occupiers of the Queen's houses were John Tarbock (34) and Hugh

Lowe (36); a century later George Tarbock had both. In a copy of a rental for 1663 the Crown had payments from Sir Peter Leycester for walling and from William Leftwich for chief rent of 12d from a wich-house.

The Preacher

One house (152) in Horsemill Street was once held by the Bromfield family but was then sold for the benefit of the minister at Witton church. According to a memorandum in the parish registers under the year 1634, this house had to be worth at least £10 a year, or else had to be made up to that amount by levies on the parish. This entry was endorsed in 1665, 1658, 1659 and 1665. In this latter year the churchwardens, Robert Nickson, Peter Leigh, Hugh Swettenham and George Amery, wrote that 'there is soe much Walleinge in a wich house Consistinge of two Bayes of buildinge in Northwich .... as is worth £2 10s which the Curate or present Incumbant there yearly gathers leavyes and receives to his own use.'[29]

The School

The Grammar school's wich-house was situated on the north side of the Leach Eye (124), sandwiched between the properties of Peter Warburton of Arley and Thomas Starkey of Stretton. The foundation charter granted by Sir John Deane in 1557 provided for a wich-house to be part of the school's endowment. The site once belonged to the chantry at Witton and was described as being 'two parts of a salt-house divided into three parts'. With the dissolution of the chantries these two-thirds, then occupied by Thomas Bromfield, 'late chantry priest' were granted by the King to Nicholas Bacon, grocer, and John Chrymes, cloth worker, both of London. About 1550 Deane purchased the wich-house from these men; it was still occupied by Bromfield at an annual rent of 16s 8d.

About 20 years after the founding of the grammar school the 'wich-house stead' was leased at 2s a year to Ellen Tarbock, which would suggest that by this time the use of the site had reverted to some purpose other than salt-making. The right to 'wall' was presumably conducted elsewhere as the school had regular income from its allocation of 'peecings'. Each year the school was allowed 12 'peecings' to be put to 'the most benefitt of the school Master', and the feoffees had the privilege of setting their own price. At the beginning these were priced at 15s 4d each, bringing in £9 a year, and then for much of the 17th century the peecings were worth £1 each. From 1632 the premises were used as a barn and regularly let to John Broome for 3s: he also leased the whole of the school's walling allocation. After the Restoration 30s a 'peecing' was a regular amount levied on various individuals but especially members of the Broome and Houghton families. In 1663 William Houghton paid £9 for half of the allocation and would have paid the remaining £9 had he not been interrupted by William Leftwich who claimed them and paid only £8 on the instruction of Peter Venables. In the 1670s the walling remained at £18 a year until 1677, after which the income ceased.

Income from the site did continue however. Whilst the rent in the 1570s was only 2s it does seem that there were some difficulties in obtaining lessees and between 1620 and 1632 the site remained vacant. It then appears as two-thirds of a barn let for 3s to John Broome and it seems to have then remained in the hands of that family until 1712: a Peter and a Katherine Broome held it in the late 17th century and were followed by Ralph Broome, one of the school trustees. By 1659 the 'stead' was described as being a dwelling house let at 3s and this rent rose to 6s 8d by the end of the century and 10s in 1703-5. In 1712 the school trustees granted Peers Massey, a collar maker, a 99-year, three-life lease on a cottage, 'formerly a wich-house' lying in Swine Market Street and to the north of Leach End.[30] This was said to be between two other one-time wich-house sites which were then described as being an old piece of building owned by the Warburtons of Winnington, and a house and garden formerly owned by Dr Bentley, and then owned by Thomas Nickson, a trustee, and occupied by John Senhouse, a salt officer. In 1760 this same cottage was leased to John Massey, saddler, who was executor of Peers' will, and to James Penkstone, baker.[31] At this time the southern boundary of the site was described as being along Fagg Lane, then the new name for what had been Leach Eye.

The Partington Family
This family resided in Witton and only acquired possession of wich-

houses in the second half of the century. John Partington, a woollen draper, had an income from property there worth £15 p.a. and had two female servants in his four-hearth house. His two sons, John and Richard Partington, both drapers, had £10 and £5 respectively from property interests in Northwich.

On 16 May 1663 John Partington made his will and mentioned that he was in possession of salt-making rights which he had purchased from persons with 'salt howses and other lands whereon noe salthowses are nowe stading' but to which 'several of the occupations of waleing belong'. These purchases were from Hugh Crosby of Whitley (147) Richard Bromfield (53), the Leftwich family (39 & 115) and William Leycester (44, 32 & 41). One of these may well have been his shop, which is referred to in his will. In addition to buying property in Northwich, John also bought two crofts, 'Howey' and 'Ridgeway', in Leftwich from Earl Rivers and had a shop and dwelling house in Nether Knutsford. He also leased a number of wich-houses. From the Warburtons of Arley he had three-life lease on a wich-house for an annual rent of £3 and four 'walmes' of salt. He leased another that had been owned by Julius Winnington of Birches for several years at an annual rent of 5s and four 'walmes' of salt (91). From Peter Venables of Kinderton he leased a dwelling house in Witton for 80 years from 1 March 1626 and the lives of himself and sons Thomas and John, for the initial sum of £46 and a rent of 13s 4d a year, two capons a year and the service of leading two cartloads of timber, stone, slate or other materials to Kinderton when required. This lease was renewed on 29 October 1653 for the lives of John, Thomas and Richard Partington. On 13 January 1627, for the sum of £23 he also obtained from Venables a parcel of ground called 'Heesomes Ground' with a barn and an ancient 'mease place' (mansion) lying near the Wade Brook and the lane to the brook, at an annual rent of 6s 8d plus a heriot.

John Partington wrote his will on 16 May 1663. The inventory of his goods amounts to the sum of £939 18s 4d, of which £600 was in 'ready money'. The rooms in his home included a 'grand chamber', 'boarded chamber', 'roome over parlour', 'chamber over kitchen' and a 'maid's chamber'.

The Occupiers

Whilst some of the proprietors did work their own houses to produce salt, most, especially the gentry, leased their 'walling' rights to 'occupiers'. These, when identifiable, are invariably local craftsmen, tradesmen and husbandmen, who, perhaps by means of their business skill and possession of leases on favourable terms, were able to invest in the salt business. In addition to the rent paid for the wich-house, these entrepreneurs were required to pay to the lord of the manor what was known as the 'lead fine' for the privilege of making salt. Whilst this fine was set on the lord's behalf by the jury at the 'Great Court' held after Easter it was not collected until the end of the year after the occupiers had had their full amount of walling. The setting of the annual fine by the burgesses would seem to suggest that it might vary, but in actual fact it was a constant 8s for four leads, and what the jury determined was the total amount due, giving due consideration to exemptions and the number of applications to 'wall'. Burgesses who occupied wich-houses were exempt, but only if they did not sub-let their entitlement to a non-burgess. As already mentioned some houses were designated as 'judger's houses' and exempt from the lead-fine, paying instead a 'judger's fine' of 2s in lieu. In respect of exemptions the onus of proof lay with the occupier and this freedom could be challenged. When Richard Starkey claimed to be free from paying the lead-fine on one of his two houses on the grounds of it being the house of the judger of Comberbach, he was required to pay the lead-fine in full until he could prove the fact.[32]

Once an occupier committed himself to rent a wich-house his interests in that property were protected against any sudden decision by the owner to terminate the lease: in essence he or she had to have 12 months notice of termination.[33] The court ruled that when a person had occupation for an indeterminable period, such as 'for life' or 'at will', then although the owner might unexpectedly terminate the lease at the end of the salt-making season, he or she was permitted to continue for a further year. The explanation given for this is that the occupier may have unwittingly made provision for wood and other materials for the following year. No such provision was open to those who had a fixed term contract for a year or a set number of years. The owner had rights too: if he wished to expel his tenant he had to make a presentation of the fact to at least two burgesses before 12 noon on 30 November. Presumably this would give the occupier sufficient time to cancel any arrangements made for the following year.

According to the only known full list of walling dated 1565, of the 71 occupiers, only ten were also owners.[34] Some of these owners also leased extra 'walling' from their colleagues: Humphrey Yate walled 28 leads of which only six were his own and Robert Winnington 'walled' 26 of which four were his own. Other large-scale producers that year were William Worrall, 24; Edward Golbourne, 22; Hugh Lowe, 20; Roger Torbock, 18; Thomas Winnington, 12; Robert Bromfield, 12; and Rondle Shaw, 10. Seven men were, however, content simply to make salt with their own leads. There were only two women occupiers. Jone Rendye worked two leads and Sibill Winnington worked six. In all that year a total of 450 leads were walled – full production was in progress (see *Appendix Two*).

Whilst the 1565 list is the only known walling list for the town, other evidence of occupation does exist, especially in probate records. Richard Holford's inventory (1605) refers to 'one lease of 8 leads occupation in Northwich for three yeres yet enduringe at the yerelie rent £5 16s', valued at £10, and also to 'one lease of an oven & tow parts of an oven wallinge in Northwich aforsaid' valued at £5: these were in addition to his own wich-house.[35] Jeffrey Harrison's inventory (1615) refers to 'two wychhouse leads' that he leased to Richard Rowe. In her will Ellen Heyes (1629) refers to the wich-house of eight leads occupied by Peter Dewsbury. George Broome (1639) mentions in his will of the £3 rent due from a wich-house. William Leftwich leased a wich-house in Yate Street to John Broome. The inventory of Mary Bromfield, spinster (1666), reveals that she rented a 'peeceinge of wallinge' for which £1 10s 0d was due when she died. She also owed the same amount for carrying salt to Frodsham, the port used for shipping salt both to the rest of England and abroad. Items listed as being in her 'Wich-house' were 'one Iron pan Iron barrs one Iron hatch one coalerake, one picke, barrowes, & other materialls belonging to the said Iron pann' which were worth £14, along with 'coales & wichwood' worth £4 10s 0d.

As Mary Bromfield's inventory suggests, occupiers had their own equipment – leads, barrows and crannocks. Thomas Pickmere (1597) had four 'wychowse leads' worth 40s, three 'Cranocke of barrowes' worth 10s and 'wychwood' both in the woods and at home worth £50. Peter Pavor (1610) had eight leads valued at £4 along with 'barrowes, leachtubbes' and other implements in both his houses worth 5s. His fuel, 'wichwood' was worth £6. Richard Holford (1605) had seven leads worth £3 10s 0d along with 10s worth of barrows. Thomas Skellhorne (1605) had four leads worth 40s, two 'leach tubes' and two 'houpes' worth 20d, 'wood standinge in the towne' worth £53 6s 6d, and 'wood standing out of the town' worth £4 -- in fact over half the value of his estate was taken with the cost of his fuel; his barrows and two axes were worth 4s 4d. Jeffrey Harrison's (1615) two leads were each worth 10s, but he does not seem to have had any other equipment. George Broome (1634) had eight leads worth £4 and barrows worth 13s 4d. Roger Pavor (1632) had 'leades, Barrowes, wood & cloth in the wichehouse' worth £3. John Johnson, mercer (1637) had wood in the streets worth £15 and eight leads, barrows and clouts worth £4.

An undated partial list of 'Peecings' from the early part of the century shows that Margaret Shakerley owned two wich-houses and occupied them both, but on one day (21 August) she actually worked 12 leads and must therefore have hired another wich-house.[36]

The Tarbock Family

The Tarbocks probably originated in south-west Lancashire around the area of Tarbock, near Huyton. The earliest known member of the family is John Tarbock who had a grant of a wich-house in c.1295: there is another reference to a John Tarbock in 1366.[37] A Roger Tarbock is listed in 1595 as occupying 18 leads. He died in 1575 and was perhaps brother of John Tarbock of Witton 'the elder', who died seven years later. John 'junior', who married Margaret Pickmere in 1561, seems to have been the head of the main line – a family prominent in the affairs of Northwich.

A Peter Tarbock, George Tarbock and their sister Ellen Heyes were part of a generation from which sprang the late 17th and early 18th cen-

```
┌─────────────────────────────────────────────────────────────────┐
│     John Tarbock  = Margaret        Roger                       │
│     m.1561          Pickmere        d. 1575                     │
│     d. 1586         d. 1593                                     │
│                                                                 │
│  Robert = Margaret   George = Elizabeth   Peter   =   Ellen     │
│  b. 1563             b. 1569              b. 1574     Heyes     │
│                      d. 1641              d. 1640               │
│  Margaret Elizabeth                                             │
│                                                                 │
│            Ellen    Peter  =  ? Thomas  ? George  Ellen  Elizabeth │
│                     b. 1636                                     │
│                                                                 │
│                       Peter                                     │
│                       b. 1671                                   │
│                                                                 │
│                   The Tarbock Family                            │
└─────────────────────────────────────────────────────────────────┘
```

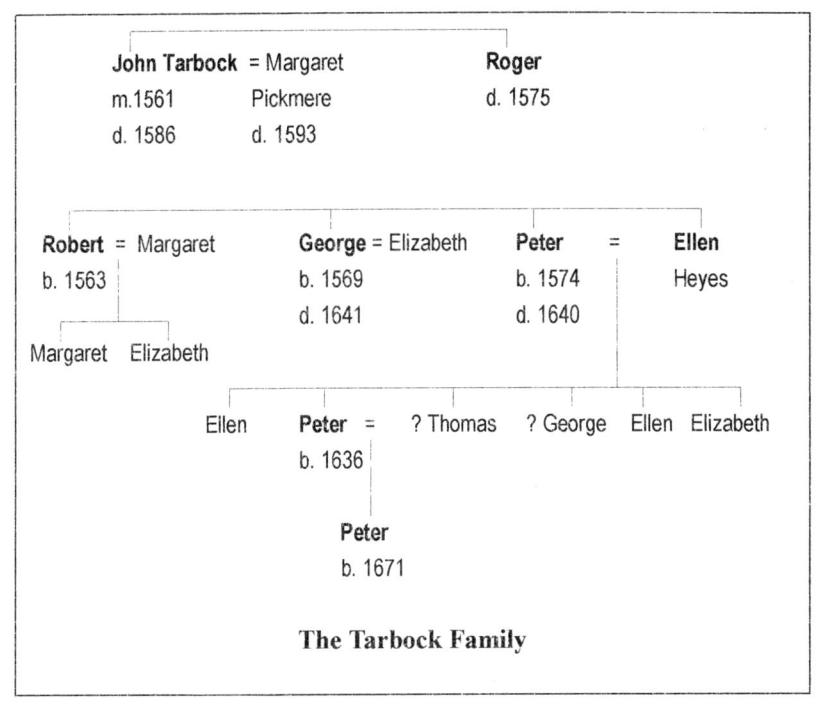

tury families. Peter Tarbock inherited all his wealth from his sister Ellen who died in 1629.

Following Peter Tarbock's death in July 1640 an *inquisition post mortem* recorded that he held property known as 'the New Swanne' from the King, which he let to John Dutton and Thomas Holford. He also had two shops leased to William Birkenhead and William Jeffery; a half share in a wich-house of six leads (34) also held from the King, which he sub-let to Alice Dewsbury; a half share in 'the Old Swanne'; half a burgage held by George Pavor; half of another wich-house occupied by Margaret Tarbock and then John Broome; half another held by Richard Newall and then John Broome; half another, of six leads, in the tenure of George Shaw and then John Ainsworth; half another held by Ralph Nickson and then by Alice Horton and finally another leased to Sir Peter Warburton and then Alice Horton. Clearly a man of some significance with interests in several key aspects of Northwich life. He left a widow, Mary, a six-year old son, also named Peter, and a daughter, Elizabeth.

In 1660, according to the Poll Tax returns, Peter Tarbock had interests in Northwich worth £10 p.a. and a further £15 in Witton. A Thomas Tarbock, husbandman, and George Tarbock, labourer, also appear in the returns. A George Tarbock was a feoffee of Witton School who was charged with usury by the ecclesiastical authorities, but in a successful defence Tarbock asserted he was acting as an executor and was employing money for the use of the poor. By 1664 there is only one of the name in the Hearth Tax returns – Thomas, who had a single-hearth home in Northwich.

The Broome Family

This family seem to appear in Northwich at the beginning of the 17th century and regularly occupied a number of wich-houses. They may be related to a family who lived in the vicinity of Lostock Gralam during the reign of Elizabeth I. According to the schedule accompanying the town plan (see *Appendix Three*) the family had a single tenement in Market Place (73) and about this time a John Broome was a churchwarden at Witton.

George Broome, husbandman, died in 1664. The inventory of his goods and chattells totalled £27 7s 10d with the sum of £30 being owed to him. His home consisted of a 'street chamber', 'garden chamber' and an 'upper chamber' and it may be that this is the house plot referred to on the town plan (133). It is known that this building was repaired in 1606 and had been previously occupied by Yeoman Gardner and then by his son-in-law Hugh Ditchfield.[38] George was certainly involved in producing salt for the list of his goods included eight leads and a number of barrows.

George Broome married Katherine and by her had five sons, George, John, Samuel, Ottiwell and Richard, and two daughters, Ursula and Ellen. The eldest son George inherited his father's home but then died relatively young in 1639, leaving the family property to his younger brother Samuel. Judging from the bequests in his will George must have presented a colourful sight as he strolled around the Market Place for he had possessed three suits, one of which had silver buttons, and three hats – one black, one white and one grey lined with green taffeta. He was an educated man as he possessed a desk (inherited from his father) and five Latin books. Interestingly the inventory only lists these items, along with a goat and his wearing apparel, which was worth £3 16s 8d, so presumably the majority of his goods had been disposed of prior to death, or at least prior to the arrival of the appraisers. A large sum of money was owed to him. Of the £117 16s 6d due, his brother John owed the 'great some' of £62 4s 0d. Like his father, George also had interests in salt-making and had possession of a wich-house in Yate Street which he had purchased from the Mainwarings of Kermincham (82) and which his mother was leasing from him when he died.

The most influential member of this family was John Broome. From an early date he was leasing the walling rights belonging to the Witton School and was also tenant of the school's wich-house site which had been converted into a barn in what became Swine Market Street. In the 1640s John was lessee of a wich-house owned by Peter Tarbock and later became the occupier of at least 16 other wich-houses of which there was a block of three along the north side of the High Street, close to the junction with Market Place (6, 7, 11, 12, 15, 18, 30, 41, 47, 76, 77, 78, 84, 90, 120, & 123). Two of his properties are known to have had specific functions: a stable (41) and a kitchen 'to his new building' (47).[39] It seems that he resided in premises that backed onto the River Dane (9). According to the Poll Tax returns John was classed as an innkeeper with an income of at least £5 a year from his business: he may also have had property in Lostock Gralam.[40] He employed six servants in a house rated at seven hearths. On these facts it would seem that he was one of the wealthiest residents.

Somewhat surprisingly, John's brother Samuel, a butcher who lived with his wife Cicelie, was listed as being exempt from paying the Hearth Tax: brother Ottiwell was also exempt.

The Houghton Family

Another family regularly engaged in occupying wich-houses were the Houghtons of Northwich. Something about this family has already been said in Chapter 3. William Houghton in the 1660s certainly leased a number of wich-house properties: one from John Swinton of Knutsford

(144), and three from Richard Bradford of Shipbrook (56, 117 & 119). His brother Thomas had one from the Pavors of Northwich (28) and one from Dr Bentley (88).[41] It is known that in addition William was a tenant of the Grammar School. In 1663 he paid £9 to the trustees and would have paid the same amount for peecings due for the year ending at Christmas 1663, but had been obstructed by William Leftwich who disposed of them 'and was to answer the schoole for them the sume of £9'. However, for some unknown reason Peter Venables, bailiff of Northwich, instructed Leftwich to set the six peecings for only £8.

Houghton's will, made in February 1664, makes no mention of his properties, but the inventory of his possessions made 18 months later does refer to salt-making. In the salt works in Leftwich, owned by Leftwich Oldfield, William had a stock of coal worth £25, half an iron pan, iron bars, barrows and other materials worth £5. In Northwich (we are not told exactly where) he had three iron walling pans with iron bars, barrows and materials worth £30, coal worth £40, 'wichwood' worth £4, and 'tacks' (leases) worth £20. It seems likely that William was both occupying and sub-letting his walling rights. In August 1668 William's widow, Margaret, died. Her will, recorded by the same William Leftwich, is quite specific and mentions her 'sixteene leads of wallinge': these were in three wich-houses owned by Richard Bradford of Shipbrook and the one owned by John Swinton of Knutsford.[42] However, according to the inventory of her goods, her walling rights were conducted elsewhere. Mention is made of the wich-house in Leach Eye (117), but this was used as a store room for coal, bricks, lime and some tubs and ladders. Walling was carried out in a wich-house known as 'Gandys' on the north side of Yate Street, though I have yet to identify it. Here she had an iron pan with bars, bearers, barrows and all the necessary equipment for making salt with a stack of wood for fuel in the High Street. Walling was also carried out in one of two wich-houses in Horsemill Street (24 & 25) both owned by Mr Marriot of Witton. In one of these she had an iron pan with bars, bearers, barrows and all the necessary equipment for making salt: it was here that she exercised her 10 years interest in the four leads of walling belonging to John Swinton which was worth £20. In the other, next door, Margaret again stored coal, bricks and old iron. In Rachel Sudlowe's wich-house on High Street (96) Margaret walled her one year's interest in 'seven leads and one third part of a lead', worth £4, and had an iron pan and the necessary equipment. The inventory also mentions that from the time of her death until the date of the appraisal walling had continued and raised £33 8s towards her estate, and that a further £6 was due on walling scheduled for the remainder of the year. Following her death Sudlowe's wich-house in High Street was worked by her son-in-law, William Swettenham the blacksmith.

Margaret's will and inventory are particularly informative for they reveal a number of facts concerning the management of the salt business. Firstly, it is clear that walling rights associated with particular premises could be, and were, carried out in other houses, and secondly that wich-houses capable of being used for walling were not kept in constant use.

The Others

There are a number of other families who, although they do not appear to have been owners or occupiers, do seem to have played a significant part in local affairs: these include the burgess families.

The Pownall Family

This family were descended from a family that had migrated from East Cheshire and settled in Witton during the late medieval period. The earliest reference to the family in the parish registers is in 1562 when George Pownall married Ellen Hewitt a few days before the christening of their daughter Elizabeth. Twenty years later there is mention of a Humphrey Pownall marrying Joan Tewe. The eldest son of each generation seems to have used the style 'yeoman'.

Ralph Pownall had a number of leasehold properties in Hartford, Winnington, Twambrook and Lostock Gralam when he died in March 1606/7 aged about 70 years. He had married Anne Ryley and had a son named Humphrey, daughters named Elizabeth (who married Richard Boote) and Margaret (married to Peter Tarbock), and four grandsons – Thomas, George, Raffe and Robert. In addition to his agricultural interests, Ralph held two wich-houses, each of four leads, on lease from Thomas Marbury and Peter Pavor that were worth £23 p.a. At the time of his death he had large quantities of wood to fuel the wich-houses. In Northwich there were several piles worth £26, sufficient for 19½ peecings, and in Witton, Marbury and 'Reddiche' there were further stocks worth the high price of £86 5s. Of course he had lead pans – 12 in number worth 10s each and barrows worth 12s. A rather interesting item in the inventory of his possessions is 'a cote for the warre' worth 2s 4d, reflecting a yeoman's military obligations

The inventory of Robert Pownall's goods amounts to £365 2s 9d of which a third consisted of his cattle (£40), other animals, crops of rye, barley, oats and corn, items of husbandry and salt-making necessities, including £20 worth of wich-wood. Another third of Robert's goods and chattells were in the form of debts and ready money, of which one man – John Gandy – owed £91 10s. The remaining third consisted of household goods contained in the house, parlour, kitchen and a room over the house.

The Birkenhead Family

Of the Birkenhead, or Berchenhead, family the most noteworthy was Sir John Birkenhead who was born in 1617. He was a member of a family that had settled in Northwich in the early 16th century, perhaps moving here as a result of some connections either with the Stanleys or else through royal service. The family may be connected to the Birkenheads of Backford near Chester, an influential family who served the Tudor monarchs by holding a number of official positions in Cheshire, Flint and Lancashire. The parish registers record the burial of a Sir Henry Birkenhead on 23 January 1562/3 who at some time prior to 1561 had been installed as curate. The next generation was that of William, born about 1550, who married Joan Bradford in December 1573 and had at least two sons, John and Randle. A William was recorded in 1629 as being one of three tenants of a burgage property called the 'New Swan'. William's son Randle Birkenhead, born in February 1581, was in 1629 recorded as lessee of burgage premises known as 'Old Swan'. There is some confusion as to where these men lived. Both the Old Swan and the New Swan were the property of Ellen Heyes, sister to Peter Tarbock of Witton. Following her death an *inquisition post mortem* declared that she held, along with many other properties, a messuage or burgage known as the 'New Swan' which was then in the occupation of William Eaton, William Birkenhead and George Amery. It also records that she held a moiety (half) of the burgage known as 'Old Swan' then occupied by Randle Birkenhead. According to her will, dated in May 1629, the New Swan, 'at or near Bridge End', was occupied by 'Randle Birkenhead, the elder, innkeeper'. It adds that William Birkenhead occupied one of two shops at 'the Bridge End'. When Ellen's nephew Peter Tarbock died in 1640 his *inquisition post mortem* records the same premises and says that the New Swan was tenanted by members of the Dutton and Holford families, and that William Birkenhead had occupied one of two shops: unfortunately whilst mention is made of the New Swan no tenant is given. It seems that William occupied a shop by the Town Bridge which adjoined the New Swan and was probably part of the same complex of buildings. As to Randle's accommodation, it might be that his inn keeping business moved from the site of the Old Swan in Market Place to the new location on the other side of the bridge at about this time.

Not only was Randle an innkeeper but he was also a saddler. He was an educated man, for he was also the parish clerk of Witton and an usher, or under-master, of the local grammar school – Sir John Deane's. His entries in the parish registers are particularly fine with a good italic style and Gothic lettering and ornamentation. Randle died in 1636 and left sons Thomas (who died in the parish of St Brides, London in 1631 aged 24), William, Randle, Roger (of Chester), John and Isaac.[43] The inventory of Randle's goods and chattells survives and probate was granted to his widow, Margaret, on 30 March 1637.

The second Randle fell on hard times during the Civil War as a supporter of the Royalist cause. In 1651 it was said that his estate was worth only £3 or £4 a year and that his family lived partly on charity.[44] When he died an inventory of his property was made on 23 November 1657 which shows that he was indeed a man of very modest means for it lists very simple furniture and basic necessities and has a total value of a mere £3 0s 2d. Probate was granted to his widow, Elizabeth, three years later. She is the only member of the family to be listed in the Hearth Tax returns: she then occupied a two-hearth house. This Randle was suc-

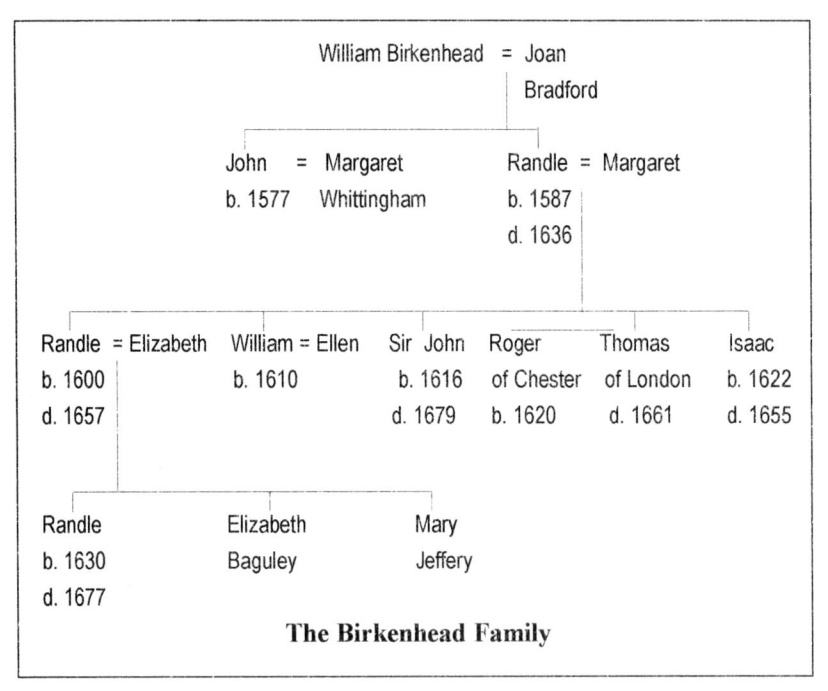

```
                    William Birkenhead = Joan
                                        Bradford
              ┌─────────────────────────┴──────────┐
          John = Margaret              Randle = Margaret
          b. 1577  Whittingham          b. 1587
                                        d. 1636
  ┌───────────────┬──────────────┬──────────┼──────────┬──────────────┐
Randle = Elizabeth  William = Ellen  Sir John   Roger       Thomas      Isaac
b. 1600           b. 1610          b. 1616   of Chester  of London    b. 1622
d. 1657                            d. 1679   b. 1620     d. 1661      d. 1655
  │
  ├──────────────┬──────────────┐
Randle         Elizabeth       Mary
b. 1630        Baguley         Jeffery
d. 1677
```

The Birkenhead Family

ceeded in the family business by yet another Randle Birkenhead who was born in 1630. His brother William was also a saddler and he occurs in the Poll Tax returns along with his wife, Ellen, and daughter Marie. In his will, this third Randle bequeathed a gold ring to his sister Elizabeth Baguley, and to his sister Mary Jefferies all his household goods and 20 yards of flaxen sheets. Cousin John Baguley received a black saddle worked with green silk, a white bridle and snaffle, a pair of girths and a pair of gloves. Cousin William Baguley had the bed in the shop and Randle's wearing apparel and work tools. Peter Tarbock had a new saddle and Ralph Leftwich a new tan bridle and saddle. His inventory which was appraised on 12 January 1677/8 only amounts to £12 and consists of shop goods worth £5. His bed and bedding worth £2, his apparel worth £2 10s and debts due to him made up the remainder.

Randle's brother John was christened at Witton on 24 March 1616 and educated at the local grammar school before going on to Oriel College, Oxford, in the early 1630s as a 'servitor' (otherwise known as a 'fag' – one who works to support himself through college). During his time at university John worked as a secretary in the offices of the university chancellor – Archbishop Laud. He graduated with a Bachelor of Arts degree in January 1637 and gained his Masters degree three years later before becoming a Fellow of All Souls College. With the onset of the Civil War the royal court was based at Oxford and John certainly espoused the King's cause. Between 1643 and 1645 he was the editor and major contributor to a weekly, anti-Parliamentary propaganda pamphlet called the *Mercurius Aulicus*. He was described by one critic as a 'lier, bold, mean and not sweet'. It has been said of John that he was the 'true father of English journalism' and that for 'wit, clarity, compactness and vigour he has rarely been surpassed'. With the fall of King Charles, John lost his university positions and left Oxford for London and travels in Europe. The Restoration in 1660 brought him back into the limelight with the award of a doctorate in Civil Laws and election to Parliament in 1661; knighthood in 1662; and then two years later the office of Master of Requests. As a founder member of the prestigious Royal Society he was elected a Fellow of that organisation. Then in 1665, perhaps not unsurprisingly, he was elected to become a feoffee (trustee) of his old school, Sir John Deane's. He died in December 1679.[45]

The Robinson Family

The Robinsons appear in local records with some regularity and were burgesses of the town. A William Robinson, who had a house in Market Place (66), was bailiff of Northwich three times between 1597 and 1612 and a feoffee of Sir John Deane's Grammar School; when he died in 1623 he was described as 'a very honourable man', 'mourned by all'. It is likely that it is he who wrote the Survey Book in 1606 which was then regularly updated; he may also be responsible for the drawing of the town plan c1610. His son Thomas was admitted to Magdalen Hall, Oxford, where he matriculated on 25 February 1581, aged 21 years, becoming a Bachelor of Arts at Brazenose College on 30 January 1583.[46] He may have been the father of another Thomas who was one of a group of devout Puritans and a particular friend of Richard Mather, curate at Witton from 1628 to 1640: in 1638 Robinson was a churchwarden. In his will Mather left Thomas a religious treatise *Elton upon the 8th of*

Romans.[47] During and after the Civil War, Robinson (along with William Leftwich and Dr Bentley) was appointed as one of the County Commissioners for Sequestration and was particularly active in that role (see *Chapter 7*). It is interesting to note, but by no means unusual, that within a small town such as this two of the prominent families, the Birkenheads and the Robinsons, were on opposing sides.

Another Thomas Robinson made his will on 1 September 1671 and being unable to write he made his mark. He left all his possessions to his 'loveing wife Elin' for the use of her and her children. To Francis, John, Edward, Katherine and Alice Chrimes and Thomas Griffith he left four pence each. Following his death in January 1675 the inventory of his possessions amounted to a very modest £6 10s. Was this the same Thomas who was Steward of Northwich in 1656 and 1671? It seems so, in which case his inability to write was probably due to his failing health rather than illiteracy.

---

[1] CRO: D4360/2; DCH/m/37/60; Calvert, pp. 1068, 1073, 1077, 1082, 1089.
[2] Calvert, pp. 1080, 1117.
[3] Calvert, pp. 1103, 1113 *et al*.
[4] The township names attached to judgers' houses were Claverton, Barterton, Leigh, Leftwich, Plumley, Lache, Tattenhall (or more likely, Cattenhall in Kingsley), Eaton, Acton, Cogshall, Little Witton, Witton, Marbury, Dunham Massey, Tatten, Winnington, Dutton, Crowton, Hartford, Lach Dennis, Comberbach, Marston and Lostock Gralam.
[5] CRO: DSS/1/1/50/1-6.
[6] Nos. 47, 50, 57, 92, 107, 108? 109, 112, 116, 145, 146, 151.
[7] Nos. 6, 19, 76, 77, 90, 120, 123.
[8] Nos. 14, 31, 97, 101.
[9] CRO: DCH/M/37/60.
[10] Nos. 36, 39, 79, 115, 127, 150.
[11] Cal. Ancient Deeds, vol vi, p. 189.
[12] Nos. 11, 12, 89.
[13] Nos. 8, 10, 103, 106, 142, 143.
[14] Nos. 9, 32, 40, 41, 44, 95.
[15] Nos 29, 33, 96, 140.

[16] Calvert, pp. 1127, etc.
[17] CRO: PR.
[18] Nos. 24, 25, 27, 45, 46. CRO: D4360/2; Calvert p. 1068-73.
[19] Cox, p. 13
[20] Cox, p. 24
[21] PRO: Calendar of State Papers 10/3, no. 9, f.33.
[22] Ormerod, ii, p. 671 and iii, p. 721.
[23] Ormerod, iii, p. 155.
[24] CRO: DSS 1/4/2/6.
[25] CRO: DSS 1/4/2/8.
[26] *Cheshire Inquisitions Post Mortem.*
[27] CRO: WS.
[28] Poll Tax and Hearth Tax.
[29] CRO: EDV 99/1.
[30] CRO: SL 300/8/61.
[31] CRO: SL300/8/63.
[32] CRO: DLT/A/2/60, p. 35.
[33] Calvert, p. 1040.
[34] Calvert, p. 1068-73.
[35] CRO: WS 1605. The following wills are all CRO: WS (date)
[36] CRO: DSS/1/4/33.
[37] CRO: DCH/J/134.
[38] CRO: DLT/A2/57.
[39] CRO: DLT/A2/49b
[40] G.O. Lawton (ed.), 'Northwich Hundred: Poll Tax 1660 and Hearth Tax 1664', *R.C.L.S.*, vol cxix (1979), pp. 145, 238.
[41] CRO: DCH/M/37/60
[42] CRO: WC 1668.
[43] From the parish registers it seems that Thomas was baptised on Christmas Day 1607 and William on 20 May 1610. It is likely that Randle, junior, was born on a date between these two, c.1608/9. John was christened on 24 March 1616, Roger was baptised on 13 August 1620 and Isaac was baptised on 13 October 1622.
[44] CCAM, part I, p. 103.
[45] Sir John's life is covered in P. W. Thomas, *Sir John Berkenhead, 1617-1679*, (1969).
[46] *Oxon*, p. 1268.
[47] Cox, p. 75.

7

RELIGION, POLITICS & CIVIL WAR

Religion
For us today it is hard to comprehend the way in which religion and religious debate occupied such a prominent place in the lives and minds of 17th century men and women. The church was a central theme of everyday life and culture. The parish, with its clergy and churchwardens, was the basic unit of civil administration. Attendance at church was compulsory, with fines for those who failed without good reason. Church courts policed the morality of the community and their records reveal many cases of drunkenness, sexual misconduct, adultery, libel, slander and blasphemy. So far as Northwich and Witton were concerned the focus of religion was the chapel of St Helen, Witton, and the parish church of St Mary and All Saints, Great Budworth. There has been a chapel in Witton since perhaps the 13th century, and many features of its present-day fabric are of the late medieval period. In 1498 Richard Winnington left 40s towards the cost of building the steeple, and in 1525 Randle Pickmere of Middlewich left 20s for 'churchwerke'. The known list of perpetual curates of Witton goes back to 1538 and the parish registers commence in 1561.

During Elizabeth's reign a settlement was established aimed at a compromise to keep both those with Catholic leanings and those with extreme Puritan ideals united within one Anglican Church. Catholicism was based on rigid principles of prescribed forms of worship and a hierarchical church with the Pope at its head and reflecting the social hierarchy of the times. This ancient and one-time traditional form of worship relied upon the Latin Mass and strict ritual procedures with particular ceremonies on particular days. To those of the Protestant persuasion the observance of these rituals and the nature of the priesthood, seen by many as corrupt and an abuse of power, interfered with worshipping God and ministering to the people. They believed that all individuals, regardless of status, could save themselves through faith and living an industrious and thrifty life rather than by means of priestly intervention. They favoured simple forms of worship based on the preacher in his pulpit, private study of the Bible, a system of church government at parish level, and rejected anything that suggested Catholicism such as the wearing of vestments, observing saints' days, and kneeling at the altar rail. Tension between these two had always existed and constantly fluctuated in its ferocity, but overall the Puritans were gaining control at parish level.

On 24 March 1603, James VI of Scotland became James I of England in succession to his distant kinswoman Queen Elizabeth who had ruled for a glorious 45 years. From her he inherited a strong and stable monarchy with a loyal and contented population. Hers had been a reign of exploration and military adventure, of culture and artistic expression through literature, music, painting and architecture. That is not to say that all was well, for James also inherited expensive wars in Ireland and the Low Countries, domestic financial problems and the same opposing religious opinions. James' accession was greeted enthusiastically, for here was a male monarch with children. He had a reputation for having ruled wayward Scotland with much success. Added to this he was a Protestant who could tolerate differing shades of religious doctrine: his mother, Mary Queen of Scots, had been a staunch Roman Catholic whilst he had been brought up in the Presbyterian Church of Scotland. His antecedents therefore gave hope to the many English Catholics who anticipated a relaxation of the punitive laws imposed against them and, at the other end of the spectrum, the Puritans had faith that the new head of the Church of England would accept some of their plans for reform. Both were disappointed.

Whilst James did initially suspend the collection of fines for recusancy, he later had to reintroduce them to acknowledge the wishes of Parliament and a need for increased income. Catholic annoyance led to the famous conspiracy we know as the Gunpowder Plot of 1605, which interestingly is referred to in the Nantwich parish registers with the comment 'Such is the fruits of popish religion'. So far as the Puritans were concerned their hopes of reform as expressed in their Millenary Petition of 1603 were rejected following the Hampton Court Conference at which the proposals were debated. Puritan ministers had called for the abolition or relaxation of certain ritualistic practises – the signing of the cross at baptism, bowing to the altar, wearing surplices, lighting candles, burning incense, etc. – but in the end they were required to conform to the rules laid down in the Book of Common Prayer, which contained some of these practices, or else lose their livings.

Over the years the King softened his policies in the interests of harmony. Puritan ministers were allowed to ignore rules and rights with which they felt uncomfortable so long as they accepted the King's authority over the church and used the Prayer Book from time to time. Recusancy fines were only applied occasionally and Catholics could worship as they pleased without too much disturbance, though they were still treated with suspicion by many. James also allowed, or rather did not interfere with, the rights of the gentry to appoint Puritan ministers to the livings of parishes nor in the practice of endowing lectures by nonparochial preachers.

On 27 March 1625 Charles became King and whilst his father had been willing to accept differing religious views, Charles' beliefs were strongly Anglican with an acceptance of good order, ritual and the sacraments. However he tended towards the view that Catholics, rather than being evil, were misguided souls. His High Church, or Arminian, attitudes led Charles to promote those within the church whose beliefs were similar. One of the leaders of the Arminian cause, William Laud was promoted from being Bishop of St David's, to Bath and Wells, London and finally Archbishop of Canterbury in the space of three years. To many in the country of Puritan persuasion it seemed that the King and his bishops were moving closer towards the Catholic church, especially since Charles was married to a French Catholic princess – Henrietta Maria.

They were repelled by the steady increase in ideas of ritual, ceremony and order within the Anglican church. They also considered the established church as an instrument of state control in religious affairs exercised through its hierarchy of bishops. Anxious at the move to the right many Puritans set up schemes to ensure that vacant parishes were filled by Puritan ministers. Conversely the more conservative members of the Church of England feared that their traditional practices were being stripped away in those parishes served by Puritan clergy. Witton chapel suffered from the Puritan influence for it lost its rood screen, stalls, glass and monuments, some of which commemorated the local families of Winnington, Pavor and Sutton and were recorded by Randle Holme in 1580. This debate between Arminianism and Puritanism rumbled on for many years.

In Cheshire since the latter years of the 16th century the popularity of the Puritan ethic had grown due to the indifference of the Bishop of Chester. In 1578 the chapelry of Witton was accused before the Archbishop of York in that 'masters and parents send not their children to be taught the catechisme'. Between 1599 and 1601 Witton chapel had a regular preacher or 'lecturer' – Thomas Pierson, a former pupil of Witton School who edited the works of William Perkins, an influential Puritan divine and 'High Priest of the Puritans'.[1] The townspeople of Northwich allocated monies from walling rights to maintain a preacher and it became one of the centres in Cheshire where preaching exercises were regularly held. The master of the grammar school, Richard Pigott, was a Puritan who was described by one of the mainstream puritanical writers, Calamy, as an 'able, prudent and religious man'.[2] In 1633 Richard Mather, who had been curate at Witton since 1628, was presented to the church authorities for not wearing a surplice, not reading prayers on Wednesdays and Fridays, and not reading the Book of Common Prayer. When he died in 1640 it was said that he was buried with 'the deepest mourning of all good men'.[3] These probably did not include John Walton, who was cited for slandering the good cleric. Allegedly he said to the rector, in the presence of a number of people gathered in the inn run by Widow Birkenhead, 'thou art a lying priest and you came thither beggarly and bare as a louse, but set a beggar on a horse and he will ride'. The case came before the Consistory Court at Chester in 1638 and evidence was given by Richard Piggot (then aged 39 years) who said he had known the curate for some nine years and that he was a man of 'honest life and conversation'. William Roe also gave evidence to say that Walton had uttered the 'popish' words in an angry and disgraceful way in front of a number of people including Ralph Leftwich, Robert Pownall and Mrs Thomas Berrington.[4]

By the end of James' reign there were several Puritan parish clergy in Cheshire; two of whom had links with Northwich – those at Weaverham and Great Budworth. The mother church at Great Budworth was served by John Ley, who published many pamphlets criticising the reforms imposed on the church by Archbishop Laud. His 1645 pamphlet defended Cromwell and his Parliament describing the leader as a 'famous Puritan divine'. Under the Protector he was chairman of the Committee for Examining and Ordaining Ministers and in 1648 he presided over a meeting of 59 ministers held in Northwich to agree modes of Puritan worship. The next incumbent, James Livesey, refused to sign the Act of Uniformity (1662) and was ejected from his living as a Dissenter. Peter Earl, the curate at Witton, left this same year. The well-known cleric, Adam Martindale, was offered Witton but took the more lucrative parish of Rostherne. Ejected ministers conducted non-conformist worship and 'lectures' in houses and open places. Martindale records that a Northwich town official issued a precept forbidding such meetings. He challenged this as unlawful and was prepared to have the matter tried in court, but Peter Earl intervened and a compromise was reached.

The Puritans believed that everyone had to accept God's discipline and live a godly life. Those who failed would incur God's wrath. Thus they interpreted every earthly event to the judgment of God, so that when James Wright of Northwich fell off his horse and broke his neck because he was drunk, his death was seen as punishment for his evil ways. Likewise, another man fell off his horse and into the 'channel of the street' (the brine channel) and dashed his head on the horns of a hide outside a tanner's shop.[5]

Whilst on the one hand Archbishop Laud was actively attempting to remove Puritan ministers from their livings and prohibiting lecturers from the preaching exercises, King Charles, on the other, despite his alleged leanings towards Catholicism, issued his 'Instructions on Papists', ordering searches for them and their suppression from the very start of his reign. Commissions were issued to county officials who in turn sent instructions to all constables for the 'Inquireing Searching & finding out the goods & Chattells Lands tenemts demises and farmes of Recusits Convict'.[6] Parish by parish returns were made by the local constables and officials. The constables of Northwich Hundred were commanded to appear at the home of 'Widdowe Berchenhed in the Northwiche upon the fifteenth daie of November next by eight of the Clocke in the afore noone' to make their returns. They reported that so far as the parish of Witton was concerned there were three Papists in 1638. Margery Billington, widow, of Witton was one – but the authorities did not know whether she was merely suspected or had been convicted and were uncertain of her estate as she was only a servant. In Hulse there were Robert Wood and his wife Ellen who had property worth £5 and a tenement worth £3 a year.[7] The certificate was signed by all the constables of the various townships, who included John Johnson and George Amery for Northwich and William Huet and Richard Hilton for Witton: the churchwardens were Thomas Robinson, John Sworton and William Bramall. On 11 May 1641, Margery, wife of William Tandy of Northwich, and Elizabeth, widow of Richard Harcourt of Wincham, were convicted of recusancy by the Quarter Sessions sitting at Northwich.[8]

Mention has been made of the Consistory Court and in any discussion about religion it would be remiss not to mention its work for it certainly had an impact on everyone. During this period the church exercised control both over the clergy and the laity through its courts. The Archdeacon, through the Consistory Court, strove to maintain ecclesiastical control over everyday life by disciplining the clergy, proving wills, awarding grants of administration and issuing licences and faculties along with other administrative matters, but, arguably, more importantly so far as the parishioners were concerned, by enquiring into complaints of immorality and matrimonial affairs. The court's jurisdiction was wide – adjudicating in tithe disputes, wills and marriage contracts; punishing those proved to have committed libel or slander; enquiring into cases of scandalous behaviour, seduction and bastardy. Even failure to attend church could bring a person before the courts. The numerous extant case papers and files of evidence testify to a community racked by niggling, back-stabbing, prying, gossiping and general meddling in other people's business. Whilst some might see the court as meddlesome, others might easily use the law to get one over on a troublesome neighbour or settle an old score. No doubt lies, perjury, prejudice and bribery played their part.

Here is a flavour of the many other cases that are recorded in the Consistory Court Books:[9]

1601(59):   *Edward Boden cites Margaret Anderton for saying he was a whoremaster and no woman would escape his hands for he kept women until they were 'distracted of her wits'.*

1606(56):   *The Office (of the Archdeacon) cites Richard France and Jane Cappel for fornication.*

1607(57):   *The Office cites Richard Fryer for saying that those who receive Communion whilst kneeling are dammned as it ought to be received sitting.*

1608(91):   *Margaret Wilbraham cites Ann Winnington for saying she was Thomas Trevis' whore.*

1608(101):   *John Winnington cites Robert Winnington over the tutorship of Ellen Winnington.*

1609(35):   *John Walker cites Thomas Percival saying that he was lewd in Julius Winnington's wich-house with a cloak to be naughty with Thomas Rogerson's wife.*

1609(34):   *Robert Walton cites John Maisterson for saying he was a drunken knave and a rascal.*

1609(36):   *Peter Tarbock cites Robert Hisham, a churchwarden, for irregularity of the accounts.*

1612(39):   *The churchwardens cite Peter Tarbock, the old warden, for presenting inaccurate accounts.*

1618(15):   *Elizabeth Tarbock cites Margery Wilbraham for saying she was naughty with a father and his two sons.*

1618(16):   *Elizabeth Tarbock cites Ellen and Mary Massey and Ann Shaw for saying she fornicated before marriage.*

1621(68):   *Katherine Broome and Elizabeth Billington cite Alice*

Rogerson for saying they were George Booth's whores.
1622(36): Elizabeth Millington cites Alice Rogerson for defamation.
1622(37): Alice Crewe cites Ann Wilkinson for defamation.
1635(143): Thomas Deane cites Peter Frodsham for saying 'at the Sign of the Swan' that he was the father of Emme Sadler's bastard.

Politics

Charles' reign began well: peace with France and Spain had been secured and finances were improving. The need for money was of course ever present and the King used a number of methods to obtain a satisfactory income. Among these were the 'Forced Loans', which were collected by local justices: anyone who failed to make a loan could be jailed. The returns for Cheshire made under the direction of the Lord Lieutenant, the Earl of Derby, were sent to London in October 1625.[10] The Northwich Hundred provided £263 6s 8d, of which payments of £10 were made by William Oldfield of Leftwich, Robert Holford of Lostock Gralam and John Warburton of Winnington, but there are no references to payments by men from Northwich or Witton. Regular subsidies were collected and in 1626, based on a fifth of income, the following Northwich men paid their dues: Roger Pavor 4s on lands he held worth 20s; John Billington paid 10s 8d on goods worth £4, and Christopher Birchall, John Broome, Thomas Harrison and William Norcott each paid 8s on goods worth £3. Richard Dean is also listed but seems to have been exempt as a cleric.[11] In Witton, Thomas Bromfield paid on lands worth 20s (i.e. 4s) and William Huet and Peter Dewsbury on goods worth £3 (8s).

Another device used by the King was 'Distraint of Knighthood', based on a medieval system of raising money. Those whose annual income from land was £40 or more were required to assume the honour of knighthood and failure to do so rendered an individual liable to a fine. In July 1632 fines were imposed on those who held such landed property and had not taken the order at Charles I's coronation. Whilst there was no one from Northwich or Witton with sufficient wealth to fall into the category, there were a few from the immediate area who paid fines for this 'oversight'. Robert Holford of Lostock and Richard Bentley of Hulse were each fined £10; William Oldfield of Leftwich was fined £14;

and Robert Venables, baron of Kinderton, was fined £60.[12]

Another method which caused serious opposition was the imposition of 'Ship Money' between 1635 and 1641. Some historians suggest that this was a major cause of the Civil War. This medieval tax was originally intended to provide ships for the Navy from contributions paid by the inhabitants of coastal counties when war was threatened. Charles' advisors suggested that on the pretext of combating piracy, which affected all subjects, and on the grounds of national defence, it would be legitimate to tax the whole country. Normally taxation was based on income and an individual assessment, but this tax was based on a required lump sum which was divided into contributions paid by each county and the residents of each city and township and members of the clergy – it affected almost everyone. On 16 October 1637, three days after taking office, Thomas Cholmondeley, sheriff of Cheshire, wrote to all head and petty constables with his instructions regarding the levying of this tax. The constables of Northwich Hundred were required to meet at 'the Signe of the Swan' in Northwich by 9 o'clock on Tuesday 30 October.[13] They were instructed to bring with them anyone who had served as constable under the previous two sheriffs and had knowledge of the assessments then made. Following this meeting Cholmondeley issued the assessments for each of the townships – the town of Northwich was to pay £20 and Witton £4 12s 2d. Having this assessment the constables were then ordered to levy 'upon the ablest men havinge goods moneyes or trade and if there be none such then upon the lands and lyvings wth in yor towne respect beinge had to the poorer sorte'. The collection of the money was a slow process and in December Cholmondeley had to threaten constables of various townships to make payment by 4 January or else face imprisonment. The following year the sheriff, then Phillip Mainwaring, also had problems and was still asking for collections to be made to him at 'the house of John Dutton the Swan in Northwich' by 14 February 1639.[14]

The Civil War

The Civil War must have had significant consequences for the people of Northwich but the details of how they fared are obscure. The apparent reduction in resident population in the parish during the middle decades of the century may relate to these troubled times, if not by reason of people moving away, then because the registers were not kept for three or four years. The registers record that 'throw civil wars, flying of ministers and Clarks, feares distractions and troubles of the tymes were lost and burned by cavaliers and others of this garrison, that their names could not be collected nor found to be inserted and engrossed in this book as formerly'.[15] Whatever the numbers of the local townspeople during these times, they will have been swelled from time to time by a transient population of soldiers, administrators, suppliers, prisoners and many others who followed the armies. Being considered of strategic importance Northwich was garrisoned, first on behalf of the lord of the manor, the Earl of Derby, a staunch Royalist, and then soon after by the Parliament-arians under Sir William Brereton, a Member of Parliament and one of the deputy lieutenants of Cheshire. He fortified the town and used it as a base for his activities in 1643 and 1644: defensive earthworks were established on Winnington Hill overlooking the Town Bridge.[16] A pamphlet published in March 1643 states that 'we (the Parliamentarians) have fortified Northwich with trenches, sconces, etc., for the securities of all those parts which have been so infected by the Commissions of Array, and the Earl of Darbies forces at Warrington, and wee have often sallied out for the clearing of those parts which were most in danger'.[17] In December 1643 Robert Lowe, commander of the Northwich Garrison, was paid for costs incurred by him for carters bringing wood to supply the sentries, and three months later Major Carrington was paid £5 for retaining Lancashire soldiers in the garrison for a further night 'for preservacion thereof from the enemy'.[18] Northwich seems to have been the base for Colonel John Leigh's regiment of foot which was formed of men from the hundreds of Bucklow, Northwich and Eddisbury. Money, horses, cattle and provisions were brought into the garrison to Captains Gerrard and Croxton from many of the surrounding villages and in particular from Over.[19] Another known Parliamentarian officer was Captain Richard Pigott, a Northwich man who was master of the Grammar School between 1625 and 1643. After his military career, in 1646, he became master of Shrewsbury School. In November 1643 he was repaid for his services in 'beinge entrusted for the securinge of that garrison, during the absence of Capt. Leigh and Capt. Gerrard'.[20] Not only was the town a garrison for Parliamentarian troops, but it was also a place of confinement for Royalist prisoners.[21]

The creation of a garrison town was bound to have caused much inconvenience, confiscation of property, lawlessness and general privations with most households providing billets. The garrisoning of nearby Over, for which detailed accounts survive, indicates the extent of the problem.[22] In a three-year period quartering of troops cost the community £268 8s 3d, losses of property amounted to £606 14s 7d and 'loans' to Parliament £360 18s 8d – a grand total of £1,236 1s 6d.

There seems to have been little military action in and around Northwich, though slightly further afield there is at least one known incident. On 18 August 1644, Colonel John Marrow led Royalist cavalry out of Chester to attack the Parliamentarian base at Northwich. At Sandiway the opposing forces met with the result that the Royalists were forced to retreat leaving their commander dead, having been shot by a sniper who was hiding under a hedge.[23] The troops garrisoned at Northwich certainly saw action elsewhere in Cheshire, for it was from the town that Brereton's force moved south to defeat the Royalist commander, Sir Thomas Aston, at the Battle of Middlewich (13 March 1643). Following this incident Brereton was appointed as Parliamentarian Commander of the Cheshire forces. By the end of the year Brereton's army came under pressure from Royalist reinforcements and he was forced to quit both Middlewich and Northwich, allowing the enemy in. At this time only Nantwich remained in Parliamentarian hands and this was subjected to a siege which lasted through December and January, being lifted as a result of the outcome of the battle of Nantwich, fought on 25 January 1644. This temporary down-turn in events for the Royalists at the beginning of 1644 probably saw Northwich change hands again for by the spring it was again garrisoned by Brereton's men. In the early summer months matters improved for the Royalist cause and Prince Rupert made a successful progress through Cheshire and South Lancashire. Parliament, alarmed by the situation in the north-west, sent orders to the midland shires, including Nottingham,

Stafford, Derby and Leicester, to send reinforcements. As a consequence an army of 12,000 men assembled at Knutsford Heath under the command of the Earl of Denbigh. However on receiving news that Prince Rupert was marching north from Shrewsbury towards York and that the King was also moving north from Oxford, the Parliamentary army split into two: Brereton led half towards Yorkshire and the other half, under Denbigh, set off for Oswestry. Before Brereton could reach Yorkshire news was received of Prince Rupert's defeat at Marston Moor (2 July), and he therefore turned to harass the Royalist flight to Chester. The City, ever loyal to the King, received the Prince and his colleagues who stayed for several weeks before fleeing further south.

In May 1644 when Prince Rupert was marching north, he and his forces camped on Rudheath for a few days. This caused some alarm in Northwich and defences along the northern boundary with Witton were established with some haste. These military activities are attested to by the sufferings of Katherine, widow of John Stubbs of Witton, who successfully petitioned the justices sitting at Middlewich in 1650 for compensation.[24] Having already lost her 'deare husband in the service' she claimed 'great losses' in that:

> *'having her habitation wthout the walles of Northwich in the tyme of the Garrison. And being her house Joyn'd unto the outmost guard upon the comeing of Prince Rupert against the towne as the Officers and souldiers within the towne suspected the Offices and gentlemen within the towne caused ffower bayes of her building to be puld downe for feare of giving advantage to ye Enimyes'.*

Fortunately, Mrs. Stubb's petition is endorsed that she be compensated. Her husband was in all probability the John Stubbs who was one of a number of men who took the 'delinquent' Robert Bromfield, 'late of Witton', to Halton Castle.[25] About the time of Prince Rupert's visit Bromfield's activities were causing the Parliamentarian authorities some concern. In May 1644 Bromfield wrote to the Governor of Chester giving details of army movements and the Northwich garrison, particularly as to how and when it might be surprised. He was later arrested and imprisoned at Halton for his contempt of the ordinance prohibiting 'spies and intelligencers'.

From the summer of 1644, Tarvin was Brereton's headquarters and remained so throughout the siege of Chester. He placed forward detachments at Huxley, Tattenhall, Aldford, Barrow and Christleton, and in support had units at Beeston, Oulton, Over and Northwich. With a force based at Farndon he protected the bridge against Royalist Wales. In November 1644, the city of Chester came under siege from his troops and neighbouring counties were urged to send men to support him and swell his insufficient forces. The Royalist commander, Byrom, repeatedly made attacks on these bases with little success. Assistance for Byrom came north from Oxford under Prince Maurice but was stopped in February 1645. Prince Rupert also attempted to put pressure on the Parliamentary forces and managed to relieve and supply Beeston Castle and give some relief to the citizens of Chester before moving south again. Brereton, with reinforcements from Yorkshire, Lancashire and Staffordshire now managed to surround the City. The state of affairs imposed by the leaguer (to use the contemporary term) was to last for a long 15 months. The conditions endured by the residents of the city need not concern us here, other than to say that they suffered great hardship. Times were also hard for the inhabitants of the surrounding villages upon whom the besieging troops imposed themselves. Further out, the villages and townships of Malpas, Tarvin and Christleton suffered the inconvenience of permanent garrisons; but the effects of the tumultuous events of 1644-45 were felt even further afield.

The King and Rupert in May 1645 marched north which prompted Parliament to order Brereton to abandon his siege. However, Royalist indecision led to their defeat at Naseby, and as a consequence Brereton returned to resume his siege of Chester. In September the City was attacked and the walls bombarded. The King himself arrived at Chester in late September as did Parliamentary forces under General Poyntz. On 24 September the armies clashed at Rowton Moor leaving about 1,000 Royalists dead or captured. The following day the King fled from the county. In December 1645, Beeston Castle fell to the Roundheads and then on 3 February 1646 Chester surrendered.

The prosecution of the war required finance. The King could use the great landowners loyal to him to raise funds in those areas under their control. Parliament had no such 'traditional' resources. In 1643 ordinances were passed authorising the confiscation of estates held by those proven to be either Royalist sympathisers or popish recusants. The process, known as sequestration, was administered and carried out by a Parliamentary Committee with sub-committees in the counties. Once a case of delinquency was proved to their satisfaction the commissioners would deprive a Royalist owner of 80% of his estate, allowing the defendant's family a tenth for their maintenance; the final part going to the informant. Those proved to be popish recusants were allowed to keep a third of their estates in accordance with legislation passed in the reign of Queen Elizabeth. Once the estates were confiscated all income – rents and profits – went into the Parliamentarian coffers. Later, the system allowed for the sale of confiscated lands in order to accumulate capital sums of money and this included sale back to the original owner on payment of a 'fine'. Such 'compounding' was based on a sliding scale dependent upon an individual's involvement in the war: a Royalist Member of Parliament could lose half the value of his estate; those who took part in both phases of the Civil War (1643-46 and 1647-51) might lose a third, and those who took part in only one phase, a sixth.

Returns and reports were regularly sent from the local county committees to the Sequestration Committee and the Committee for Compounding that sat in Goldsmith's Hall, London. The Cheshire meetings were often held in Northwich due to its central position and Thomas Robinson seems to have been a prominent member: having been appointed as a Commissioner in May 1650 he seems to have acted as secretary, as much of the correspondence between the county and London was from him.[26] In the summer of 1651 Robinson was paid 10s by the feoffees of the grammar school 'when hee came from London' having delivered a petition to Parliament. On 6 June 1654, Robinson wrote to the Commissioners for Sequestrations in London seeking permission to pay £5 to the steward of Northwich court and costs for dinners for the steward, burgesses and attendants on the occasion of the two annual fairs, charges which had been paid previously 'with care to avoid extravagance'. He also added that at the fair courts more was extracted than the cost of the dinners. A reply dated 9 June allowed payment. It seems that Robinson was particularly active in 1654 and 1655 in examining papists and other delinquents for the purpose of sequestration of their estates. In a letter dated 8 June, Robinson accepted that he should work with a justice of the peace to examine witnesses, remarking that such men were 'far above me' and offered the name of William Leftwich who was 'honest and rational', not so 'high a quality as the justices of the peace' but better than men of inferior quality who 'could not afford the pains and receive only their charges'.[27] His nomination was approved on 8 July. Leftwich had previously served Parliament as a sequestration commissioner prior to 1649. As such, like Robinson after him, he administered the estates of local Royalist landowners and accounted for income from their properties and any necessary expenditure: for example, payments for a new millstone at Witton Mill from Venables' rents; repairs to the Court House, and the purchase of scales for use by the Market-Lookers from the Earl of Derby's income.[28]

Being a prominent Royalist, Derby's Northwich properties were sequestrated and administered on behalf of Parliament by the local commissioners: Bentley, Leftwich and Robinson.[29] His salt rights were sold by them to a Mr Starkey; a shop and house in the Market Place were bought by Joshua Hodgkis of London and the manor of Northwich was purchased by Thomas Boswell on behalf of the Countess of Lincoln and her two sons.[30] The estates of the Venables family of Kinderton in Northwich and Witton were also seized by Parliament. Peter Venables (the Baron of Kinderton), his wife and their son Thomas all travelled to London in April 1646 to learn of their fate. Peter, a one-time member of the Long Parliament, adhered to the King in the initial stages but did not bear arms against Parliament, and Thomas stated that he had given up his arms a year previously. Peter was fined £9,800 based on a third of the value of his estate and his son £2,500 as a sixth part; presumably the Committee were satisfied that Peter had been involved in both phases of the Civil War and that Thomas had only taken part in one phase. Eventually, following appeals, the total fine for both men was reduced to £6,150.[31] Other men with property in Northwich included Peter Leycester of Tabley who was fined £747 10s 0d in January 1647, and Thomas Cholmondeley who was fined £1,200, later reduced to £450.[32] As one might expect, the 'spy' Robert Bromfield also suffered sequestration. In his defence, on 3 February 1649, he stated that although he had initially adhered to the King he did fight for Parliament under the commands of Sir Thomas Middleton and Major General Mytton: he was fined £57 3s 0d. It seems that Bromfield was unable to pay as in August 1651 he was charged £25 for non-payment of the second half of his fine – at this time he was serving under General Whalley. Others who had to compound with Parliament included Robert Holford of Lostock Gralam and Richard Bentley of Hulse, who were both fined £10, and William Oldfield of Leftwich, who was fined £14.[33]

It was not just the landed gentry who stood to suffer such losses. In 1651 the Cheshire Commissioners for Sequestration wrote to London to say that Randle Birkenhead's estate was worth less than £200 with an income of only £3 or £4 a year and that his family lived partly on charity. Accordingly they recommended that he be discharged from sequestration.[34] The reason he had come to notice was the fact that he was bailiff to the Earl of Derby and was with him at the rout in Wigan (August 1650). It seems that at one time Randle was of sufficient means to raise his own small company of foot to serve the Royalist cause. He fought at Edgehill (October 1642) and continued in the King's service throughout the war 'suffering imprisonment, plunder and sequestration'.[35] At the battle of Worcester (August 1650) he received wounds which were to be the death of him. Randle's brother Isaac also served the Earl and was captured in 1651 but decided to confess what he knew of his master's activities and later gave evidence against him. Isaac then worked for the Parliamentarian party and became adjutant-general to Colonel Robert Venables on his expedition to the West Indies. He died on the return voyage in 1655.[36]

Following the King's execution on 30 January 1649, the monarchy and the House of Lords were officially abolished and England was declared a Commonwealth. During the Interregnum there is little to say of Northwich and the surrounding area save for the fact that Charles II's army, under the Duke of Buckingham, stayed in the town in August 1651 on its way south to the battle of Worcester (September 1651).[37] There are suggestions that King Charles stayed in the town. Eight years later, Northwich was again garrisoned by Royalists at the time of the

Booth Rebellion. The Presbyterian Parliamentarian, Sir George Booth, led a Cheshire rising of a coalition of Royalists and disillusioned Parliamentarians as part of a national plan of action organised by the Sealed Knot. Parliament got wind of the rising, arrested many of its ringleaders and notified local military authorities of what was afoot. Consequently the Sealed Knot abandoned the enterprise but was not quick enough to warn Booth and his colleagues who represented some ardent Royalists – Cholmondeley, Massey, Grosvenor and Stanley. From his base near Chester, Booth moved across the county with a force of nearly 5,000 men, forcing Colonel Lambert, marching towards Chester from Nantwich, to alter his route to intercept Booth. On the night of 18 August, Booth's army garrisoned Northwich whilst Lambert lay at Weaverham. The following morning Booth sallied out to face Lambert at Hartford, but after a brief skirmish moved north to a more favourable position on the other side of the Weaver at Winnington. Despite a position on high ground overlooking the narrow Winnington Bridge, Booth was unable to hold off Lambert's assault and his forces were routed – his cavalry being pursued in all directions by Lambert's experienced horsemen of the New Model Army. Eventually Booth and the other leaders were arrested and sent to the Tower of London, but charges were never brought against them and they were eventually released. Following the battle of Winnington Bridge, Lambert occupied Northwich for Parliament.

---

[1] C. Hill, *Society & Puritanism in Pre-Revolutionary England*, 1964, p. 113.
[2] Cox, p. 74.
[3] Cox, p. 75.
[4] CRO; EDC 1638/49.
[5] J. Hall, (ed.) *The Civil War in Cheshire*, LCRS, vol 19 (1889), p. 8.
[6] CRO: DSS/1/4/22.
[7] CRO/1/4/22/6.
[8] CRO: CR 63/2/7/1.
[9] CRO: EDC 5. The numbers in brackets refer to the file for that particular

year.

[10] CRO: CR63/2/6.
[11] CRO: CR63/2/5/1.
[12] CRO: D4923/1, fo. 32.
[13] CRO: DSS/1/4/21/1.
[14] CRO: DSS/1/4/21/6.
[15] Witton Parish Registers, f. 105v.
[16] The defences on Winnington Hill are described in Ormerod, vol iii, p. 162.
[17] Cox, p. 87.
[18] Cox, p. 94, citing Harleian 1999.
[19] Harleian Mss 2126.
[20] Cox, pp. 53, 56, 57, 74-76.
[21] Hall, p. 38-9.
[22] Harleian MSS. 2126, ff. 3-39. See also Bostock A.J., '17th Century Over', *The Winsford Record*, 1998.
[23] R.N. Dore (ed.), *The Letter Books of Sir William Brereton*, volume I, R.S.L.C. (1984), p. 284.
[24] *Cheshire Quarter Sessions Records, 1559–1760*, Lancashire & Cheshire Record Society, 94, p. 141.
[25] Cox, p. 88, citing Harl. 1999, f. 329.
[26] *CCC, 1643-60*, part I, p. 212, etc.
[27] *CCC, 1643-60*, part I, p. 685.
[28] Cox, p. 94.
[29] *CCC, 1643-60*, part I, p. 685.
[30] *CCC, 1643-60*, part II, pp. 1116, 1118.
[31] *CCC, 1643-60*, Pt II, p. 1183.
[32] *CCC, 1643-60*, Pt II, pp. 1232, 1286.
[33] CRO: D4923/1, f. 32.
[34] *CCAM, 1642-56*, Pt 1, 103.
[35] Cal. Sate Papers (Domestic) 1672-3, p. 104; P.W. Thomas, *Sir John Berkenhead, 1617–1679*, p. 4.
[36] *CCC, 1643-60*, Pt I, 685; P.W. Thomas, pp. 10-12.
[37] CCAM, 1642–56, Pt III, p. 1444.

8

CONTINUITY AND CHANGE: THE DAWN OF A NEW ERA

THE foregoing chapters have taken a snapshot of life in Northwich during the 17th century and have suggested that there was much in common with the centuries that went before: for the town and its people, centuries of continuity. Despite many changes to the town and the way of life experienced by its people there was much that remained the same until almost the present day.

There can be little doubt as to the importance of Northwich in 17th century Cheshire: the contemporary writers were quite clear on that and not only due to the existence of the brine pit, but also to its central location and as a venue for economic, commercial and judicial affairs. These characteristics had existed since at least the time of the Domesday Survey when, along with the city of Chester and the other two wiches, the town merited a special description of its laws and customs. The town's importance continued by being one of a number of centres at which courts of Quarter Sessions were held, now succeeded by the County and Magistrates courts which are held regularly in the town; as an administrative centre for the hundred of Northwich and later the Northwich Rural and Urban District Councils; as a focus for the chemical industries in central Cheshire; and, lastly, as a commercial and trading centre, its position and convenient transport facilities making it an ideal place – factors which William Webb commented upon almost 400 years ago.

Continuity as a town is reflected in the townscape, for even today its layout and building plots portray a ghost of the ancient town. As late as the 1780s it was said that the building plots were principally salt-houses, but not used as such for about a century, and during the late 19th century it was said that the town contained many ancient buildings, all of which are now long since gone due to the subsidence caused by salt mining and the constant extraction of brine. The streets of 19th century Northwich were described as being particularly narrow and inconvenient. Apple Market Street, originally intended just for the sale of fruit and vegetables but later a variety of goods, was only 12 feet wide, just as it is today and much as it would have been throughout the 17th century and even earlier. The streets were regularly visited by those selling agricultural produce, fruit, vegetables and livestock, and by pedlars selling their wares – shoes, woollens, linen and hardware. On market days, Apple Market Street, Swine Market Street and Cross Street were virtually impassable as a result of congestion due to baskets of wares being laid out along the sides of streets, covered stalls being erected blocking out the light from the windows of adjacent properties and carts being parked outside premises so that the occupants were interrupted in their free passage to and from their homes and places of business. In order to relieve congestion in the late 18th century the lord of the manor provided a butchers' shambles along what is now High Street, that then being the widest thoroughfare. By 1817 this was insufficient for half the butchers who had meat to sell, so a new shambles was set up in Swine Market Street, the predecessor of today's market place.

Continuity exists too amongst the modern townspeople. Life for its residents will have continued in much the same way as it always had. Population levels in Northwich diminished in the late 18th century due to the erection of a number of warehouses along the River Weaver, whereas that of Witton increased and continued to increase beyond the figures for Northwich. Though the 19th and 20th centuries witnessed a large influx of people in search of job opportunities that were provided by the chemical industries, the old Northwich families survived and continued to live and work in the same or neighbouring townships. Just as the 17th century residents, like their predecessors before them, busied themselves in producing salt, so did those who followed them. Many had other interests too – in the trades and businesses which were typical of any small town which serviced the needs of the surrounding rural economy: butchery and its associated skills of leather craft; cloth working; metal working; building and carpentry; whilst the food and drinks trade serviced the needs of visitors, businessmen and traders from near and far. These commercial activities which exist today clearly had ancient roots.

The town was a mix of large village, with its typical rural characteristics, and a small urban and industrial centre, but it is perhaps true to say that it had much more in common with rural manors than any borough. Northwich people not only had family links with the surrounding countryside, but also had smallholdings in the neighbouring townships for their subsistence as well as to produce goods for market. Whilst the town's prosperity certainly depended upon salt, it also depended upon the countryside.

There was much continuity then, but there were changes too, which was hardly surprising for the century was one of great change in England – social, economic, political and religious – and these matters naturally affected the people of Northwich. The late 17th century was the dawn of Northwich's economic expansion that was to take place throughout the next century.

There were changes to the overall administration of the town. In 1784 the Earl of Derby sold the manor to James Mort of Witton House. Living locally this new lord of the manor took a more active interest in the affairs of the town and was instrumental in improving the market conditions. James handed the lordship over to his son, Jonadab who died in 1799 and was succeeded by his sister Anne, who then sold the manor to the Heywood family. For much of the 19th century the lord of the manor was James Pemberton Heywood, a barrister, of Wakefield. In 1871 he sold his interests to the Northwich Local Board, the forerunner of the Northwich Urban District Council and predecessor of today's Winsford Town Council and Vale Royal Borough Council. The ancient courts and the town's jury of burgesses continued until replaced by the functions of the Urban District Council and the Magistrates courts.

CONTINUITY AND CHANGE

Changes in the salt industry were the most profound. Whilst the town lost its salt-making to neighbouring townships, it enjoyed something of a Renaissance during the 18th century with improvements made to the river which, though intended as an aid for salt manufacturers, also became an asset to the town in bringing new prosperity to its traders and businessmen. The Weaver Navigation Act, 1721, allowed for the passage of shipping along the river between Winsford and Frodsham, and for a short stretch of the Witton Brook. The scheme was first mooted in the 1660s to relieve the burden of traffic on the road to Frodsham. Initially there were spells of activity in improving the river and then in 1710 a bill to make the river navigable was introduced by a Liverpool Member of Parliament. This was opposed by Cheshire land-owning society on the grounds that its proposer was not a Cheshire man and was only serving his own interests of shipping rock salt to Ireland and Denmark. Opposition came from the local tenantry who made money from carting coal and rock salt and from the brine pit owners on the grounds that the scheme favoured the rock salt industry. As a consequence of this opposition the bill did not become law until 1721. The Weaver Navigation did not operate fully until 1733, but by the middle of the century it showed substantial profit. Shipments of rock salt quadrupled from 13,000 tons to 54,000 tons between 1747 and 1777; the produce of a dozen rock salt workings in Witton, Marston and Wincham. Shipments of white salt from the brine pits doubled during the same period from 16,000 to 31,000 tons, but increased dramatically by the end of the century to 100,000 tons. The salt industry had now passed from its ancient 'domestic' stage to become a full-scale industrial operation – from part-time working to full-time industry. Whilst salt was no longer being produced within the town it became the recognised focus of activities that were carried out in the surrounding townships: the heart of Cheshire's salt industry. The town had emerged from the medieval world and had come to terms with the new industrial and commercial practices.

Besides coal and salt, the Weaver Navigation also provided a means for the transport of Cheshire cheese, corn, stone, timber and cotton. The local markets also benefited and the annual fairs were extended to last two weeks. Goods from Manchester and Yorkshire, Irish linen, Sheffield and Birmingham wares were all available at the Friday market. Pressure on the town's facilities was so intense that a suggestion was made to hold the markets in a neighbouring township: in fact the annual fairs were held on the other side of the river in Leftwich. By the end of the 18th century there were several merchants and tradesmen of independent fortunes living in close proximity to the town. Tunnicliffe's Topographical Survey of Cheshire lists seven principal merchants and salt proprietors in the town. Increased prosperity was not realised by all. In 1713 Ralph Broom fled following bankruptcy when his salt pit failed, and Ralph and Thomas Nickson emigrated to America when their businesses failed.

So much for Northwich, but what of the other two wiches? They fared somewhat differently. In fact salt production declined during the 18th century leaving Northwich to assume its dominant position. Middlewich hoped to gain from improvements to the River Dane between Northwich and its confluence with the Wheelock Brook but these never occurred and caused particular difficulties with the production of salt and its transportation to the Weaver through Winsford. It was at Winsford in the late 18th century that salt production started, first by means of sinking brine pits and then by mining rock salt. Production of both was in such quantities that numerous salt works were established along the banks of the Weaver, which eventually eclipsed Northwich's production levels. An extension of the Weaver Navigation between Winsford and Nantwich was planned to assist the latter town's salt businesses. Though enacted in 1734, it never materialised and this, added to the restrictive practices in salt production which continued in the town, led to the demise of the industry there. The problems experienced by Middlewich and Nantwich certainly facilitated Northwich's dominant position.

Northwich's reputation as an industrial and commercial centre attracted new people to the town resulting in a considerable increase in population. At the end of the 17th century there had been about 600 residents in Northwich. Fifty years later this figure had increased by a further 50% but by 1778 had more than doubled to around 1,300. At the turn of the next century the population increase had slowed somewhat with 1,338 people living in the town. Consistently Northwich's population had represented about a third of the whole parish of Witton, but as the nineteenth century progressed Witton itself became the dominant residential area. In 1801 there were 1,531 people in Witton, ten years later this had risen to 1,966 at a time when there were only 1,382 people in Northwich. In 1821 the figures for the two townships were 2,405 and 1,490 respectively.

Today Northwich is an attractive, busy and prosperous market town. It has a long and fascinating history and the black and white buildings, which are a feature of its centre, give the streets a far older appearance than is the case. Over the centuries the town and its people have witnessed many changes – and will no doubt continue to do so. And whilst there is something of a continuity in the townscape today this may shortly become less so with the plans to redevelop the town centre following a major land stabilization programme.

APPENDIX ONE
16TH CENTURY RESIDENTS OF NORTHWICH AND WITTON
1. Muster Roll 1548

Northwich
Billmen with harness
Robert Holford	J, S, B, Sp.
Humphrey Holford	J, S, B, Sp
Robert Winnington	J, S, B, Sp
William Pickmere	J, S, B, Sp

Able men without harness
Edward Golbourne
Peter Pavor
Richard Walton
Phillip Antrobus
John
Thomas Winnington, sen[r].
John Ywers
John Tarbock
William Percival
Hugh Minshull
George Wood
Thomas Wood
Robert Pickmere
Humphrey Yate
Henry Bostock
Thomas Winnington, jun[r].
George Holford
John Miles
Hugh Rowe
Geoffrey Gardener
Richard Norcott
William Bailey

Men unable to serve
George Pickering	J, Sp
John Venables	J, S, P
Robert Massey	J, S, B, Sp

Witton
Archers
John Baxter
Randolph Shack[erley]
William Stubbs
Robert Shack[erley]

Billmen with harness
William Somerford	J, S, B, Sp.
Nicholas Warburton	J, S, B, Sp.
Richard Venables	J, S, Sp.
Lawrence Bailey	J, S, P
George Sudlow	J, S, B
Hugh Rowe	J, S, P, Sp.
Richard Bromfield	J, S, P, Sp.
William Calley	J, S, Sp.
George Tarbock	J, S, B, Sp.
William Sudlow	J, S, B, Sp.
Robert	J, S, B, Sp.
Randle Tarbock	J, S, B, Sp.
Thomas	J, S, P
Peter Venables	J, S, P, Sp.
Mathew Stubbs	J, S, B, Sp.

Able men without harness
Edmond
William Minshull
Thomas Birchwood
Henry Venables
Humphrey Bromfield
Robert Birchwood
John Venables
James Johnson
George Bass

Men unable to serve
Thomas Bromfield	J, S, P, Sp.
Randle Bote	J, S
Roger Mottershead	J, S, P, Sp.
John Benett	J, Sp.

'Harness' refers to arms and armour. The following abbreviations are used: J = Jack (a padded jerkin); S = Sallet (a steel helmet); P = poleaxe (a long-handled military axe); B = Bill (a long-handled axe with two sharp points); Sp = splints (armour for the elbows)

16TH CENTURY RESIDENTS

2. Subsidy Roll, 1593

Name	Land or Goods	Taxable Value	Tax due
Northwich			
Hugh Winnington, gent.	land	20s	4s
Ralph Yate	land	20s	4s
Richard Bromfield	land	20s	4s
Richard Holford's heirs	land	20s	4s
Thomas Norcroft	land	20s	4s
Phillip Downes	goods	£5	13s 4d
William Golbourne	goods	£3	10s 8d
Edward Wood	goods	£3	8s
Ralph Nickson	goods	£3	8s
Witton			
Robert Bromfield	land	30s	6s
Richard Wood	goods	£3	8s
Richard Hewitt	goods	£3	8s

APPENDIX TWO
ELIZABETHAN SALT OWNERS & OCCUPIERS

The following is taken from CRO: D4368/2. The text has been modernised. In each case the occupier for the year 1565 is followed by a list of the owners from whom he or she leased their leads.

Edward Golborne 22 leads:
8 leads of Dutton lands
4 leads of Mr Wilbraham's of Woodhey
4 leads of Mr Sutton of Sutton
4 leads of Mr Ireland's
2 leads of Peter Paver's lands

William Pickmere 8 leads:
4 leads of Mr Sutton's lands
4 leads of Mr Leftwich's lands

Raffe Vernon 6 leads:
4 leads of Mr Wilbraham's lands
2 leads of Sr. John Warburton's lands

Richard Wilbraham 4:
4 leads of Mr Raffe Done's lands

Robert Massey 4:
4 leads of Sr. John Warburton's lands

Edward Sudlowe 4:
4 leads of Sr. John Deane's lands

John Masterton 10:
4 leads of Lord Derby's lands
6 leads of Mr Starkeys of Darley

Robert Henshawe 4:
4 leads of Mr Dutton of Dutton's lands

Randle Shaw 10:
4 leads of Mr Holford's lands
2 leads of Mr Hase's lands of Littley
2 leads of Sr. John Deane's land
2 leads of Mr Starkey's lands of Darley

George Bromfield 6:
6 leads of Adlington's land

Robt. Harrison 4:
4 leads of Sr. John Warburton's land

John Huet 6 & 3rd part:
3 leads & the 3rd part of Dutton's lands
1 leade of Arley lands
2 leads of Kinderton lands

Sibill Winnington 6:
2 leads of Mr Paver's lands
2 leads of Mr Horton's lands
2 leads of Mr Curie's lands

Thomas Winnington 12:
3 leads of Mr Paver's lands
2 leads of Mr Leftwich's lands
2 leads of Sr. John Warburton's land
2 leads of Mr Winnington's land of Hermitage
2 leads of Mr Robert Pickmere's of Leftwich
1 lead of Mr Horton's land

William Sudlow 6:
4 leads of Sr. John Deane's lands
2 leads of John Horton's land

George Sudlowe 2:
2 leads of John Horton's land

Thomas Newhall 4:
4 leads of Mr Starkey's land of Darley

Raffe Pownall 4:
2 leads of Sr. Thomas Venables land
2 leads of Sr. John Deane's land

ELIZABETHAN SALT OWNERS & OCCUPIERS

John Tarbock 6:
6 leads of the Queen

Mr William Marbury 12:
12 leads of his own land

James Ward 4:
4 leads of Lord of Derby's land

John Paver 6:
4 leads of Mr Legh of Adlington
2 leads of Mr Heyes of Littley lands

Nicholas Warton 6:
6 leads of Mr Starkey's land of Darley

Raffe Bradford 4:
4 leads of Hugh Mere's land of Rostherne

Christopher Birchall 4:
4 leads of Mr Winnington's land of Birches

Philip Downs 7:
6 leads of Dutton's land
1 lead of Mr Sutton's land

John Warburton 6:
6 leads of Sr. William Brereton of Brereton's land

William Roe 6:
4 leads of Sr. John Holcroft's land
2 leads of Mr Sutton's land

John Mainwaring 4:
4 leads of Sr. Raffe Leycester's land

Laurence Winnington 6:
6 leads of his own lands

William Cowley 6:
6 leads of Mr Egerton's land of Ridley

Laurence Bromfield 6:
4 leads of Sr. Thomas Venables' land
2 leads of William Worrall's land late of the Vale Royal

John Walley 6:
4 leads of Robert Bromfield's land
2 leads of Humphrey Walley's land

John Bould 4:
4 leads of Mr Holford's lands of Holford

Humphrey Yate 28:
10 leads of Sutton lands
6 leads of his own lands
3 leads of Mr Paver's land
3 leads of Sr. John Warburton's lands
2 leads of Mr Starkey's land of Stretton
4 leads of Sr. John Warburton's lands

John Nickall 4:
4 leads of Lord Derby's land

Richard Walton 8:
4 leads of Sr. Arthur Mainwaring's land
4 leads of John Fovell's land

Robert Shaw 4:
4 leads of Mr Leftwich's land

William Worrall 24:
4 leads of Mr Venables' land of Antrobus
4 leads of the Hermitage land
6 leads of Sr. John Warburton's land
2 leads of his own lands
2 leads of Dutton lands
2 leads of Kinderton land
2 leads of Raffe Bromfield
2 leads of James Paver

George Johnson 4:
4 leads of his father's land

OWNERS, OCCUPIERS AND OTHERS

Hugh Lowe [20]
4 leads of the Queen's land
4 leads of Raffe Bostock of Moulton
2 leads of Richard Littler's land
2 leads of Kinderton land
2 leads of Mr Winnington's land of Hermitage
2 leads of Kinderton land
2 leads of Sutton land
2 leads of Mr Holfords land

Robert Winnington 26:
16 leads of Sutton land
4 leads of Hermitage land
4 leads of his own land
2 leads of Sutton land by Humphrey Walley
(Here there is a note *"Querey whether the particulars be not mistaken in the original"*)

Roger Tarbock 18:
4 leads of Mr Thomas Grimsdich's land
4 leads of Mr Legh's land
4 leads of Lord Derby's land
(Here there is a note *"Querey whether this is not wrongly inserted. W.H."*)
2 leads of Lord Derby's land
2 leads of Mr Paver's land
2 leads of Mr Sutton's land
2 lead of Mr Starkey's land of Darley

Robert Jefferson 6:
4 leads of Mr Starky's land of Stretton
2 leads of Robert Bromfield's land

Alexander Taylor 8:
4 leads of Sr. Rafe Leycester's land
2 leads of Mr Paver's land
2 leads of Mr Leftwich's land

William Venables 4:
4 leads of Sr. John Warburton's land

Raffe Bromfield 6:
6 leads of his own lands

Robert Bromfield 12:
4 leads of Kinderton land
4 leads of Leftwich land
2 leads of Robert Pickmere's land of Bostock
2 leads of Adlington land

John French 4:
4 leads of Hugh Crosby's land

John Forest 6:
4 leads of Leftwich land
2 leads of Mr Breretons land of Tatton

Thomas Trewe 4:
4 leads of Mr Fox's land

Thoms Venables, gent. 4:
4 leads of his own land

Thomas Bromfield 6:
2 leads of Mr Brereton's land of Tatton
2 leads of Leftwich land by Mr Leigh of Ridge
2 leads of Robert Bromfield's lands

Oliver Fox 4:
2 leads of Mr Starky's land of Stretton
1 lead of Leftwich land
1 lead of Mr Richard Sutton's land

William Clotton 2:
2 leads of his own land

George Holford 2:
2 leads of Mr Sutton's land

Peter Venables 2
2 leads of his own land

Jone Rendye 2:
2 leads of Winnington's land of Hermitage

ELIZABETHAN SALT OWNERS & OCCUPIERS

William Tewe 2:
2 leads of Mr William Holford's lands

Peter Pavor 2:
2 leads of his own land

Peter Winnington, senior 1:
1 lead of Mr James Paver's land.

Thomas Worral of Witton Heath 3:
2 lead of Sr. Thomas Venables' land
1 lead of Leftwich land.

John Winnington of Pickmere:
2 lead of Mr Leftwich's land

Robert Hickcock 1:
1 lead of Mr Huxley's land

Richard Winnington: 1
1 lead of Mr James Paver's land

Thomas Bostock:
3rd part of 2 leads of Mr Dutton's land

George Winnington:
1 lead of Mr Roger Horton's land

Peter Winnington, junior:
1 lead of Mr William Marbury's land

The School land is 2 parts of 4 leads.

James Winnington:
2 leads of Mr Laurence Winnington of the Hermitage

William held 1 & 3rd part:
1 lead & the 3rd part of one lead of Mr James Paver's land.

Humphrey Holford 8:
4 leads of Lord Derby's land
4 leads of Mr James Pavor's land

Total: Five score & thirteen salthouses & one lead.

Lead lookers this present year 1565:
Laurence Bromfield, the foreign lead looker.
Richard Walton. Richard Winnington.

APPENDIX THREE
References to the Northwich Town Plan
(Harleian MSS 2073, f.114/115)
Entries shown in bold refer to particular town buildings.
The map is shown as *Figure Three*

1. Cholmondeley, late Holford
2. Cholmondeley, late John Dutton
3. Hase of Little Legh
4. Holford's land
5. **The Brine Pit**
6. Arley's land
7. Sir Peter Warburton
8. Armitage's land
9. Leicester of Tabley
10. Armitage
11. Lord Gerrard
12. Lord Gerrard
13. Harcourt and Litler
14. Earl of Derby
15. Earl of Bridgewater
16. John Deane
17. Widow Deane
18. Sir Peter Warburton
19. Peter Warburton of Arley, Esq.
20. Wilbram of Witton, late Done's
21. Sir Richard Wilbraham
22. Sir Richard Wilbraham
23. **The Horsemill**. Huxley has 1 lead.
24. Mr Duncombe and Stepney,
25. Paver's heirs
26. Thomas Bromfield of Witton
27. Mr Duncombe and Stepney
28. Roger Paver
29. Thomas Marbury, Esq.
30. Sir Peter Warburton, Justice

78. Crosby
79. Leftwich, late Mainwaring
80. Land of Leftwich
81. Walton's
82. Henry Mainwaring, Esq.
83. Peter Venables, Esq.
84. Sir Ralph Egerton
85. Ralph Leicester of Toft, Esq.
86. Lady Mary Cholmondley
87. Thomas Marbury of Marbury, Esq.
88. Sir William Brereton
89. Lord Gerrard, late Dutton's
90. Arley's land
91. Julius Winnington
92. Richard Sutton's heirs
93. Sir Gilbert Ireland
94. Mere of Rostherne
95. Leicester of Tabley
96. Thomas Marbury of Marbury, Esq.
97. Earl of Derby
98. **The Shops**
99. Raphe Bostock of Moulton
100. Margaret Shakerley
101. William, Earl of Derby
102. Robert Venables
103. Hugh Winnington, Esq.
104. Margaret Shakerley
105. Horton of Coole
106. Leftwich of Leftwich
107. Sutton's heirs

REFERENCES TO THE NORTHWICH TOWN PLAN

31. Earl of Derby
32. Leicester of Tabley
33. Thomas Marbury, Esq.
34. King James
35. Leftwich of Leftwich
36. Peter Venables, baron of Kinderton
37. Harcourt of Winnington
38. Cholmondeley, late Dutton
39. King James
40. Leftwich of Leftwich
41. Leicester of Tabley
42.   "   "
43. Thomas Sudlow of Witton
44. Leicester of ....
45. Duncombe and Stepney
46.   "   "
47. Sutton's heirs
48.   "   "
49. Mere
50. Sutton's heirs
51. Sutton's heirs
52. Bostock
53. Thomas Bromfield
54. ....
55. Peter Venables, esq.
56. Pickmere
57. Sutton's heirs
58. **The Court House,** Leicester of Toft
59. Richard Jackson
60. Leicester of Toft
61. The House of Correction
62. Thomas Leftwich
63. Land of Thomas Leftwich
64. **The Swan**
65. Land of Duncombe and Stepney
66. William Robinson
67. Willington

108. Richard Newhall
109. Sutton's heirs
110. Starkey of Stretton
111. Arley lands – Joan Paver
112. Sutton's heirs
113. Arley – Rogerson
114. **The Leadsmithy**
115. Leftwich
116. Sutton's heirs, alias Salmon
117. George Bradford
118. Sir Peter Warburton
119. Horton of Aldersey
120. George Bradford's land
121. Peter Warburton, Esq.
122. Peter Leicester of Toft, Esq.
123. Peter Warburton, Esq.'s land
124. School land, & Paver's heirs
125. Thomas Starkey of Stretton
126. Hugh Winnington, esq.
127. Leftwich of Leftwich
128. **The Backhouse,** Earl of Derby
129. Grimsditch of Appleton
130. Toft & Ainsworth
131. Sutton's heirs
132.   "   "
133. Leicester of Tabley's land – Broome
134. Bromfield & Ridgeway
135. Pickmere – Derby
136. Roger Paver's land
137. Toft & Ainsworth
138. Armitage
139. ....
140. Thomas Marbury, esq.
141. Robert Venables, gent.
142. Hugh Winnington, esq.
143.   "   "
144. Maras, Foxley

195

OWNERS, OCCUPIERS AND OTHERS

68. Land of Peter Venables, baron Kinderton
69. Leicester of Tabley
70. Grant, anciently late Wrench
71. Earl of Derby Peter Venables
72. George Marbury
73. Broome
74. John Johnson
75. Thomas Marbury, Esq.
76. Arley
77. "

145. Sutton's heirs
146. "   "
147. Crosby
148. Peter Venables
149. Robert Mainwaring of Marton, 1619
150. William Leftwich's land
151. Sutton's heirs
152. Church land
153. Edward Mainwaring

APPENDIX FOUR

POLL TAX RETURNS, 1660

Taken from Lawton, G.O. (ed.), 'Northwich Hundred: Poll Tax 1660 and Hearth Tax 1664' LCRS (1979), vol cxix. Names and occupations have been modernised and the tax paid has been omitted.

NORTHWICH

Willam Bentley, gent, £10 pa
Peter Venables, lab.
John Mosse, lab.
Jane Parker, sp.
Susanna Woodworth, sp.

William Leftwich, gent. £5 pa
George Leftwich, sgl.
Cutbeard Smith, lab.
Ann Crimes, sp.

Margaret Maddocke, sp.

John Norcott, sherman, married
Samuell Norcott, sherman
John Vernon, sherman
Marie Norcott, sp.

Thomas Norcott & Marie his wife
William Fairebrother, lab.
James Gefferey, lab.
Elizabeth Worrall, sp.
Elizabeth Johnson, sp.

George Barker, barber, & Katherine his w.
Elizabeth Barker, sp.

George Dewsbury, draper, £5 pa
Issabell Heath, sp.

Raph Cheney, blacksmith, & Christian his w.
Raph Nixon, blacksmith
Ann Whaley, sp.

Ellin Finney, sp.
Thomas Simnor, lab., & Jone his w.
Katherine Stones, sp.

John Newall, tailor, & Margaret his w.
William Newall, tailor

Roger Cooke, husb., & Isabell his w.
Ralph Cooke, lab.
Margaret Cooke, sp.

John Cooper, shoemaker, & Marie his w.
Raph Kilshaw, shoemaker
Henrie Frodsham, shoemaker
Marie Chow, sp.

Edward Gefferey, butcher, & Elizabeth his w.
Edward Gefferey, jn., butcher
Richard Gefferey, shoemaker
Katherine Rogerson, sp.

James Gerrard, tinker, & Thomasen his w.

Samuel Gefferey, butcher, & Ellin his w.
John Gefferey, butcher
Marie Baguley, wid.
Elizabeth Hornby, sp.

Ottiwell Rogerson, lab., & Margerie his w.

Elizabeth Rogerson, sp.
Richard Rogerson, lab., & Elizabeth his w.

Mathew Helsby, butcher, & Elizabeth his w.

Thomas Harrison, husb., & Katherine his w.

OWNERS, OCCUPIERS AND OTHERS

Ann Mathewes, sp.

John Perrian, lab., & Ellin his w.

Franncis Trevis, barrow maker & Elizabeth his w.
Thomas Hilton, barrow maker

Roger Phithean, shoemaker & Ellin his w.

William Tanner, feltmaker, & Margaret his w.
Phillip Low, feltmaker

Raph Nixon, butcher, £5 pa
Robert Nixon, butcher, & Elizabeth his w.
Katherine Davies sp.

William Birkenhead, saddler, & Ellin his w.
Marie Birkenhead, sp.

Ann Toverton, wid.
Ann Page, sp.

Alice Lowton, wid.
Elizabeth Lowton, sp.

John Broome, innkeeper, £5 pa
Richard Simnor, lab.
Richard Swarprick, lab.
Marie Arrow, sp.
Elizabeth Shaw, sp.
Alice Dewsbury, sp.
Marie Bradshaw, sp.
William Sidon lab., & Alice his w.

Hamnet Bowden, lab., & Katherine his w.
John Oulton, carpenter

Daniell Radford, grocer
Marie Radford, sp.

Ellinor Exeter, wid.
Susanna Exeter, sp.
John Horten, shoemaker, & Elizabeth his w.

Thomas Horten, tailor
Alice Horten, sp.
Margaret Horten, sp.

Thomas Alexander, tailor, & Alice his w.

Peter Paver, husb., & Elizabeth his w.
Margaret Bossen
Richard Dod, lab., & Ann his w.

William Haughton, lab. & Margerie his w.

George Dobson, lab. & Margerie his w.
Marie Dobson, sp.

William Gefferey, butcher, & Elizabeth his w.

Mathew Moores, tailor, & Ann his w.

Samuell Broome, butcher, & Cicelie his w.

James Moores, lab., & Katherine his w.
Ann Moores, sp.

Ann Ditchfeild, sp.

Phillip Basnet, lab.

William Swynton, grocer
Ann Swynton sp.

Joseph Leath, cooper, & Jane his w.

Thomas Trevis, lab., & Jone his w.

Randle Lamb lab., & Elizabeth his w.

John Ratcliffe lab., & Ellin his w.

Thomas Sidon lab., & Alice his w.
Susanna Sidon married
Katherine Sefton, sp.

Elizabeth Royle, wid.

POLL TAX RETURNS 1660

Ellin Royle sp.

John Wrench, grocer, & Maude his w.
Sarah Raneker, sp.

Robert Barlow, innkeeper, & Elizabeth his w.
John Barlow, blacksmith
Ann Broome, sp.
Marie Weedoe, sp.

Henrie Smith, innkeeper, & Elizabeth his w.
Margaret Weedoe, marryed her husband living in another town

Thomas Robinson & Margaret his w.
Margaret Robinson, sp.

Raph Leftwich, gent., £5 pa
William Robinson, tailor
Marie Dod, sp.

Gefferey Haughton, lab., & Margery his w.
Elizabeth Haughton, sp.
Thomas Haughton, lab. & Ann his w.

Richard Rice, lab. & Ellin his w.

Richard Church, lab. & Alice his w.

John Jackson, glover, & Marie his w.

William Parcivall, butcher, & Ellin his w.

Elizabeth Herbert, wid.
Marie Leftwich, sp.

Raph Dobson, lab., & Katherine his w.

James Gefferey, butcher, & Marie his w.
Margaret Gefferey, sp.
Jone Birchall, wid.

Lawrence Birchall, lab., & Elizabeth his w.
Ann Robinson, sp.

Thomas Weedoe, lab. & Jone his w.

Thomas Malbone, lab., & Alice his w.

Peter Emsworth, lab.,& Ellin his w.
Randle Fox, lab.

Richard Heesome, lab & Emm his w.

George Stubbs, lab. & Ann his w.

John Gefferey, butcher, & Elizabeth his w.

Raph Weedall, lab. & Ellin his w.
Raph Weedall, barrow maker

Robert Ditchfeild, barrow maker, & Ann his w.
Robert Ditchfeild, barrow maker

Thomas Lamb, lab., & Margerie his w.

Peter Tarbock, gent. £10 pa

Edward Mariott, gent. £5 pa

Richard Bradford, yeo. £5 pa

John Partington, draper £10 pa

Richard Partington, draper £5 pa

Robert Warburton, gent. £7 10 0 pa

William Harcourt, gent. £5 pa

William Row, yeo. £5 pa

Mrs Ann Moseley £5 pa

Joshua Hodgkis £5 pa

Peter Venables £5 pa

OWNERS, OCCUPIERS AND OTHERS

WITTON

Susanna Bromfield, wid., £30 pa
Susanna Bromfield, sp.

Richard Hilton, husb. £10 pa.

Mr Raph Horton, £7 10 0 pa.

George Deakin, wheelwright

Richard Rogerson, lab.

Thomas Alexander, tailor, & Jone his w.

Thomas Alexander, carpenter, & Elizabeth his w.

Peter Weedall, carrier, & Marie his w.
Edmund Knight, lab.

John Stubbs, miller, & Ann his w.
Katherine Stubbs, sp.

George Ellams, glazier, & Rebecca his w.
Thomas Swinton, schoolmaster
John Sunderland, blacksmith
Liddia Sunderland, sp.
Elizabeth Jackson, sp.

Hugh Bosson, joiner, & Margaret his w.

Richard Stubbs, husb., & Ellin his w.

Jone Platt, sp.

Katherine Wilcoxon, sp.
Katherine Cooper, sp.

Robert Jackson, husb., & Arrabella his w.

Jone Maddocke, sp.
Elizabeth Johnson, sp.

Ellin Birtles, sp., £5 pa.
Marie Birtles, sp.

Richard Cawley, mercer, & Marie his w.

Raph Tench, tanner
Jane Tench, sp.

Margaret Wilbraham, sp.
John Wilbraham, husb.

Richard Bradford, husb., & Marie his w.

Peter Tarbock, gent., £15 pa

Richard Pownall, shoemaker, & Marie his w.

Alice Boote, sp.

John Sworton, blacksmith, & Ann his w.

Edward Mariott, gent., £5 pa.
John Mariott, shoemaker

John Partington, yeo., £15 pa
Ellin Paton, sp.
Elizabeth Robinson, sp.

William Becket, husb., & Ellinor his w.
John Becket, lab.
Marie Becket, sp.

Thomas Pownall, husb., & Margaret his w.
Elizabeth Sworton, sp.

Margaret Hooley, sp., & Thomas Ackson, collarmaker £5 pa
John Jackson, collarmaker

Thomas Sudlow, yeo., & Rachell his w.
Margaret Nixon, sp.

Thomas Pownall, shoemaker

POLL TAX RETURNS 1660

Thomas Tarbock, husb.
George Tarbock lab.

John Worsley, husb., & Jone his w.

Peter Leigh, blacksmith, & Ellin his w.

Ellin Leigh, sp.

Robert Birchwood, husb., & Margaret his w.

Thomas Blease, lab., & Marie his w.

Ottiwell Broome, lab., & Elizabeth his w.

Thomas Worsley, tailor

Marie Pownall, sp.
Elizabeth Birtles, sp.

Humfrey Pownall, husb. & Elizabeth his w.
Margaret Weedall, sp.
Raph Pownall, shoemaker

George Venables, husb., & Elizabeth his w.

William Green, husb., & Elizabeth his w.
Marie Green, sp.
Elizabeth Green, sp.

Marie Green, sp.

Peter Tovie, husb. & Margaret his w.

William Martin, husb. & Margerie his w.

Thomas Wharmby, glazier, & Marie his w.

Thomas Hewit, husb. & Margaret his w.

Robert Worrall, carpenter, & Jane his w.

George Martin, lab.

George Percivall, lab., & Ellin his w.

William Sudlow, tailor, & Ann his w.

Jone Birchall, sp., £7 10 0 pa

Lawrence Birchall, husb., £5 pa

William Harcourt, gent., £15 pa

APPENDIX FIVE

HEARTH TAX RETURNS, 1664

Taken from Lawton. G.O. (ed.) 'Northwich Hundred: Poll Tax 1660 and Hearth Tax 1664', LRCS (1979), vol cxix. Names and occupations have been modernised and the tax paid has been omitted.

NORTHWICH

Name	Hearths
Dorothy Bentley	7
William Leftwich	3
Thomas Harrison	3
John Perrisan	2
Thomas Norcot	3
Thomas Jackson	2
George Dewsbury	2
Raphe Cheney	2
Thomas Sumner	1
Widdow Cooke	2
Peter Venables	2
John Coopper	2
Thomas Holford	7
Raph Nickson	6
William Birkenhead	2
William Swinton	2
Samuell Jefferey	2
John Broome	7
Shusanna Leftwich	5
Elizabeth Royle	3
Elin Leftwich	5
Daniel Radford	4
James Moores	3
John Wrench	2
George Simson	2
Robert Barlow	4
Richard Galley	1
Thomas Robinson	4
Jeffrey Houghton	1
Thomas Houghton	1
Richard Jackson	2
William Sudlow	2
Elizabeth Birkenhead	2
William Houghton	2
John Hill	2
Thomas Alexander	1
Peter Paver	2
John Horton	2
Robert Wright	4
Thomas Robinson	2
Peter Weedall	3
Lawrence Birch	2
Peter Ainsworth	2
John Jackson	1
George Barker	1
William Mourton	2
	120

Not Chargeable

Name	Hearths
George Leftwich	1
Widdow Treance	2
Roger Phythian	1
Mathew Helsby	1
Ann Tarton	2
William Percivall	1
Raph Dobson	1
James Jefferys	1
Samuell Broome	1
Ottiwell Rodgerson	1
Richard Rodgerson	1
William Amery	1
John Jefferys	1
Thomas Horton	1
George Stubbs	1

HEARTH TAX RETURNS 1664

William Holt	1	Robert Ditchfeild	1
Elizabeth Bradshaw	1	Thomas Lamb	1
Thomas Siddow	1	Peter Leigh	1
Hamnet Boden	1	Jone Nickcowe	1
Randle Lamb	1	Alice Feouchild	1
John Barlow	1	John Ratcliffe	1
Margret Teator	1	Raphe Malbone	1
Alice Lawton	1	Robert Gorse	1
Katherina Sefton	1	Elizabeth Malbone	1
Richard Church	1	Thomas Malbone	1
George Dobson	1	Randle Oulton	1
William Miller	1	Thomas Treanch	1
Richard Dodds	1	Margaret Sudlow	1
Anne Weedall	1	William Rodgerson	1
Ellin Leighe	1	John Rodgerson	1
William Jefferys	1	William Barlow	1
William Shaw	1	George Ditchfield	1
Ottiwell Broome	1	John Madson	1
Mathew Moores	1	Edward Highson	1
Katherin Wainwright	1	Peter Broome	1
Michael Saintlawrance	1	Thomas Worall	1
John Abraham	1	Ann Jefferys	1
James Dalton	1	Thomas Wrench	1
Willam Yate	2	John Nors	1
Thomas Weedall	1	Elizabeth Jefferys	1
Jeffrey Jackson	1		
Margret Yate	2		**86**
Thomas Weedall	1		
Jeffrey Jackson	1		
Margaret Yate	1		
Elizabeth Moores	1		
Ralph Ditchfeild	1		
Phillip Basnet	1		
James Field	1		
Randle Fox	1		
Katherina Stones	1		
Richard Highsom	1		
Richard Feyey	1		
William Blackey	1		
Richard Treanit	1		
Robert Birchfeild	1		
Raphe Weedall	1		

OWNERS, OCCUPIERS AND OTHERS

WITTON

Mr Bromfeild	3
Richard Hilton	1
Richard Fryer	1
George Deacon	1
Richard Bradford	1
Peter Weedall	1
Richard Walley	1
Katherina Stubbs	1
Thomas Blease	5
Hughe Bosson	1
Run Stubes	1
John Harper	1
Robert Jackson	1
Elin Bertles	1
Jone Maddock	1
Raphe Tench	2
Richard Cauley	2
Isabell Norcott	3
John Wilbraham	2
Alice Boote	1
Ann Surton	1
Mr Mariott	1
John Partington	4
Humphey Fodon	1
Thomas Pennall	1
Thomas Pownall	1
Richard Bennitt	1
John Acson	1
Richard Sudlow	1
Thomas Tarbox	1
John Worsley	1
Peter Leigh	1
Robert Berchwood	1
Thomas Jackson	1
Ottiwell Broome	1
Houmpherey Pownall	1
Mary Pownall	1
Woods House	1
Peter Toues	1
George Venables	1
Williarn Martin	1

Thomas Warmbey	1
Mary Green	2
Thomas Wilt	2
Ellin Perceivall	1

61

Not Chargeable

Elizabeth Rodgerson	1
Margret Eaton	1
Elizabeth Barker	1
William Blacker	1
Raphe Ashley	1
Richard Jackson	1
John Bennitt	1
Thomas [Swinton?] schoolhouse	1
Katherina Penne	1
Lawrence [Birchall?]'s house	1
Thomas Alexander	1
Katherina Key	1
Elizabeth Bromfield	1
John Parr	1
Ann Malbone	1
John Salford	1
Margerey Teloor	1
Richard Stoneley	1
Richard Worsley	1
Margaret Venables	1
Katherina Davenport	1
Katherina Blour	1
Raphe Bristow	1
Elizabeth Rodgerson	1
William Greene	1
William Beckitt	1
Jone Moores	1
John Hall	1
Moses Acson	1
Thomas Walton	1
Robert Worrall	1

APPENDIX SIX

Size of Houses from Northwich Inventories

(Taken from 40 Northwich inventories which list rooms. The dates refer to the year the inventory was taken. Rooms in italics refer to those not specifically mentioned but inferred by names of other rooms)

1 Roomed Houses

House	Birchall, 1624
House	Woodier, 1665
Shop	Birkenhead, 1678

2 Roomed Houses

Shop, Chamber over shop	Norcott, 1665
House, Chamber over house	Lawton, 1689

3 Roomed Houses

House, Parlour, Buttery	Venables, 1621
House, Middle chamber, Green chamber	Venables, 1631
Street Chamber, Garden chamber, Upper chamber	Broom, 1634
House, Parlour, Chamber over parlour	Houghton, 1665
Shop, Chamber over shop, Cockloft	Johnson, 1637
House, Chamber, Garret	Bostock, 1699
House, Shop, Chamber over shop.	Higginson, 1682

4 Roomed Houses

House, Parlour, Buttery, Upper chamber	Horton, 1616
Hall, Parlour, Chamber over parlour, Man's chamber	Paver, 1631
House, Parlour, Buttery, Backhouse	Birkenhead, 1660
House, Shop, Chamber over house, Upper chamber	Cooper, 1667
House, Buttery, Great room above, Little room above	Jeffereys, 1683
House, Buttery, Chamber over house, Little chamber	Houghton, 1669
House, Parlour, Chamber, Chamber over house	Lord, 1687

5 Roomed Houses

House, Parlour, Kitchen, Chamber over house, Chamber over parlour.	Cheney, 1625
House, Shop, Chamber over shop, Chamber next shop, Chamber at stairhead	Bromfield, 1667
House, Buttery, Shop, Chamber over shop, Little chamber	Swettenham, 1671

OWNERS, OCCUPIERS AND OTHERS

House, Kitchen, Buttery, Chamber over house,
Chamber over kitchen   Church, 1688
House, Parlour, Chamber over house, Chamber over parlour,
Cross chamber   Leftwich, 1692
House, Kitchen, Chamber over house, Chamber over Kitchen,
Cockloft   Hasselgreave, 1699

6 Roomed Houses
House, Buttery, Kitchen, Chamber over house, Chamber over buttery
Lower chamber.   Singleton, 1673
House, Parlour, Little buttery, New chamber above stairs,
Chamber over parlour, Miller's chamber (Barn, Mill)   Pavor, 1610
House, Parlour, Chamber below 'going out of the dwelling house',
Chamber over house, Middle chamber over house,
Chamber over parlour. (Barn)   Birchall, 1668
House, Parlour, *Buttery*, New chamber, Room over house,
Room over parlor, Room over buttery.   Pavor, 1680
House, Parlour, Room over house, Upper chamber, Lower chamber
Another room.   Houghton, 1683

7 Roomed Houses
Hall, Parlour, Chamber over hall, Chamber over parlour, Maid's chamber,
Middle chamber, Near chamber (Parlour without, Stable)   Holford 1605
House, Parlour, Buttery, *Shop*, Chamber over house, Chamber over
parlour, Chamber over shop.   Royle, 1669
House, Parlour, Kitchen, Closet, Chamber, Street chamber,
Store chamber   Nield, 1678
House, Buttery, Kitchen, Parlour next the stable,
Parlour next 'Higlake', Chamber over house, Chamber over parlour,
Chamber over parlour. (Stable)   Harper, 1691

9 Roomed Houses
House, *Parlour*, Little shop, Shop, Mr Littler's chamber, Great chamber,
Street chamber, Chamber over parlour, Further chamber.   Leftwich, 1661
                                                  (filed as Leftwich 1686)
House, Buttery, Kitchen, Dining room, Passage room, Best room,
Shop, Red chamber, Chamber over shop.   Eaton, 1697

10 Roomed Houses
House, Parlour, Buttery, Closet, Chamber over house, Cockloft,
Cheese loft, Malt loft, Corn loft, Store (Barn, Mill)   Leftwich, 1641

12 Roomed Houses
Hall, Buttery, Hall buttery, 'Oell buttery', Kitchen, Kitchen buttery,

SIZE OF HOUSES FROM NORTHWICH INVENTORIES

Blue chamber, Samuel's chamber, Cheese chamber, Boarded chamber,
Gallery, Cockloft. (Barn, Stable)   Norcott 1679

14 Roomed Houses
Hall, Parlour, Buttery, Kitchen, Dining room, Chamber over hall,
Chamber over parlour, Chamber over buttery, Kitchen chamber,
Passage room, Closet over the hall, Cock loft over parlour chamber,
Cock loft, Little room in new building.   Bentley, 1680

15 Roomed Houses
House, New parlour, Old parlour, Chamber over new parlour,
Old parlour chamber, Blue chamber, House chamber,
Ralph's chamber, Servant's chamber, Maiden's chamber,
Chamber over cellar, Cellar, Garret, brewhouse, dayhouse.   Nixon, 1679

Appendix Seven
WICH-HOUSES AND THEIR OWNERS

The numbers in the first column refer to the early 17th century town plan (Appendix Three).

No. of Leads	House of the Judger of …	1595 (CRO: DLT/A/2/60, pp27-30; Calvert, pp 1112-1118)	1619 (CRO: D4360/2; Calvert, pp 1077-1082)	c.1660 (CRO: DCH/M/37/60)
		Seath Street – South Side		
1	4	Lache	Sir Hugh Cholmondeley	Cholmondeley	Cholmondeley
2	4		Sir Hugh Cholmondeley	Cholmondeley	Cholmondeley & Rossendale
3	4		John Heyes of Litley	Newall of Chester	Bentley
4	4		Sir Hugh Cholmondeley	Cholmondeley	Cholmondeley
6	4		Peter Warburton of Arley	Warburton of Arley	Warburton of Arley
7	4		Th. Leigh of Adlington	Judge Warburton	Stanley of Alderley
8	4		Hugh Winnington of Hermitage	Winnington of Hermitage	Raphe Nickson
9	4		Peter Leycester of Tabley	Leicester of Tabley	Leicester of Tabley & Leicester of Newcastle
10	4	Leftwich	Hugh Winnington of Hermitage	Winnington of Hermitage	Raphe Nickson
11	4	Little Legh	John Dutton of Dutton	Lord Gerard	Cholmondeley & Rossendale
12	4	Barterton	John Dutton of Dutton	Lord Gerard	Cholmondeley & Rossendale
13	4		Ralph Leftwich & Richard Litler	Harcourt & Litler	Norcott & Deane
14	4		The Earl of Derby	The Earl of Derby	Richard Carter & Richard Litler
15	4		Richard Brereton of Tatton	Lord Bridgewater	Lord Bridgewater
16	4		Heirs of Sir John Deane	Deane of Shurlach	Richard Deane of Shurlach
18	4	Claverton	Thomas Leigh of Adlington	Judge Warburton	Stanley of Alderley

WICH-HOUSES AND THEIR OWNERS

#	No.	Location	Owner	Owner	Owner	Owner
19	4		Peter Warburton of Arley	Warburton of Arley	Warburton of Arley	Warburton of Arley
20	4		Richard Wilbraham of Witton	Wilbraham of Witton	Wilbraham of Witton	Peter Tarbock
21	4		Thomas Wilbraham of Woodhey	Wilbraham of Woodhey	Wilbraham of Woodhey	Wilbraham of Woodhey
22	4		Thomas Wilbraham of Woodhey	Wilbraham of Woodhey	Wilbraham of Woodhey	Wilbraham of Woodhey

Part of Little Street (Horsemill St)

#	No.	Location	Owner	Owner	Owner	Owner
23	1		Huxley of Brindley	Huxley of Brindley	Huxley of Brindley	Huxley of Brindley
24	4		Heirs of James Pavor of Watford	Duncombe & Stepney	Duncombe & Stepney	Tarbock & Marriot
25	4		Heirs of James Pavor of Watford	Duncombe & Stepney	Duncombe & Stepney	Tarbock & Marriot
26	4		Robert Bromfield of Witton	Bromfield of Witton	Bromfield of Witton	Bromfield of Witton
27	4		Heirs of James Pavor of Watford	Duncombe & Stepney	Duncombe & Stepney	Tarbock & Marriot

Seath Street – North side

#	No.	Location	Owner	Owner	Owner	Owner
28	4		Peter Pavor of Northwich	Pavor of Northwich		Raphe Winnington
29	4	Marbury	Marbury of Marbury	Marbury of Marbury	Marbury of Marbury	Cholmondeley
30	4		Thomas Leigh of Adlington	Judge Warburton		Stanley of Alderley
31	4		The Earl of Derby	The Earl of Derby		Hodgkis of London
32	4	Little Witton	Peter Leicester of Tabley	Leicester of Tabley	Leicester of Tabley	Leicester of Newcastle
33	4		Thomas Marbury of Marbury	Marbury of Marbury		Cholmondeley
34	4		The Queen	The King		The King
35	6		Ralph Leftwich of Leftwich	Richard Harcourt of Wincham		Norcott
36	4	Witton	Thomas Venables of Kinderton	Venables of Kinderton	Venables of Kinderton	Venables of Kinderton
38	6	Acton	Sir Hugh Cholmondeley	Cholmondeley		Cholmondley & Rossendale
39	4	Cogshall	The Queen	The King		The King
40	4	Eaton	Ralph Leftwich of Leftwich	Leftwich of Leftwich		John Partington

OWNERS, OCCUPIERS AND OTHERS

41	4		Peter Leicester of Tabley	Leicester of Tabley	Leicester of Tabley
42	4		Peter Leicester of Tabley	Leicester of Tabley	Leicester of Tabley & Leicester of Newcastle
43	4		Heirs of Sir John Deane	Deane of Shurlach	Deane of Shurlach
44	4	Tattenhall	Peter Leicester of Tabley	Thomas Sudlow of Witton Leicester of Tabley	George Simcock of Shipbrook Leicester of Newcastle
45	4		Heirs of James Pavor of Watford	Duncombe & Stepney	Tarbock & Mariott
46	4		Heirs of James Pavor of Watford	Duncombe & Stepney	Tarbock & Mariott
47	4		Richard Sutton of Sutton	Heirs of Sutton	Lady Davenport
50	4		Richard Sutton of Sutton	Heirs of Sutton	Lady Davenport
53	4		Richard Bromfield of Northwich	Bromfield of Northwich	Robinson Rowe/Partington
56	4		Robert Pickmere of Hulse	Pickmere of Hulse	Richard Bradford of Shipbrook
57	4		Richard Sutton of Sutton	Heirs of Sutton	Earl Rivers
		High Street – North side			
76	4	Winnington	Peter Warburton of Arley	Warburton of Arley	Warburton of Arley
77	4		Peter Warburton of Arley	Warburton of Arley	Warburton of Arley
78	4		John Crosby of Whiteley	Crosby of Whitely	Crosby of Whitely
79	4		Ralph Leftwich of Leftwich	Leftwich of Leftwich	Leftwich of Leftwich & Northwich
		Yate Street – South side			
82	4		Henry Mainwaring of Carincham	Mainwaring of Carincham	George Broome
83	4		Thomas Venables of Kinderton	Venables of Kinderton	Venables of Kinderton
84	6		Ralph Egerton of Ridley	Sir Richard Egerton	Warburton of Helferston

210

WICH-HOUSES AND THEIR OWNERS

85	4	Lostock Gralam	George Leycester of Toft	Leycester of Toft	Leycester of Toft
86	4	Lach Dennis	Sir Hugh Cholmondeley	Lady Mary Cholmondeley	Cholmondeley
87	4	Hartford	Thomas Marbury of Marbury	Marbury of Marbury	Mr Davies of Ashton
88	6	Crowton	Sir William Brereton of Brereton	Brereton of Brereton	Dr William Bentley
89	6	Dutton	John Dutton of Dutton	Lord Gerard	Cholmondeley & Rossendale
90	6		Peter Warburton of Arley	Warburton of Arley	Warburton of Arley
91	4	Tatton	Julius Winnington of Birches	Winnington of Birches	Starkey of Stretton
92	6	Dunham Massey	Richard Sutton of Sutton	Heirs of Sutton	Lady Davenport
93	4		George Ireland of Crowton	Ireland of Crowton	Hatton of Crowton
94	4		Hugh Mere of Rostherne	Allen of Mobberly	Allen of Mobberly
95	4		Peter Leicester of Tabley	Leicester of Tabley	Leicester of Tabley
96	4		Thomas Marbury of Marbury	Marbury of Marbury	Cholmondeley
97	4		The Earl of Derby	The Earl of Derby	Hodgkis of London
		Yate Street – North side (Leach Eye)			
99	4		Ralph Bostock of Moulton	Bostock of Moulton	Bostock of Moulton
100	4		George Johnson of Lostock	Shakerley	Shakerley
101	4		The Earl of Derby	The Earl of Derby	Hodgkis of London
102	4		Robert Venables of Antrobus	Venables of Antrobus	Venables of Antrobus
103	4		Hugh Winnington of Hermitage	Winnington of Hermitage	John Reed
104	4		Fovell of Middlewich	Shakerley	Shakerley
105	4		John Horton of Cowlane	Horton of Cow Lane	Horton of Cow Lane
106	4		Hugh Winnington of Hermitage	Winnington of Hermitage	Leftwich of Northwich
107	4		Richard Sutton of Sutton	Heirs of Sutton	Moseley
108	6		Randoll Yate of Northwich	Robinson - Newall	Bentley
109	6		Richard Sutton of Sutton	Monkton	Earl Rivers

211

OWNERS, OCCUPIERS AND OTHERS

110	4		Thomas Starkey of Stretton	Starkey of Stretton	Mackworth - Bentley
112	4		Richard Sutton of Sutton	Heirs of Sutton	Monkton - Earl Rivers
115	4		Ralph Leftwich of Leftwich	Leftwich of Leftwich	John Partington's shop
116	4		Richard Sutton of Sutton	Heirs of Sutton	Monkton - Earl Rivers
		Leach Eye			
117	4		George Bradford of Shipbrook	George Bradford	Bradford of Shipbrook
118	4		Judge Peter Warburton of Chester	Judge Warburton	Stanley of Alderley
119	4		Horton of Aldersey	Horton of Aldersey	Bradford of Shipbrook
121	4		Peter Warburton of Arley	Warburton of Arley	Warburton of Arley
122	4		George Leycester of Toft	Leycester of Toft	Leycester of Toft
123	4		Peter Warburton of Arley	Warburton of Arley	Warburton of Arley
124	4		The School & the heirs of James Pavor of Watford	The School and Duncombe & Stepney	The School and Tarbock & Marriot
125	4		Thomas Starkey of Stretton	Starkey of Stretton	Mackworth - Bentley
126	4	Comerbach	Hugh Winnington of Hermitage	Winnington of Hermitage	Ralph Nickson's barn
127	4		Ralph Leftwich of Leftwich	Leftwich of Leftwich	Leftwich Oldfield
129	4		Thomas Grimsditch	Grimsditch	Thomas Appleton
		Little Street - East side (Horsemill Street.)			
140	4		Thomas Marbury of Marbury	Marbury of Marbury	Cholmondeley
141	4		Robert Venables of Antrobus	Venables of Antrobus	Cholmondeley
142	4		Hugh Winnington of Hermitage	Winnington of Hermitage	George Leftwich of Northwich
143	6		Hugh Winnington of Hermitage	Winnington of Hermitage	Peter Venables
144	4		William Foxley of Pickmere	Foxley of Pickmere	John Swinton of Knutsford
145	4		Richard Sutton of Sutton	Heirs of Sutton	Mrs Moseley
146	4		Richard Sutton of Sutton	Heirs of Sutton	Lady Davenport

Little Street – West side (Horsemill Street.)

		Marston			John Partington
147	4		Hugh Crosby of Lostock	Crosby of Lostock	
148	4		Robert Bromfield of Witton	Bromfield of Witton	Bromfield of Witton
149	4		Lady Julian Holcroft of Vale Royal	Mainwaring of Merton	Hughson - Rowe of Hartford
150	4		Ralph Leftwich of Leftwich	Leftwich of Leftwich	Leftwich Oldfield
151	4		Richard Sutton of Sutton	Heirs of Sutton	Moseley
152	4		The Preacher at Witton	The Preacher at Witton	The Preacher at Witton

Notes: There are 108 wich-houses listed above and they include a total of 453 leads (98 x 4, 10 x 6, and 1 x 1) which equates to 113 houses of 4 leads plus 1 lead which was the ancient method of assessment.

No. 46 was known as 'The Pavement House'.
No. 53 was the 'Horsemill'.
No. 97 was known as 'The Shops'.
No. 96 was a house occupied by Margaret Sudlow, c. 1660
No. 110 had a house built by Mrs Mary Venables.
No. 47 became a kitchen in John Broom's new building, c.1660.
No. 50 became a parlour in the same new building, c.1660.

Appendix Eight
OWNERS AND THEIR ALLOCATION OF LEADS & HOUSES

OWNERS, OCCUPIERS AND OTHERS

1604 (Calvert 1119–21)	Leads	Houses	1637 (Calvert pp 1082-3)	Leads	Houses	c. 1660 (CRO: DCH/M/37/60)	Leads	Houses
The King	10	2	The King	10	2	The King	10	2
The Earl of Derby	*20	*4	The Earl of Derby	*20	*4	The Earl of Derby	*20	*4
Peter Warburton of Arley	30	7	Peter Warburton of Arley	30	7	Sir George Warburton of Arley	30	7
John Dutton of Dutton	14	3	Lord Gerrard	14	3	Lord Cholmondeley & Thomas Rossendale	20	4
Sir Hugh Cholmondeley	22	5	Robert, Lord Cholmondeley	22	5	Lord Cholmondeley	16	4
Richard Sutton of Sutton	50	11	Sir Humphrey Davenport	50	11	The co-heirs of Sutton	32	7
						Earl Rivers	14	3.5
						Mrs Heyes	2	0.5
Thomas Venables of Kinderton	8	2	Peter Venables of Kinderton	8	2	Peter Venables of Kinderton	12	3
Sir William Brereton of Brereton	6	1	William, Lord Brereton	6	1	Dr William Bentley	6	1
Raffe Leftwich of Leftwich	24	6	William Oldfield	8	2	Leftwich Oldfield	8	2
			Raffe Leftwich	16	4	John Partington	8	2
						Raffe & William Leftwich	8	2
Raffe Egerton of Ridley	6	1	Richard Egerton	6	1	Robert Warburton	6	1

214

OWNERS AND THEIR ALLOCATION OF LEADS & HOUSES

Owner					
Sir George Leicester of Toft (prev. of Walton)	8	2 Raffe Leicester of Toft	8	2 Raffe Leicester	8	2
Sir Thomas Holcroft of Vale Royal	8	2 John Huson	4	1 Thomas Rowe John Huson	44	11
Thomas Marbury of Marbury	20	5 William Marbury	20	5 Thomas Cholmondeley	16	4
Thomas Wilbraham of Woodhey	8	2 Sir Richard Wilbraham	8	2 Sir Thomas Wilbraham	8	2
Sir Urian Leigh of Adlington	12	3 Sir Peter Warburton	12	3 Sir Thomas Stanley	16	4
Judge Warburton	4	1 Judge Warburton	4	1		
Peter Leicester of Tabley	24	6 Peter Leicester of Tabley	24	6 Sir Peter Leicester	12	3
				William Leicester of Newcastle then John Partington	12	3
Hugh Winnington of Hermitage	26	6 Lawrence Winnington	26	6 George Leftwich	12	3
				Raffe Nickson	4	1
				Peter Venables	6	1
				John Read	4	1
John Heyes of Little Leigh	4	1 Richard Newall	4	1 Dr William Bentley	6	1
Richard Wilbraham of Witton (prev. of Done of Utkinton)	4	1 John Wilbraham	4	1 Peter Tarbock	4	1
Sir John Egerton (prev. Brereton of Tatton)	4	1 Richard Egerton	4	1 John, Earl of Bridgewater	4	1

215

OWNERS, OCCUPIERS AND OTHERS

James Pavor of Watford	21	Peter Tarbock & William Faldoe	21	Peter Tarbock & Edw. Marriot	5
The School	2.6	The School	2.6	The School	1
John Ireland of Hutt	4	Sir Gilbert Ireland	4	Hatton of Crowton	1
Richard Venables of Antrobus	8	Mrs Mary Venables	8	Colonel Venables	2
Thomas Starkey of Stretton	8	Thomas Starkey	8	Mrs Venables & Mrs Mackworth	2
Raffe Littler of Wallerscote	2	Raffe Litler of Wallerscote	2	Raffe Litler of Wallerscote	0.5
Richard Harcourt of Wincham	6	William Harcourt	6	Thomas Norcott	1.5
Julius Winnington of Birches	4	Paul Winnington of Birches	4	Raffe Starkey	1
Roger Deane of Shurlach	8	Richard Deane of Shurlach	8	Richard Deane of Shurlach	2
George Simcock of Shipbrook	4	Thomas Sudlow	4	John Sudlow	1
John Horton of Coole	4	John Horton of Coole	4	John Horton of Coole	1
John Allen of Rostherne	4	William Allen of Rostherne	4	William Allen of Rostherne	1
Henry Mainwaring of Kermincham (late Bromfield's)	4	Henry Mainwaring of Kermincham	4	George Broome	1
Peter Paver of Northwich	4	Richard Paver of Northwich	4	Mrs Winnington	1
Richard Yate	4	John Heyes of Little Legh	4	Dr William Bentley	1

216

OWNERS AND THEIR ALLOCATION OF LEADS & HOUSES

John Horton of Aldersey	4	1	John Horton of Aldersey	4	1	Richard Bradford	12	3
Robert Pickmere of Hulse (late Bostock of Moulton)	4	1	Henry Pickmere of Hulse	4	1			
George Bradford of Shipbrook (prev. Clotton of Northwich)	4	1	Richard Bradford	4	1			
William Foxley of Pickmere	4	1	Richard Swinton	4	1	John Swinton	4	1
Raffe Bostock of Moulton	4	1	Raffe Bostock of Moulton	4	1	Raffe Bostock of Moulton	4	1
Folville of Middlewich	4	1	Mrs Margaret Shakerley	4	1	Sir Geoffrey Shakerely	8	2
Thomas Ireland of Bewsey	4	1						
John Crosby of Whitley	4	1	Richard Crosby	4	1	John Crosby	4	1
Thomas Grimsditch of Appleton (late Johnsons of Lostock)	4	1	Richard Grimsditch	4	1	Joseph Watt	4	1
Richard Bromfield of Northwich	8	2	Richard Bromfield Witton Church	4	1	John Partington & Th. Rowe Witton Church	4	1
George Huxley of Brindley	1	1	George Huxley of Brindley	1	1	George Huxley of Brindley	1	1
Hugh Crosby	4	1	Richard Crosby	4	1	John Crosby	4	1
Thomas Bromfield of Witton	4	1	Thomas Bromfield	4	1	Thomas Bromfield	4	1
	453	108		453	108		453	108

Notes: The leads of the Earl of Derby were in reality 16 within four houses; the other four leads were an allocation of salt-making rights without an actual house.

The total number of actual houses should be 108 containing a total of 449 leads (97 x 4, 10 x 6 and 1 x 1).

217

BIBLIOGRAPHY

A   MANUSCRIPT SOURCES

Cheshire and Chester Archives:
- i) Cholmondeley Mss. (DCH)
- ii) Vernon and Warren Mss (DVE)
- iii) Leicester of Tabley Mss. (DLT)
- iv) Shakerley Mss. (DSS)
- v) Wilbraham Tollemache Mss. (DTW)
- vi) Northwich Urban District Records (LuNo)
- vii) Ecclesiastical Records (EDA - EDC)
- viii) Parish registers of St Helen's Church, Northwich, formerly Witton Chapel (P53)
- ix) Wills and Probate Records (WC, WI, WS)

Public Record Office, London: State Papers: SP/10

British Library: Harleian Mss 2126

Derbyshire County Record Office: D3155/CROXALL XI

Wirral Archives: Macclesfield Collection: MA/T/1/124

B   CALENDARS AND PRINTED SOURCES

Bennett, J.H.E. and Dewhurst, J.C. (eds.) *Cheshire Quarter Sessions Records, 1559-1760*, Record Society of Lancashire & Cheshire, 94 (1940).

Booth, P.H.W. & Carr, A.D. (eds.) *Chester Chamberlain's Account, 1361-62*, Record Society of Lancashire and Cheshire, vol. 125, (1991).

Brownbill J. (ed.), *The Ledger Book of Vale Royal Abbey*, Record Society of Lancashire and Cheshire, vol. 68, (1914).

Calendar of the Committee for the Advance of Money

Calendar of the Committee for Compounding.

Calendar of Close Rolls

Calendar of Charter Rolls

BIBLIOGRAPHY

Calendar of Miscellaneous Inquisitions
Calendar of Letters and Papers, Henry VIII
Calendar of Liberate Rolls
Calendar of Patent Rolls
Calendar of State Papers Domestic
Camden, *Brittania*, (1607) ed. by P. Holland
Cooke, J.H., *Bibliotheca Cestriensis* , (1904)
Dawes, M.C.B. (ed.), *Register of Edward the Black Prince,* four volumes (1930-33).
Deputy Keeper of the Public Records Reports
Dore, R.N. (ed.), *The Letter Books of Sir William Brereton*, vols. 123 & 128, Record Society of Lancashire and Cheshire (1984)
Foster, J., *Alumni Oxonienses*, (1887-88 and 1891-92)
Hall, J. (ed.), *The Civil War in Cheshire*, Record Society of Lancashire and Cheshire, vol 19, (1889).
Gastrell, F., *Notitia Cestriensis,* Chetham Society
John Rylands catalogue no. 456
Lawton, G.O. (ed.) *Northwich Hundred: Poll Tax 1660 and Hearth Tax 1664*, Record Society of Lancashire and Cheshire, vol 109, 91979).
Leland, J., *Itinerary of England*, 1535-1543 (ed. Smith, L.T., 1907, five volumes)
Morgan, P. (ed.), *Domesday Book: Cheshire*, (1978)
Morris, C., (ed.) *The Journeys of Celia Fiennes*, (1947)
Parkinson, Rev. R. (ed.) *The Life of Adam Martindale, written by Himself*, Chetham Society, old series vol. 4, (1845)
Stewart-Brown, R. (ed.), *Accounts of the Chamberlains and other officers of the County of Chester, 1301-1360*, Record Society of Lancashire and Cheshire, vol 59, (1910).
Stewart-Brown, R. (ed.), *Calendar of County Court, City Court and Eyre Rolls of Chester,1259-1297, with an Inquest of Military Service*, Chetham Soc., N.S., vol 84 (1925).
Stewart-Brown, R. and Mills, M. (eds.), *Cheshire in the Pipe Rolls,1158-1301*, Record Society of Lancashire and Cheshire, vol 92, (1925)
Varley, J (ed.), *A Middlewich Chartulary, Chetham Society,* new series vol 105, (1944)
Venn, J and J.A., *Alumni Cantabrigienses*
Inquisitions Post Mortem 1603-1660, Record Society of Lancashire and Cheshire, vol 91, 1938

OWNERS, OCCUPIERS AND OTHERS

C SECONDARY SOURCES

Beck, J,	*Tudor Cheshire* (1969)
Bostock A.J.,	'17th Century Over', *The Winsford Record*, (1998). 'Owners, Occupiers and Others', *Cheshire History*, vol. 41 (2001)
Calvert, A.F.,	*Salt in Cheshire*, (1915)
Chaloner, W.H.,	*Salt in Cheshire 1600 – 1870*, Lancashire and Cheshire Antiquarian Society, vol. 71, (1951), and also in Ward W.R. (ed.) *Palatinate Studies*, Chetham Society, vol 36 (1992)
Collins, J.,	*Salt and Fisheries* (1682)
Cox, M.,	*A History of Sir John Deane's Grammar School, Northwich* (1975)
Crump, W.B.,	'Saltways from the Cheshire Wiches', *Lancashire and Cheshire Antiquarian Society*, vol. 40 (1939)
Curzon, J.B.,	'Paying for the Invasion', *Cheshire History*, 40, (2000).
Dore, R.N.,	*The Civil Wars in Cheshire* (1966)
Hall, J.,	*History of the Town and Parish of Nantwich*, (1883).
Harris, B.E., & Clayton, D.J.	*Criminal Procedure in Cheshire in the Mid-Fifteenth Century*, Transactions of the Historical Society of Lancashire and Cheshire, vol. 128 1978
Hewitt, H.J.,	'Mediaeval Cheshire', *Chetham Society*, n.s. 88 (1929).
Hill, C.,	*Society & Puritanism in Pre-Revolutionary England*, (1964).
Hodson, J.H.	*Cheshire 1660 – 1780: Restoration to Industrial Revolution* (1978)
Hoskins, W.G.,	*Local History in England* (1972).
Howard Hudson, J.,	*Cheshire 1660 – 1780: Restoration to Industrial Revolution*, (Chester, 1978)
Hurst, J.D.,	*Savouring the Past: The Droitwich Salt Industry* (1992)
McNeil, R.,	*Two medieval wich-houses excavated in Wood Street, Nantwich - 1980;* Salt Museum Publications. *1980*
Ormerod, G.,	*History of the County Palatine and City of Chester,* second edition, ed. T. Helsby (1882)

BIBLIOGRAPHY

Phillips, C.B. & Smith, J.H. — *Lancashire and Cheshire from AD 1540* (1994).
Richards, R, — *Old Cheshire Churches*, (1973)
Sylvester D., & Nulty, G., (eds.) — *The Historical Atlas of Cheshire*, (1958).
Thomas, P.W., — *Sir John Berkenhead, 1617-1679*, (1969)
Vale Royal B.C. — *Cheshire Historic Towns Survey*, Part 1

INDEX

Note: A single name does not necessarily imply a particular individual (there may be several with the same name). Appendices have not been indexed.

A

Abbot of Vale Royal 19
Abbreviations xiii
Ackson, John 82, 83
Ackson, Moses 82
Ackson, Thomas 56, 81, 82, 83
Act of Uniformity (1662) 168
Acton 12, 141
Acton, Alan 19
Adam the Salter 9
Adlington 140
Administration, Civil 164
Ainsworth, John 153
Alderley 140
Aldford 176
Ale 126
Ale brewing 24
Ale-tasters 101, 113
Alexander, Thomas 83
All Souls College, Oxford 161
Allen, William 33
Amery, George 147, 159, 169
Anderton, Margaret 170
Angel Hotel 39
Anglican Church 164
Antrobus 33, 94
Antrobus, James 100
Apple Market Street 32, 34, 40, 45, 183
Archdeacon 169
Arley 147, 149
Arminianism 166, 167
Ascension Day 7
Asshal, Thomas 100
Aston Grange 141
Aston, Sir Thomas 174
Ati's Cross 8
Axstuth 18

Aynsworth, Robert 145

B

Backhouse Street 40. See also Leach End
Backside 82
Bacon, Nicholas 147
Baguley, Alice 87
Baguley, Elizabeth 82, 160
Baguley, Ellen 87
Baguley, John 82, 160
Baguley, Margaret 85
Baguley, Randle 82
Baguley, William 82, 99, 160
Bailiff 19, 20, 156, 161, 179
Bakehouse 32, 34, 40, 104, 141
Baker 148
Baker, Thomas 67, 98
Baptisms 49, 50, 51, 52, 143, 166
Barber 84
Barker, Daniel 99
Barker, George 82, 84
Barlow, George 99
Barlow, Robert 73
Barlow, Thomas 67, 100
Barons of Kinderton 131, 178. See Kinderton
Barrow xv, 67, 78, 119, 121, 127, 151, 152, 154, 156, 158, 176
Barrow makers 84
Barterton 12
Bartington 141
Basingwerk Abbey 23, 26
Bassmith, Raph 99
Bateson, William 20
Battle of Middlewich 174

222

INDEX

Battle of Nantwich 174
Battle of Rowton Moor 176
Battle of Winnington Bridge 180
Battles. See also Edgehill, Marston Moor, Naseby and Worcester
Baxter 104
Beds and bedding 59, 60, 61, 68, 69, 77, 78, 82, 83, 86, 89, 112, 160
Beeston 176
Beeston Castle 176
Bentley family 59
Bentley, Dr William 33, 55, 65, 66, 69, 85, 139, 148, 156, 162
Bentley, Mrs Dorothy 69
Bentley, Richard 171, 179
Berchenhead family. See Birkenhead family
Berrington, Mrs Thomas 168
Bigge, Richard 23
Billington, Elizabeth 170
Billington, John 171
Billington, Margery 169
Billington, Richard 63
Birchall, Christopher 171
Birchall, Jone 56
Birchall, Lawrence 56, 125. See Witton
Birches 142, 144, 149
Birkenhead family 158
Birkenhead, Elizabeth 159. See also Baguley, Elizabeth
Birkenhead, Ellen 160
Birkenhead, Isaac 159, 179
Birkenhead, John 158, 159, 160, 161
Birkenhead, John (Sir) 84, 158, 161
Birkenhead, Margaret 159
Birkenhead, Marie 160
Birkenhead, Mary 160. See also Jefferies, Mary
Birkenhead, Ralph 81, 82
Birkenhead, Randle 158, 159, 160, 179
Birkenhead, Roger 159
Birkenhead, Sir Henry. See Birkenhead family
Birkenhead, Thomas 159
Birkenhead, Widow 167, 169
Birkenhead, William 68, 81, 153, 158, 159, 160
Biron, Geoffrey 19
Birth out of wedlock 111
Black Death 18
Black Prince, The 16, 20, 21, 23
Blacksmith 73, 79, 80, 83, 88, 157
Blood 126
Blundeville, Randolph (1181-1232) 15
Bochelau 8
Boden, Edward 170
Book of Common Prayer 166
Book of Customs 102, 124
Books 69, 77, 80, 102, 144, 155
Boote, Richard 157
Booth Rebellion 179
Booth, George 139
Booth, Sir George 139, 180
Bordarius 13
Borough xv, 4, 14
Bostock 12, 145
Bostock family 19, 94
Bostock, George 65
Bostock, John 84
Bostock, Mr 39
Boswell, Thomas 178
Bounds of Northwich 24
Bradford, Joan 158
Bradford, Margaret 143
Bradford, Richard 85, 86, 156
Bradford, Robert 156
Bradshaw, Ralph 34
Bradwell, Richard 19
Bragg and puglement 108
Bramall, William 169
Brass 16, 60, 67, 77, 83, 86, 88
Bread baking 24, 104
Brereton 12
Brereton, Lord William 130, 131

OWNERS, OCCUPIERS AND OTHERS

Brereton, Sir William 173
Brewhouse 62
Brewing 24, 62, 73, 97
Bridge End, The 159
Bridge, The Town 16, 20, 21, 30, 98, 132, 173
Brine xv, 9, 15, 18, 97, 101, 105, 107, 114, 115, 119, 121, 122, 124, 126, 129, 130, 132, 133, 183
    Strength 129
Brine channel 97, 101, 107, 122, 124, 168
Brine-pit 2, 21, 32, 39, 108, 118, 121, 131, 132, 133, 182, 185, 186
Broken Cross house 67
Bromfield family 25, 59, 74, 147
Bromfield, Geoffrey 66, 68
Bromfield, Mary 151, 152
Bromfield, Mrs Susanna 56, 66, 78
Bromfield, Richard 149
Bromfield, Robert 66, 151, 175, 178
Bromfield, Thomas 26, 33, 118, 147, 171
Brook, Mr 131
Broom, Ralph 186
Broome family 59, 94, 148, 154
Broome, Cicelie 155
Broome, Ellen 154
Broome, George 34, 63, 65, 151, 152, 154
Broome, John 33, 56, 67, 72, 74, 100, 131, 148, 151, 153, 154, 155, 171
Broome, Katherine 148, 154, 170
Broome, Ottiwell 88, 102, 154, 155
Broome, Peter 148
Broome, Ralph 148
Broome, Richard 154
Broome, Samuel 73, 154, 155
Broome, Ursula 154
Brough, Robert 81
Brownslane 94
Broxton 8
Buckingham, Duke of 179

Bucklow East 8
Bucklow West 8
Bulkeley (Family) 20, 22
Bulkeley, Richard 19
Bulkeley, Robert 19
Bull Ring 6, 32, 39
Burgage 153, 158
Burgage plots 14, 68
Burgess 14, 16, 92, 102, 104, 109, 132, 139, 140, 150, 151, 161, 184
    Burgess Families 95, 157
    Foreign 93
Burgess, Francis 83
Burgess, Joseph 69
Burghal status 16
Burleyman 102
Burroughs, William 99
Bushell, Sir Edward 84
Butcher 72, 73, 155
Butchers' shambles 183
Byrom 176

C

Calveley, Peter 20
Camden 121
Candle maker 83
Cappel, Jane 170
Carpenter 71, 83, 85
Carriers 84, 104
Carrington, Major 173
Carterstuth 18
Castell, Robert 24
Castle 3, 6, 49, 53. See Witton
Castle Hill 30
Castle Street 41
Cattenhall 12
Cavaliers 173
Cavalry 174, 180
Cawley, John 76, 87, 88
Cawley, Mary 88
Cawley, Richard 87

INDEX

Chair 86, 88, 89
Chamberlain 108
Channel-lookers 113
Channels. See Brine channels
Chapel of St Helen 37, 49, 164, 167. See also St Helen's Church
Chapelry of Witton 49
Chappell Croft 82
Charter 14, 15
Chemical industry 183
Cheney, Ralph 76, 80, 84
Cheney, Raphe 33, 61, 72
Cheshire 92
    Deputy lieutenant 173
    Earls of 17
    Lords Lieutenants 4, 92, 171
    Sheriff 141, 172
Cheshire cheese 3, 16, 62, 67, 80, 185
Chester 9, 78, 97, 175, 180
    Bishop of 167
    Black Death 20
    Bridge Street 78
    Burgesses 24
    Earl Hugh, Earl of 11
    Earls of 13, 15, 16, 20, 24
    Governor 175
    Nuns 19
    Siege of 176
    Surrender 176
Chesterton 3
Chests and coffers 61, 89
Chief rent 138
Cholmondeley family 117, 141, 180
Cholmondeley, Sir Hugh 122, 138
Cholmondeley, Sir Robert 129
Cholmondeley, Thomas 132, 142, 172, 178
Cholmondeley, Viscount 131, 141
Chow, Marie 81
Chrimes, Alice 162
Christleton 176
Chrymes, John 147

Chrymes, Richard 132
Church Street 32, 34
Church, Richard 66, 70
Civil War, The 161, 172
Clarification 126
Claverton 11, 12
Clergy 164
Clive 12
Cloth 76
Cloth industry 80
Clothing 63
Coal 130, 156
Coats of arms 65
Cockloft 67, 77
Cogshall 12
Collar makers 80, 83, 148
Comberbach 12, 94, 150
Commission of Sequestration 69, 162, 179
Commissions of Array 173
Committee for Compounding 177
Committee for Examining and Ordaining Ministers 168
Common Bell 129
Common Leads 100
Common oven 22, 24, 104
Congleton 1, 4, 9
Conquest, Norman 7
Consistory Court 83, 87, 97, 168, 169, 170
Constable 94, 113, 169, 172
Cook 72, 73
Cook, Peter 99
Coole 23, 118
Cooper 71
Cooper, John 81
Copper 5, 16, 62, 86, 89
Corn 103
Corn mill 37
Coroner 106, 107
Coton, John 19, 24
Cotton, Mr 131

OWNERS, OCCUPIERS AND OTHERS

County court 24, 25
Court 12, 14, 18, 96, 102, 182
   Perquisites 18, 22, 97
   Rolls 24, 93, 97, 112
Court Baron xv, 97
Court House 32, 33, 39, 98, 102, 103, 106, 178
Court Leet xv, 97
Court of Assize 97
Court of Augmentations 143
Court of Wards 25
Court, The Great 97, 100
Cranage 12, 142
Cranage, Richard 74
Crannock 127, 152
Creditors 65
Crewe, Alice 171
Cromwell 168
Crosby, Hugh 138, 149
Cross Street 32, 183
Crowfoot, John 74
Crown Street 32
Crown, The 7, 14, 19, 137, 146, 147, 153. See also Specific Kings and Queens
Crowton 12
Croxton 12
Croxton, Captain 173
Crumbhill 84
Crume Hills 21, 32, 41, 105, 110
Cupboard 61, 62, 88
Customs of the Town 102

D

Dane Bridge, The 39, 105
Davenham 53, 141
Davenport, Lady 140
Davenport, Richard 144
Davenport, Sir Humphrey 140
Davies Street 32
Dean, Richard 171

Deane, Agnes 143
Deane, Anne 143
Deane, John 26, 99, 143
Deane, Richard 26
Deane, Sir John 37, 143, 147
Deane, Thomas 171
Debtors 65
Delves, Sir Thomas 131
Demesne 15
Denbigh, Earl of 175
Derby, Earls of 2, 4, 22, 25, 33, 37, 68, 115, 118, 137, 140, 171, 173, 178, 179, 184
   Steward 92, 96
Dewsbury, Alice 68, 153
Dewsbury, George 56, 74
Dewsbury, Peter 151, 171
Dissolution of the monasteries 26, 141, 142, 147
Distraint of Knighthood 171
Ditchfield, George 101
Ditchfield, Hugh 34, 154
Ditchfield, Robert 84
Dobson, Mrs 132
Dobson, Richard 99
Domesday Book 6, 7, 9, 12, 13, 14, 18, 27, 37, 182
Done Family 22, 25
Done, Sir John 143
Dorfold 139
Dorton, Samual 101
Dot, Saxon Thane 13
Downes, Mr 106
Draper, Hugh 22
Draper, John 20
Drapers 74, 149
Dressmakers 78
Drink trade 72
Droitwich, Staffordshire 121, 128, 130
Dudestan 8
Dungeon 133
Dunham Massey 12, 139

226

INDEX

Dutton 12, 141
Dutton family 22, 137, 141, 159
Dutton, Eleanor 141
Dutton, Gilbert 26
Dutton, John 153, 172
Dutton, Margaret 68
Dutton, Thomas 26, 118, 141
Dutton, William 23

E

Eagle and Child 41
Earl Rivers 131, 132, 140, 149
Earl, Peter 168
East Indies 69
Eaton 12, 141
Eaton, William 80, 159
Eddeson, John 22
Eddisbury North 8
Edgar, Constable Thomas 99
Edgar, Thomas 101
Edgehill, Battle of 179
Edward the Confessor 7, 11, 13, 17
Egg white 126
Ellams, George 84
Ernesilver 18
Exeter, Duke of 21

F

Fabrics 76
Fagg Lane 32. See also Leach Eye
Fair 1, 4, 16, 177, 185
Farmer 16, 18, 19, 20, 72, 108
Farrington, Hugh 145
Farrington, William 145
Fashion 76
Fee farm 14
Felt maker 80, 81
Feoffee 143, 148, 154, 161, 177
Feremon, Ciceley 20
Feremon, Hugh 20, 23
Feremon, John 20, 23

Fiennes, Celia 2, 5, 53, 114, 131, 133
Fighting 108
Fire-looker 113
Fires 19, 106
Fisher, Richard 83
Flood Defences 105
Floods 19
Food and Drink Trades 72
Foodstuff 62
Forced Loans 171
Forestalling 103
Fovell, John 23
Fovell, Maria 118
Fovell, Thomas 23
Fox family 93
Fox, Robert 50, 62, 99
Foxley, Margaret 138
France, Richard 170
Franchises 15
Freedoms 14
Friday boilings 7
Frodsham 3, 12, 93, 133, 151, 185
Frodsham deanery 51
Frodsham, Henry 81
Frodsham, Peter 171
Fryer, Mary 87
Fryer, Richard 73, 87, 170
Fuel, cost of 126
Furniture 60

G

Gadbrook 73
Gandy, John 158
Gandy, William 99
Gandys wich-house 156
Gardner, Yeoman 154
Geffery, Edward 73
Geffery, James 73
Geffery, John 73
Geffery, Samuel 73
Geffrey, John 73

OWNERS, OCCUPIERS AND OTHERS

Geffrey, William 73
Gentlemen 56, 66, 67, 70, 74, 77, 83, 88, 145
Gerard, Sir Gilbert 141
Gerard, William 19
Gerrard, Captain 173
Gerrard, James 84
Glazier 84
Glossary xv
Glover 73, 81
Golborne, Edward 144
Golbourne family 25
Golbourne, Edward 118, 151
Gorst, James 99
Grammar School 37, 69, 137, 147, 156, 160, 161, 167, 177
    Master 148, 167, 173
    Usher 159
Great Budworth 2, 37, 49, 164, 168
    St Mary and All Saints Church 164
Great Courts, The 97, 150
Green, William 78
Griffith, Thomas 162
Gripyard 48
Grocer 74, 147
Grosvenor family 180
Gunpowder Plot 166
Gutters 122. See also Brine Channels
Gutter-viewers 101

H

Halton 11, 12
Halton Castle 175
Hammeson, Hugh 20
Hampton Court Conference 166
Hanmere, Ralph 117
Harcourt family 141
Harcourt, Elizabeth 169
Harcourt, Raphe 141
Harcourt, William 56
Harrison, Geoffrey 72, 74

Harrison, Jeffrey 151, 152
Harrison, Thomas 171
Hartford 11, 12, 25, 49, 53, 56, 72, 94, 157, 180
Hearth Tax 51, 53, 54, 85, 88, 154, 155, 159
Heath, Isabell 74
Heesomes Ground 149
Helsby, Mathew 73
Helsby, Robert 101
Helsby, William 33
Heriot xv, 146, 149
Hermitage, Cranage 23, 118, 142
Herneway, Pymme 23
Hewitt family 25
Hewitt, Ellen 157
Hewitt, John 99
Hewitt, William 76
Heyes, Ellen (née Tarbock) 65, 68, 151, 152, 153, 158
Heyes, Mistress 140
Heyes, Thomas 118
Heywood family 184
Heywood, Adam 83
Heywood, James Pemberton 184
Hickock, Widow 34
Higginson, Samuel 76
High Street 22, 30, 32, 34, 40, 41, 45, 53, 76, 115, 118, 145, 155, 156, 157
Hignett, William 82
Hilton, Richard 56, 169
Hilton, Thomas 84
Hindley 9
Hisham, Robert 170
Hodgkis, Joshua 56, 140, 178
Holcroft, Lady Julian 138
Holford 73
Holford family 22, 25, 59, 159
Holford, Christopher 138
Holford, Mary 138
Holford, Richard 50, 65, 70, 151, 152
Holford, Robert 171, 179

INDEX

Holford, Thomas 68, 117, 118, 153
Holland, Sir John 21
Holme, Randle 167
Holmes Chapel 9
Horsemill 21, 32, 34, 72, 74, 115, 145, 146
Horsemill Street 32, 40, 115, 139, 143, 147, 156
Horten, John 81
Horton, Alice 153
Horton, Ralph 56, 66
Horton, Roger 23, 85, 118
Horton, Thomas 83
Houghton family 148, 155
Houghton, Ann 85
Houghton, Elizabeth 85
Houghton, Henry 22
Houghton, Jeffrey 84, 85, 86, 87, 88, 100
Houghton, Margaret 22, 85, 86, 156
Houghton, Margery 85
Houghton, Roger 23
Houghton, Thomas 85, 86, 87, 156
Houghton, William 22, 72, 85, 148, 155, 156
House of Correction 32, 40, 45
House of Lords 179
Howey Croft 149
Huet, William 169, 171
Hugh, son of Geoffrey of Northwich 19
Hulme 23
Hulme Hall 138
Hulse 56, 69, 169, 171, 179
Hundred xv, 2, 4
    Bucklow 4, 173
    Eddisbury 4, 173
    Northwich 4, 69, 169, 171, 172, 173, 182
Hunt, John 99, 101
Hunter, Elizabeth 88
Hunter, Ellen 86
Hunter, Samuel 88
Huntingdon, Earl of 21

Huntington, Countess of 22
Husbandman 70, 72, 79, 80, 85, 143, 150, 154
Huxley 176
Huxley family 74
Huxley, Ralph 74
Hyde, William 93, 94, 96

I

Immorality 169
Inmates 111, 112
Innkeeper 72, 73, 155, 159
Inquisition post mortem xvi, 22, 68, 141, 142, 145, 153, 158
Inventory 58
Ireland, Sir Thomas 137
Iron pans 130, 156, 157
Ironmonger 76, 80

J

Jackson, Dr William 121, 126, 129
Jackson, John 81, 133
Jefferies, Mary 82, 160
Jeffery, William 68, 153
Jeffrey, William 101
Jenkinson, William 100
John, Jackson 73
Johnson family 59
Johnson, John 76, 152, 169
Judger 12, 13, 24, 41, 138, 139, 141, 142, 150
    Fine 150

K

Kelsall 77, 94
Kelsall Hill 9
Kennerly, Edward 99
Kennerly, Josiah 99
Kent, Mr (Schoolmaster) 144
Kermincham 155
Killers of Salt 101, 127

OWNERS, OCCUPIERS AND OTHERS

Kiln Orchard 26, 41, 106
Kilshall, Ralph 81
Kinderton 12, 13, 23, 142, 149
    Barons of 37, 172
King Charles I 161, 166, 169, 171, 176
King Charles II 179
King Edward I 23, 143
King Edward III 9
King Henry IV 22
King Henry V 24
King Henry VII 92
King Henry VIII 25, 26, 58
King James I 165
King Richard II 21, 142, 143
King Richard III 22, 92
King Street 3
Kingesmol 18, 22
Knight, Thomas 99
Knutsford 85, 155
Knutsford Heath 175

L

Lach Dennis 12, 56, 69
Lache 12
Ladders 106
Lamb, Randle 86
Lambert, Colonel 180
Lancashire 92
    Lords Lieutenant 92
Lancaster, Duke of 24
Lathom, Samuel 101
Latin Mass 165
Laud, Archbishop William 161, 166, 168
le Scot, John 17
Leach End 32, 40, 148
Leach Eye 32, 40, 104, 115, 118, 139, 147, 148, 156. See also Fagg Lane
Lead fine 138, 150
Lead-looker xvi, 100, 125, 128
Leads xvi, 78, 100, 114, 115, 124, 128, 140, 146, 151, 152, 153, 154, 157

    numbers of 130
Leadsmithy 23, 32, 34, 40, 47, 106, 124
Leather Industry 81
Leave-looker 113
Lee, Elizabeth 87
Leftwich 3, 12, 53, 67, 69, 72, 132, 142, 146, 171, 179
    Hall Orchard 67
    Long Meadow 67
    Manor of 141
    Near Meadow 67
Leftwich family 22, 25, 137, 141, 149
Leftwich, George 142
Leftwich, Nathaniel 99
Leftwich, Ralph 33, 34, 56, 66, 82, 83, 96, 160, 168
Leftwich, Richard 141
Leftwich, Thomas 118
Leftwich, William 33, 56, 61, 65, 66, 69, 78, 84, 86, 87, 88, 139, 147, 148, 151, 156, 162, 178
Legh family of Adlington 140
Legh, John 19, 24
Leigh 12
Leigh, Colonel John 173
Leigh, Ellen 86, 88
Leigh, John 34
Leigh, Peter 84, 147
Leigh, William 84
Leland, John 1, 4, 114, 117, 121, 122
Lewis, Brother John 20
Ley, John 168
Leycester family 26, 34, 137, 142
Leycester, Peter 34, 118, 139, 142, 178
Leycester, Piers 26
Leycester, Sir George 33
Leycester, Sir Peter 147
Leycester, William 85, 138, 142, 149
Lichfield 78
Lime 156
Lincoln, Countess of 178
Lindsey, Robert 99

INDEX

Lindsey, Roger 101
Litler, Robert 96
Little Legh 141
Little Street 23, 32, 34, 118, 139
Little Witton 12, 142
Littler, Robert 101
Liverpool 133
Livesey, James 168
Lock-up 98
Lodgers 111
Lodporne Stone 33
Lodstone 106
London 56, 74, 81, 147
Long Parliament, The 178
Lord of the Manor 92, 132, 138, 140, 150, 183. See also Derby, The Earls of
Lord of the Seath. See Seath, Lord of the
Lord Stanley 22
Lord Strange 22
Lostock 49, 171
Lostock Gralam 12, 53, 56, 94, 142, 154, 155, 157, 171, 179
Low, Phillip 81
Lowe, Hugh 147, 151
Lowe, Josiah 99
Lowe, Robert 173
Lower Keuper Saliferous Beds 3

M

Macclesfield 9
Magdalen Hall, Oxford 161
Magistrates courts 184
Mainwaring family 131, 155
Mainwaring, Phillip 172
Maisterson, John 170
Malbank, William 11
Malbon, John 99
Malpas 144, 176
Manor xvi, 178

Manorial tenants 14
Marbury 12, 133, 142, 158
Marbury family 137, 142
Marbury, Mr 131
Marbury, Thomas 157
Marbury, William 133
Mariott, Edward 56, 66, 69
Market 1, 4, 15, 16, 97
Market Hall 40
Market Place 30, 32, 39, 41, 76, 98, 103, 143, 154, 155, 159, 161, 178
Market Street 34, 40
Market-looker 101, 103, 113, 178
Marriot, Mr 156
Marrow, Colonel John 174
Marston 12, 185
Marston Moor, Battle of 175
Martindale, Adam 168
Martinmas 7
Mary Queen of Scots 165
Massey family 180
Massey, Ellen 170
Massey, John 148
Massey, Mary 170
Massey, Peers 148
Master of Requests 161
Mather, Richard 161, 167
Matrimonial affairs 169
Meat 103
Meat preservation 7
Mechanical pumps 121
Medieval period 14
Mercer 74, 76, 152
Merchant guilds 93
Mercia, Earl of 7
Mercia, The Earl of 14
Mercurius Aulicus 161
Mere, William 33
Mershton 88
Middleton, Sir Thomas 179
Middlewich 4, 7, 9, 11, 13, 15, 19, 23, 37, 77, 94, 99, 113, 118, 121, 126, 128,

231

OWNERS, OCCUPIERS AND OTHERS

129, 130, 164, 175, 186
   Battle of 174
Military obligation 15, 158
Millenary Petition 166
Miller 72, 74, 104
Miller, William 101
Millington, Elizabeth 171
Mills 21, 22, 74
Minshull Vernon 12
Monckton, Sir Francis 140
Monckton, Sir Philip 140
Moore, William 101
Moores, Constable William 99, 100
Moores, Mathew 83, 100
Morality 164
Moriss, Phillip 101
Morris, Phillip 99
Mort, Anne 184
Mort, James 184
Mort, Jonadab 184
Moseley, Mrs Ann 56
Moseley, Mrs Anne (née Sutton) 140
Moseley, Roland 140
Mottershead family 25
Musical instruments 63
Muster Rolls 25, 50, 144
Mytton, Major General 179

N

Nantwich 7, 9, 11, 12, 13, 70, 113, 115, 118, 119, 121, 126, 128, 129, 130, 131, 144, 166, 174, 180, 186
   Battle of 174
   School 144
Naseby, Battle of 176
Nether Knutsford 149
New Model Army 180
New Swan 68, 158, 172
New Swanne 68, 153
Newall, John 83
Newall, Richard 153

Newall, William 83
Newcastle 142
Newchurch 82
Newton 12, 80
Nickson, Ralph 63, 142, 153, 186
Nickson, Robert 147
Nickson, Thomas 63, 148, 186
Nield, Thomas 88
Nixon, Elizabeth 73
Nixon, Katherine 73
Nixon, Ralph 56, 73
Nixon, Robert 73
Nixon, Thomas 73, 133
Norcott family 25, 59
Norcott, John 81
Norcott, Marie 67
Norcott, Samuel 81
Norcott, Thomas 66, 67
Norcott, William 67, 171
Norman Conquest 14
Northwich 24, 171, 172, 175, 176, 180
   Bounds 24
   Garrison 173, 174, 175
   Lordship 92, 184
   Steward. See also Steward, Derby (Earl of)
Northwich Borough Court 52
Northwich Local Board 184
Northwich Rural District Council 182
Northwich Urban District Council 182, 184
Northwich, Hugh 23
Northwich, Lucas 23
Norton Abbey 26
Norton Priory 23
Nuns 19, 141

O

Occleston 12
Occupations 66
Occupiers, The 150
Old Swan 33, 158, 159

INDEX

Old Swanne 68
Oldfield family 141
Oldfield, Leftwich 132, 156
Oldfield, Mr 131
Oldfield, William 138, 171, 179
Olton 26
Order of St John of Jerusalem 23, 34, 141
Oriel College, Oxford 160
Oswestry 175
Others, The 157
Oulton 176
Over 9, 112, 173, 174, 176
Overseers of the Poor 109
Overton 144
Owners, The 137
Oxford 161, 175
    All Souls College 161
    Balliol College 69
    Brazenose College 161
    Magdelen Hall 161
    Oriel College 160

P

Pan-cutters 101
Parish 49, 50, 51, 54, 57, 58, 66, 109, 110, 134, 137, 141, 145, 147, 157, 158, 159, 164, 165, 166, 167, 168, 169
Parker, Adam 19
Parliament 166, 173
Parliamentarians 140, 161, 168, 173, 175, 180
Parsefull, Thomas 101
Partington family 141. See also Leach Eye
Partington, John 56, 72, 74, 138, 149
Partington, Richard 56, 74, 149
Partington, Thomas 149
Partington, William 74
Pavage 21
Pavement House, The 39

Pavor family 25, 39, 74, 85, 137, 143, 156, 167
Pavor, Dame Dorothy 143
Pavor, Elizabeth 146
Pavor, Ellen 143, 144
Pavor, Emme 144
Pavor, George 68, 153
Pavor, Helen 145
Pavor, James 138, 143
Pavor, Joan 146
Pavor, John 22, 143, 144
Pavor, Jone 144
Pavor, Jonet 144
Pavor, Margaret 146
Pavor, Mary 68
Pavor, Peter 34, 65, 68, 72, 78, 84, 86, 87, 143, 144, 145, 152, 157
Pavor, Rafe 144
Pavor, Roger 144, 145, 146, 152, 171
Pavor, William 143
Peacock, Samuel 99
Peckham, Edmund 26
Peecing xvi, 109, 128, 129, 147, 152, 158
Pemberton 9
Penkstone, James 148
Pennines 9
Percival, Thomas 170
Percival, William 73
Perkins, William 167
Pewter 60, 88
Phithean, Roger 81
Phitheon, Humphrey 50
Pickmere (Family) 25, 106
Pickmere, Joan 33
Pickmere, Margaret 152
Pickmere, Randle 164
Pickmere, Robert 33
Pickmere, William 33
Pierson, Thomas 167
Piggon 89
Piggot, Richard 168

OWNERS, OCCUPIERS AND OTHERS

Pigott, Richard (Captain) 167, 173
Pipe Rolls 17, 27
Piracy 172
Plague 50, 83
Ploughland 13
Plumley 12, 94, 117
Politics 171
Poll Tax 51, 53, 54, 74, 84, 85, 146, 154, 155, 160
Pontage 9, 21, 28
Poor Rate 109
Poor relief 54
Pope, The 165
Population 49, 186
Posnett 88
Poverty 109
Pownall family 25, 157
Pownall, Anne 157
Pownall, Elizabeth 157
Pownall, George 157
Pownall, Humphrey 157
Pownall, Margaret 157
Pownall, Raffe 157
Pownall, Ralph 125, 157
Pownall, Robert 157, 158, 168
Pownall, Thomas 157
Poyntz, General 176
Preacher, The 147
Prince Maurice 176
Prince Rupert 174, 176
Princes of Wales 17
Priory of St Bartholomew, Smithfield 143
Prison 33, 40
Protestants 165
Pull, James 19
Pumps 130
Puritans 161, 164, 165, 167, 168

Q

Quarter Sessions 4, 97, 169, 182
Queen Elizabeth I 26, 146, 154, 165, 177

Queen's Peace 99

R

Radford, Daniel 76, 78
Radford, John 78
Radford, Nathaniel 78
Radford, Robert 78
Radford, Samuel 78
Radnor 143
Ratcliffe, John 86, 88
Ravenscroft, Henry 24
Read, John 142
Recusancy 165, 166, 169, 177
Red Lion 34, 40
Reddiche 158
Regrating 103
Religion 164
Rendye, Jone 151
Restoration, The 161
Retailing 74
Rich, Sir Richard 143
Ridgeway Croft 149
River Dane 1, 2, 6, 9, 18, 21, 22, 32, 37, 41, 106, 121, 155, 186
River Weaver 2, 3, 6, 18, 20, 26, 30, 34, 40, 41, 106, 121, 132, 141, 180, 183
Navigation 133
Roberts, Jonathon 99
Robinson family 161
Robinson, Edward 162
Robinson, Elin 162
Robinson, Francis 162
Robinson, James 98
Robinson, John 162
Robinson, Katherine 162
Robinson, Mary 98
Robinson, Thomas 69, 96, 161, 162, 169, 177, 178
Robinson, Wareing 99
Robinson, William 137, 140, 161
Rock salt 133, 185, 186

INDEX

Roe, William 168
Roelau 8
Rogerson, Alice 171
Rogerson, Thomas 170
Rogerson, William 83
Roman Catholicism 164, 166, 169
Roman Northwich 6
Rossendale, Thomas 141
Rostherne 33
Rowe family 25
Rowe, Richard 151
Rowe, William 56
Royal Society 121, 161
Royalist 159, 174, 180
    Prisoners 174
Royle, Joseph 83
Royle, Thomas 83
Rudheath 9, 37, 49, 56, 69, 94, 175
Rued, Hugh 22
Rulers of Walling 100, 113
Running House 115, 140
Ryley, Anne 157

S

Saddler 81, 148, 159, 160
Sadler, Emme 171
Salinae 11
Salt boilings 110
Salt industry 185
Salteresford 9
Saltern 2, 114
Salters 1, 128
Saltersbridge 9
Saltersbrook 9
Saltersford 9
Saltersford Bridge 9
Saltersgate 9
Salterswall 9
Saltersway 9
Salterswell House 9
Salt-making 102, 119, 128

Amounts produced 129, 185
Customs 102
Process 121
Salt-viewer 101
Sandbach 4, 12
Sankey 133
Saxon 14, 15
Scavenger 100, 107, 113
School 77, 147
School-house 54
Sealed Knot 180
Sealers of leather 101
Seamstresses 76
Seath Dealer 113
Seath Street 34, 39, 115, 117, 118, 139, 143, 144, 146
Seath, Lord of the 108, 122
Senhouse, John 148
Sequestration 177
Sequestration Commissioner 177, 178
Sequestration Committee 177
Shakerley family 23
Shakerley, Jeffery 138
Shakerley, Margaret 152
Shakerley, Mrs Margaret 137, 138, 139
Shaw, Ann 170
Shaw, George 153
Shaw, Richard 99
Shaw, Rondle 151
Shermen 80, 81
Ship (Brine store) 117, 119, 124
Ship Money 172
Shipbrook 13, 85, 94, 156
Shoemaker 75, 76, 81, 104
Shopkeeper 78
Shops 15, 23, 26, 32, 34, 39, 40, 59, 68, 77, 80, 81, 82, 103, 118, 142, 149, 153, 159, 168
Shrewsbury 175
Shrewsbury School 173
Shurlach 53, 94
Silk weaver 80

OWNERS, OCCUPIERS AND OTHERS

Silk weaving 83
Silver plate 60
Singleton, Robert 73
Sir John Deane's school 143. See Grammar School
Skelhorne, Thomas 70, 125
Skellett 88
Skellhorne, Thomas 152
Smith, Henry 73
Smith, Richard 101
Smith, Thomas 99
Smith, William 1, 2, 4, 37
Specialist Services 83
Spices 76
Sproston 12
St Helen's church 41, 139, 147. See also
    Chapel of St Helen
    Churchwarden 147, 154, 161, 170
    Curate 147, 167
    Minister 147
    Parish registers 164
    Perpetual curates 164
    Steeple 164
St. Ives, Huntingdonshire 98
Stafford, Sir Richard 21
Stanley family 22, 92, 180
    Derby, Earl of. See also
Stanley, Sir Thomas 92, 140
Stanlow Abbey 23
Stanthorne 12, 145, 146
Starkey family 19, 20, 24, 26, 142
Starkey, Hugh 26
Starkey, John 20
Starkey, Lawrence 24
Starkey, Mr 178
Starkey, Peter 20
Starkey, Raphe 142
Starkey, Richard 20, 150
Starkey, Samuel 132
Starkey, Thomas 20, 147
Starkey, William 20, 24
Steven, John 23

Stevene, John 23
Steward xvi, 102, 108, 125, 126, 128, 162
Stockport 9
Stocks 108
Stones, John 34
Stretton 147
Stubbs, John 74, 175
Stubbs, Katherine 175
Stuth 18
Subsidence 40, 41, 183
Subsidy Rolls 25
Sudlow family 25
Sudlow, George 26
Sudlow, Joseph 99
Sudlow, Robert 63
Sudlow, Samuel 99
Sudlow, Thomas 26, 62, 63, 72, 99
Sudlow, William 26, 83
Sudlowe, Rachel 157
Suit Roll 52
Sumner, John 65
Sumner, Thomas 72
Sunderland, John 84
Survey 1606 33, 161
Sutton family 33, 137, 139, 167
Sutton, Anne 140
Sutton, Margaret 140
Sutton, Mary 140
Sutton, near Macclesfield 12, 139
Sutton, Richard 99, 139
Swan, The 32, 41
Swanlow Lane, Over 77
Swetbrun, Randolph 23
Swettenham, Hugh 147
Swettenham, Margery 86, 88
Swettenham, William 84, 87, 88, 157
Swine Market 34
Swine Market Street 32, 34, 40, 85, 148, 155, 183
Swinton, John 85, 155, 156
Swinton, William 33, 76, 82

236

INDEX

Sworton, Elizabeth 84
Sworton, John 84, 169
Sworton, Katherine 84
Sworton, Margaret 84
Sworton, Mrs Elizabeth 84

T

Tables 61, 88
Tabley 34, 139, 142
Tailors 75, 76, 83
Tandy, Margery 169
Tandy, William 169
Tanner 81, 168
Tanner, William 81
Tarbock family 25, 94, 152
Tarbock, Elizabeth 153, 170
Tarbock, Ellen 147
Tarbock, George 147, 152, 154
Tarbock, John 22, 23, 146, 152
Tarbock, Margaret 153, 157
Tarbock, Mary 153
Tarbock, Peter 56, 65, 66, 68, 82, 132, 140, 152, 153, 154, 155, 158, 159, 160, 170
Tarbock, Richard 157
Tarbock, Roger 152
Tarbock, Thomas 154
Tarporley 9, 112
Tarvin 94, 175, 176
Tattenhall 142, 176
Tatton 11, 12, 142
Tax on Goods 16
Taxes 21
    Pavage 21
    Pontage 21
Tench, Ralph 65
Tench, William 81
Termination of wich-house leases 150
Tetton 12
Tewe, Joan 157
Thanes 7, 11

Time limits on salt production 128
Tinker 84
Toft 142
Toft, William 22
Tolls 7, 14, 22, 97
    Northwich 8
    Production 7
    Toll gatherers 108
    Transport 7, 18
Toproud family 19
Toproud, Roger 19
Torbock, Roger 151
Tower of London 180
Town Bridge. See Bridge, The Town
Town Officials 100
Town plan 161
Travis, Elizabeth 87, 128
Travis, Richard 83, 87
Trevis, Francis 84
Trevis, Thomas 170
Trustee 161. See also Feoffee
Tunendune 8
Turnell 89
Twambrook 78, 157
Twembrokes, Alice 22
Twembrokes, Robert 22
Twembrook. See also Witton
Twemlow, Joseph 100, 101
Twenbrook. See also Witton

U

Usher or Under-Master 159
Usury 154
Utkinton 143

V

Vale Royal Abbey 19, 20, 23, 26, 142
    Abbot of 19
Vale Royal Borough Council 184
Venables family 19, 22, 23, 26, 37, 59, 74, 122, 142, 178

OWNERS, OCCUPIERS AND OTHERS

Venables, Anne 132
Venables, Colonel Robert 179
Venables, Gilbert 13
Venables, John 50
Venables, Peter 33, 34, 94, 96, 98, 99, 139, 142, 148, 149, 156, 178
Venables, Robert 33, 50, 56, 172
Venables, Sir Thomas 2
Venables, Thomas 122, 124, 178
Venables, William 19
Vernon family 13, 22, 143
Vernon, John 81
Vernon, Richard 23

W

Wade Brook 149
Wades Brook 37
Walker, John 170
Waller 66, 124, 127, 128
Walling xvi, 126, 128, 140, 147, 148, 149, 150, 151, 155
   Full list 151
   Rights 132, 140, 146, 155, 156, 157, 167
Walmes 127, 149
Walton family 23, 25
Walton, Elizabeth 23
Walton, John 99, 167
Walton, Oliver 25
Walton, Richard 23, 87, 118
Walton, Robert 23, 66, 170
Walton, Roger 23
Warburton family 22, 137, 140, 148, 149
Warburton, John 69, 171
Warburton, Justice Peter 33, 137, 140
Warburton, Peter 102, 147
Warburton, Robert 56
Warburton, Sir Peter 153
Warburton, Sir Thomas 133
Warrington 98
Water-mill 21

Waterworth, Stephen 102
Watford 143
Watford, Hertfordshire 143
Watling Street 39
Weaver 12
Weaver Navigation 185, 186
Weaver Navigation Act 185
Weaverham 11, 12, 23, 99, 168, 180
Weaverham,James 19
Webb, William 2, 4, 37, 182
Webster 80
Weedall, Peter 84
Weltrogh, Siddington 144
Whalley 23
Whalley Abbey 23, 139, 142
Whalley, General 179
Wharton 12
Wheelock Brook 186
Whitchurch 9
Whitegate 82
Whitley 149
Wich-house xvi, 11, 23, 26, 67, 68, 69, 73, 78, 84, 85, 89, 97, 100, 105, 106, 107, 114, 117, 118, 125, 128, 130, 131, 132, 137, 138, 139, 140, 141, 142, 143, 144, 145, 146, 147, 148, 153, 154, 155, 157, 170. See also Derby, The Earls of
   description of 117
   Termination of leases 150
Wich-wood 151, 156, 158
Wickstead, Mr 144
Wigan 9, 179
Wilbraham family 94, 106, 143
Wilbraham, Margaret 170
Wilbraham, Margery 170
Wilbraham, Roger 139
Wilbraham, Sir Richard 143
Wilderspool 3
Wilkinson, Ann 171
William, King 11, 13
Williamson, Josiah 99

238

INDEX

Wills 56
Wincham 11, 13, 56, 141, 169, 185
Winnington 3, 12, 49, 53, 68, 69, 72, 148, 157, 171, 180
Winnington Bridge 180
Winnington family 19, 20, 22, 25, 137, 141, 142, 167
Winnington Hill 30, 69, 173
Winnington, Ann 170
Winnington, Elizabeth 83
Winnington, Ellen 83, 170
Winnington, George 33
Winnington, Hugh 33, 50, 83, 144
Winnington, John 83, 170
Winnington, Julius 34, 149, 170
Winnington, Lawrence 23, 118
Winnington, Mrs Ellen 83
Winnington, Paul 142
Winnington, Peter 99
Winnington, Richard 24, 164
Winnington, Robert 33, 83, 99, 151, 170
Winnington, Sibill 151
Winnington, Thomas 99, 151
Winsford 185, 186
Winsford Town Council 184
Wirrall, Richard 16
Witton 2, 3, 12, 13, 25, 30, 37, 69, 72, 74, 76, 83, 94, 110, 138, 143, 148, 149, 152, 154, 156, 157, 158, 169, 171, 172, 183, 185, 187
  Curate 161
  Parish Clerk 159
Witton Brook 3, 37, 74, 185
Witton Chantry 147
Witton church. See St Helen's Church
Witton Cross 37
Witton Grammar School 154, 155. See Grammar School
Witton House 184
Witton Mill 178
Witton registers 50
Witton Street 37, 41

Wood as fuel 125, 158
Wood, Ellen 144, 169
Wood, John 99
Wood, Richard 144
Wood, Robert 169
Woodhey 143
Wood-tender 101
Wool 61, 63, 74, 80
Woollen draper 72, 138, 149
Worcester, Battle of 179
Worrall, William 151
Worsley, Thomas 83
Wrench, John 76
Wright, James 138, 168
Wright, Richard 83

Y

Yanning, Peter 102
Yate family 25, 106
Yate Street 23, 32, 34, 40, 45, 67, 85, 115, 118, 139, 151, 155, 156
Yate, Hukin 25
Yate, Humphrey 151
Yeomen 70, 73, 157
York 175
York, Archbishop of 167
Young, Peter 99

Léonie Press publishes local history, social history & autobiography, including:

MEMORIES OF A CHESHIRE CHILDHOOD
by LENNA BICKERTON
(ISBN 1 901253 00 7)
Price £4.99

'WE'LL GATHER LILACS...'
LENNA BICKERTON
(ISBN 1 901253 21X)
Price £5.99

NELLIE'S STORY — A LIFE OF SERVICE
ELIZABETH ELLEN OSBORNE
(ISBN 1 901253 15 5)
Price £5.99

A HOUSE WITH SPIRIT
JACKIE HAMLETT
CHRISTINE HAMLETT
(ISBN 1 901253 01 5)
Price £8.99

MID-CHESHIRE MEMORIES
(ISBN 1 901253 28 7)
Price £8.99

KNUTSFORD PRISON — The Inside Story
DAVID WOODLEY
(ISBN 1 901253 27 9)
Price £5.99

UPTON PARK CHESTER — A community for 150 years
Phil Pearn
(ISBN 1 901253 25 2)
Price £10

TALES FROM A SPORTING LIFE
Percy Yeud (1879-1963)
(ISBN 1 901253 31 7)
Price £8.99

Léonie Press
13 Vale Rd
Hartford
Northwich
Cheshire
CW8 1PL

Tel 01606 75660
Fax 01606 77609
anne@leoniepress.com

ELIZABETH ANNE GALTON (1808-1906)
(ISBN 1 901253 36 8)
Price £10.99

WOOLLYBACK
ALAN FLEET
(ISBN 1 901253 18 X)
Price £8.99

THE WAY WE WERE
(ISBN 1 901253 01 5)
Price £7.99

To see our full range of more than 40 books, visit www.leoniepress.com